# PRISON TORTURE

## IN AMERICA

## Shocking Tales
## from the Inside

# PAUL SINGH

**SCIENCE
LITERARY
BOOKS**
*A Singh Global Initiative*

Menlo Park / San Francisco

*Published by:*
Science Literacy Books
Menlo Park   San Francisco

To contact the publisher, please email
Paul@ScienceLiteracyBooks.com

Or write to: Singh Global Initiatives/Science Literacy Books
P.O. Box 7716
Menlo Park, CA-94026

Science Literacy Books website address:
www.ScienceLiteracyBooks.com

Printed and bound in Great Britain by Marston Book Services Ltd, Oxfordshire

Paperback Edition ISBN 978-1-949454-00-0

Library of congress has catalogued the paperback Edition as follows:
Library of Congress Control Number: 2018908682
Includes Bibliographical references and Index

*Mankind's inhumanity to mankind*
*makes countless thousands mourn ... and yet humanity persists.*
—Robert Burns, 1784

From the mother of an inmate who died after years of getting no medical care, despite spending all her life's savings and court orders that he receive it:

*Americans would be outraged if they learned people were treating their pets as poorly, but nobody advocates for the rights of prisoners because prisoners are viewed as less than human. I know our country is no better than third world nations when it comes to human rights violations and denial of medical care for those who are in prison.*

—Nora Weber
Bakersfield, California

Author's Note

This is a book of non-fiction and is based on my own personal experience, the research and investigation that I conducted from inside the prison, court records, and media reports. It is a book of reporting and commentary on an issue of urgent and enduring public interest – the maltreatment of inmates in American jails and prisons.

Individuals who worked in prisons and other public employees and officials are identified by their real names. All inmates, however, are identified only by a fictional first name. Any resemblance between these fictional first names and any real person is strictly coincidental.

All medical information and all medical records about inmates that are mentioned in this book has been accessed and used with their prior written and verbal consent. The wording of the written consent is published at the end of this book in a typewritten form, while the original handwritten version of the consent is published in *Prison Papers,* its companion book, with inmates' signatures and identities carefully redacted.

This book is an investigative report on the medical cruelty and human rights abuses that are faced by inmates in our prison system. I am a physician, and I learned a great deal about the law while in confinement. However, this is not a book of medical or legal advice, and it does not take the place of consultation with an appropriate professional about medical or legal issues that the readers of my book may be facing.

# CONTENTS

## SECTION V: CONCLUSION

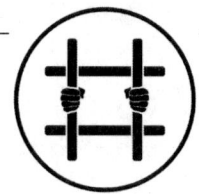

# PREFACE

*PRISON TORTURE IN AMERICA* IS THE SECOND OF TWO books that I wrote during my incarceration. The first book, *Guilty at Gunpoint: How the Government Framed Me*, explains how I spent six months in Lompoc Prison in California for a crime I never committed. The tagline of *Guilty at Gunpoint* reads "Crime and Corruption in the Department of Justice, the FDA and Big Pharma"—as you can see, the title speaks for itself. Both books were simultaneously launched on January 1, 2019, the morning after the completion of my prison sentence.

*Prison Torture* is based on a covert investigation that I undertook during my incarceration in 2016. I am a 57-year-old physician and scientist who eye-witnessed inhumane treatment of nonviolent American prisoners who have been locked up for decades in various federal prisons across the country. Many of these prisoners took enormous risk in actively assisting me in making this investigation possible so that the hidden facts about healthcare in our prisons, which has long been kept a secret, can be revealed to the American people.

This book is divided into six sections. Section I is introductory and includes the chapters, What Prompted the Covert Investigation? and Planning an Undercover Operation. In this section, I describe my first few weeks of observations in prison, which horrified me to my inner core. The events I observed intrigued me enough that I wanted to conduct a full undercover investigation of the prison torture that I was observing firsthand. I noted that the most vulnerable and the sickest of prisoners were denied the most basic medical attention and subjected to medical cruelty, emotional violence, mental torture, and abuse. Every day, I noted something new, something worse, something more unconscionable than what I had witnessed the day before. My desire and motivation to delve deeper into this prison life increased daily.

Section II, "The Trail of Tears," includes heart-wrenching testimonies written by prisoners themselves as well as the stories of some prisoners that I wrote for those who were unable to write on their own or who were not willing to write because they feared retaliation from prison officials. The handwritten testimonies of prisoners are published as is, without making any grammatical corrections or editing with the exception of making some unavoidable grammatical corrections to make their written English understandable. I used inmates' prison records, both medical and administrative, to write these stories, mainly by utilizing the prison's internal documents that never become visible to the outside world even in the best of litigations. Also included in this section is a typewritten version of entries from a prisoner's journal.

Some of these internal documents, although technically not designated as classified by the government, are worse than any classified information. About 20 percent of the government's classified information become declassified every 40 years or so when the National Archives forces the government to declassify information after the elapse of a certain period. The internal prison documents will *never* become declassified. The Federal Bureau of Prisons does not want to risk this hidden information being leaked to the public, because it is made nonexistent before it would have any chance of getting leaked; it is done verbally and ensured that it does not become part of any written records. To avoid making this book unmanageable in length, I have published the original documents in a separate, companion book, *Prison Papers*, which was simultaneously launched with the book in your hands.

The title of Section III, "Reminiscent of War Crimes," is, I feel, an appropriate title for this section. The chapters within will remind you of war crimes and human rights abuses as they have been historically observed under brutal regimes, totalitarian governments' military rules, and police states. The chapters in this section describe how prison officials manufacture, rewrite, and distort prisoners' medical records. Documents show how prison officials run a fraudulent "Sick-Call" scam. The Sick-Call system in prison, as the name suggests, is by definition meant to take care of a prisoner's medical emergency needs, but this is the biggest charade that I came across in prison. These chapters show how prison doctors, nurses, and officials withhold life-saving medications and neglect those who are most ill who find themselves caught in a self-propelling bureaucratic machine custom designed to deny medical attention. It seems that most prison officials honestly believe that anyone who is placed in jail has lost all civil rights and deserves more punishment in the form of torture than what was handed down to him by the criminal justice system. In other words, incarceration is not punishment enough.

The conclusions drawn in this section are essentially the result of a medical audit of thousands of pages of prisoners' medical and administrative records. Having been a physician, surgeon, and a biochemist for 25 years, I was uniquely qualified for being just the right person to audit these records. Everything in this section can be independently verified by delving deeply into the original medical and administrative records published in *Prison Papers*, which I have managed to smuggle out of the prison for you, the reader, to see them for yourself. "Reminiscent of War Crimes" is a critical analysis of the underlying government's official strategies of providing "medical care" in the prison system as reflected in The Trail of Tears. My critical analysis throws light on how our government forges prisoners' medical records in legal preparation for defense in case a prisoner was to sue the Federal Bureau of Prisons for cruel and unusual punishment.

"Reminiscent of War Crimes" illuminates how the prison Sick-Call system is used as a device to distract, confuse, and obfuscate the most vulnerable in prison—a device skillfully crafted to confuse the court system if the court were ever to get involved in any given case. It was critically important for me to write this section to simplify for my readers the technical nature of health-related medical information incorporated in The Trail of Tears and the originals published in the companion book, *Prison Papers*. My critical analysis shows how the Department of Justice's (DOJ) double standard of saying one thing and doing another inside the four walls of the federal prisons has caused so much pain in the lives of so many. Prisoners who complain too much are often transferred from facility to facility so that the prisons can avoid providing them medical treatment. Those who are very firm or sometimes aggressive in demanding treatment or show signs of any threat of lawsuit against the prison end up in solitary confinement under the pretext of "prison security" or "prison safety" when clearly the issue at hand is not security or safety but the urgent medical needs of critically ill patients. You will learn how the prison industry has devised deceptive methods over a century of experience to con the American public in terms of what goes on inside the federal prisons by withholding the truth from the American people.

Section IV, Legal Considerations and the Case Law, is a brief summary of many important legal cases of denial of healthcare in federal and state prisons, of prison abuse, and of violation of human rights in the United States in the last several decades. I hope this information will be of value to human rights activists and public service attorneys who are working to bring about reform in the current business of incarceration.

The Conclusion sums up the salient points, with additional supportive statistical data and some expert editorial comments.

While I have published the names of the prison officials and guards engaged in corruption and crime, I have carefully blocked out the names and registration numbers of the prisoner patients, and other information that may allow them to be identified, for their privacy and to maintain compliance with HIPAA (Health Insurance Portability and Accountability Act.) More importantly, I have done this to minimize retaliation against these prisoners by the FBOP after the publication of this book despite the fact that prisoners have given me written permission to make their names and prison records public in order to expose the medical cruelty that they are being subjected to on a daily basis [see this authorization at the end of this book].

The names used for all inmates in describing their horror stories are single names and are fictional, such as Pete or Samuel to protect them against revenge from prison authorities. The actual names of the inmates whose prison records are published in *Prison Papers* will be made available to any civil rights or human rights organization, domestic or international, that is engaged in fighting against human rights abuses of prisoners in the United States, or anywhere else in the world for that matter. Medical cruelty in many cases is tantamount to medical experimentation on humans to test their limits for torture and neglect.

Let me now ease into the introductory section of the book, which explains what prompted me to conduct a covert investigation and how I planned an undercover operation to access internal documents and prison records that I needed to fulfill this dangerous mission at the risk of my own life and the lives of many others. I believe it was worth it because the American people deserve to know the truth about what goes on inside the four walls of our prisons.

# SECTION I
# INTRODUCTION

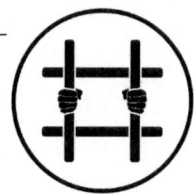

## CHAPTER 1

# WHAT PROMPTED THE COVERT INVESTIGATION?

I T WAS A SUDDEN LOCKDOWN. I HAD JUST SELF-SURREN-dered to the prison a week prior. Everything happening before my eyes was a new experience. Later that evening, I learned the cause for the lockdown. A 75-year-old man had escaped the North Prison Camp at Lompoc; he was driven off the site by his family. This elderly man with a heart condition had had heart attacks while in custody. He had been asking for medical help but received little. A prisoner told me that he would be caught and brought back and locked up in higher security and his sentence will be prolonged. Other prisoners told me that he would probably be transferred to low security from his current minimum security when he was caught and brought back, but in the words of one prisoner "at least he will be able to

ED LEISURE+CULTURE

see a doctor before they catch up to him. He has nothing to lose by escaping; he is 75, he is going to die in prison anyway."

It has now been three months since I surrendered to the prison camp at Lompoc. I have just finished writing my book, *Guilty at Gunpoint: How the Government Framed Me*, which is my personal story describing how I was sent to prison, thanks to "a coterie of vicious and unethical prosecutors harbored within and enabled by now ironically named the Department of Justice" (words of law ethics professor William Hodes.) I intend to spend the rest of my time in prison conducting my investigation and putting pieces of the puzzle together to complete this book, *Prison Torture in America: Shocking Tales from the Inside.*

When I heard the story of this 75-year-old man, it rang a bell about my own Health Screening Intake at the prison clinic on June 22, two days after I arrived here. I saw the prison physician, Jaspal Dhaliwal. He spent 30 minutes with me in his office of which he spent 28 minutes putting data into the computer. I thought he was putting information related to my health into the computer, but then I wondered what he could be typing on the keypad for such a long time if he had not taken a moment of his time to take my medical history or conduct a physical exam on me. Having been a physician myself for decades, I knew something was wrong. He spent the remaining two minutes taking my blood pressure and weight without making any eye contact, and he took my blood pressure with the wrong size cuff. My guess is that Dhaliwal probably used the same cuff on every patient. A cuff, as you know, is what a physician wraps around your upper arm to measure your blood pressure, and the size of the cuff has to match the patient size to get an accurate reading. For obvious reasons, the sphygmomanometer was showing erroneous systolic and diastolic blood pressure, numbers due to the very large size of the cuff he was using on my relatively small arm. He asked what my usual blood pressure was. I told him that my blood pressure was always normal, generally in the 118/76 range and I believe he recorded a number into his computer that reflected what I told him. He apparently knew that I was a physician because he asked me what my specialty was.

When I sensed that he was not interested in taking my medical history, I unilaterally started giving him history of my medical condition as he punched away some mysterious data into his computer. His response to the verbalization of my medical condition was simply to ignore me. He continued with his electronic paperwork. Following is a short one-sided conversation I had with him when he finally turned his attention to me two minutes before my departure from his office.

I repeated: "I hope you have had a chance to look at my medical records that were sent to you two weeks prior to my surrender? The Acknowledgment Receipt of my medical records was confirmed by the Bureau of Prisons with its signature on the Return Receipt Green Acknowledgment Card." I informed him that the Federal Bureau of Prisons (FBOP) also confirmed with my attorney in a phone call that they had received my medical records. His response was still the same silence, ignoring me as though I had not spoken at all. He continued to do his little computer-related chores in-between taking my blood pressure and weight.

I stated, "My medical records contain a letter from my medical examiner, a physiatrist [a physician who specializes in physical medicine and rehabilitation], describing what I need for continued rehabilitation in prison and a list of medications that I am currently on. Have you had a chance to review the medical examiner's report? I suffer from myelopathy, thoracic outlet syndrome, and partial paralysis of my right arm and hand." Dhaliwal ignored me again and kept looking at something on his large screen desktop computer.

He finally turned around and looked me in the eye for only a flick of a second and then gave me a derisive smirk. This was when I knew that he had not reviewed my medical records, nor did he intend to. But I did not stop talking and continued to unilaterally give him my history of illness. I was a physician and thought I could make his job easier by giving him a synopsis of my medical history, especially because he did not seem to be interested in reviewing it himself, which I found a bit odd. I informed him that my physicians had sent several hundred pages of my medical records that explained my right arm and hand paralysis, severe stenosis of my cervical spine, and severe osteoporosis. I told him that I was recommended continued physical rehab and drug therapy because I chose not to take the risk of surgical complications due to my severe osteoporosis in counseling with the two neurosurgeons who took care of me prior to imprisonment. He did not say a word and did not remove his face from the computer screen. It was clear to me at this moment that the data he continued to punch into that computer could not possibly have been anything directly related to my medical history. I had no way of knowing as to why exactly he was spending so much time on the computer during my medical visit at his office.

As I got up to leave, I tried my luck again in asking him if I could at least continue to get my medications as requested by my medical examiner, and I repeated the list of my six current medications, to which he replied, "I will give you metformin. We do not have your other medications. I will give you a substitute for the rest." He proceeded, "Well, you have to pay for your sins." Then he started telling me a story about his nephew who was criminally charged for IRS fraud and sentenced to jail for nine years. I was not paying attention to his story. He followed me to the door on my way out and yelled, "next," to the patients in the waiting room.

I will skip for now the gory details of how my own healthcare was handled at the prison. Instead I will focus on what prompted me to start conducting a covert investigation into what was going on inside the prison with regard to the sickest of all people that I have ever seen in my twenty-year career as a physician primarily handling emergency medical situations. The investigative and research skills I had developed as a scientist, researcher, freelance journalist, and author were to come in handy at the strangest of all times and places in my life. What I was about to discover in prison is so valuable that an investigative journalist would pay out of his pocket to have the privilege to go to a low-security prison to have access to the kind of information that I was able to access, except that our government would never afford any journalist such a luxury. Gleaning this information from the jail was not easy, however. It was not without risk—a risk to my own life and the lives of many others who cooperated with me in this undercover operation.

The morning after the 75-year-old escaped the prison, something interesting happened. Two bunks away from me, a man would not wake up, and it was already 7:30 a.m., the time when everyone was required to leave the dorm for work and for the cleaning crew of prisoners to step in. The rule was strict. Everyone must leave the dorm by 7:30 a.m. including those who were severely disabled, in wheelchairs, or ill. My neighboring inmates told me that the man was a type I diabetic and such incidents had occurred before, and at times it had been difficult to wake him up in the mornings. They also informed me that he (the prisoner) regularly went to pill-call line for insulin injections. Prisoners knew by now that I was a physician, so their natural response was to ask if I could help in any way. I tried to shake the patient aggressively and asked him if he had a glucometer. After violent shaking, he woke up, vomited on my green prison uniform shirt and black work-boots, and then pointed to his pillow. Underneath his pillow I found the glucometer and some diabetic supplies. I tested his sugar and it was 448.

The prisoners told me that the pill-call window at the clinic was only open from 7:00 a.m. to 8:00 a.m. I suggested to his neighbors to take him to the clinic right away before the window closed. I did not want to get directly involved with this; I was keeping a low profile to accomplish my own goals that I had set. Prisoners told me that other physician-inmates in the past had been punished for trying to help prisoners. They had been warned that they were not allowed to practice medicine in prison. Two guys, close friends of this diabetic, took him to the clinic in a wheelchair. I told the diabetic inmate to show the nurse at the window the number 448 as it showed on the glucometer screen. I quickly reviewed the previous recordings from days and weeks as he was getting ready to leave the dorm in his wheelchair. The numbers ranged from as low as 20 to as high as 500. (The glucometer does not record numbers above 500 or below 20.) Later in this book, this diabetic prisoner would be one of the prisoners who describes his story in his own words. I also publish some entries from his personal diary and his medical records. But for now, I will continue to discuss the triggers that motivated me to play with fire with others who helped excavate hidden and proscribed documentation from within the four walls of the prison.

Three weeks after this incident, I witnessed an unfortunate event that literally broke my heart. I choke just thinking about it. I had to walk away from writing this and go out for a two-hour walk before feeling emotionally stable enough to come back and start writing again. A 77-year-old inmate, who was an oral and maxillofacial surgeon, a DDS (Doctor of Dental Surgery), and who could barely walk or talk due to his age and debilitating medical conditions, was upset with his correctional counselor and case worker, Ms. T. DuBose. This prisoner, Walter, had gone to her office to file a BP-9 (BP-9 refers to a second-tier complaint to the warden for an Administrative Remedy). I do not know much about what transpired between the prisoner and the counselor, but other prisoners and I witnessed DuBose yelling at the old man because he seemed to have "accused her" of something. I knew this dental surgeon well because he had been talking to me about his health issues that were not being addressed. He had also given me some documentation about his deteriorating health condition during the week preceding this episode. This prisoner was very fragile and could not hear well despite his hearing aids. Sometimes I had to utter words directly in his ears. I guess his age and medical condition might have been the reason I reacted emotionally to the incident because it reminded me of elder abuse for which I am a mandatory reporter as a physician in the outside civilian world.

The next thing many prisoners and I saw was that DuBose had called prison guards on him, and the old man was escorted away from the dormitory toward the offices of the prison officials. Other prisoners told me that the old man was being taken to the hole. I did not know what "the hole" meant. I learned later that in prison language the hole meant solitary confinement. Within half an hour we saw the old man's locker being wheeled to the office of the correction officer (CO) in charge of the dormitory.

We could all see a CO searching the locker in his office item by item. My heart was racing that the CO would find my name on a piece of paper in health-related documents from his locker, which I had traded with him. If they found my name on any documents recovered from his locker, I would have been in serious trouble. I feared less going into solitary confinement and feared more that I would then not be able to continue this investigation, which I had just begun, losing an opportunity of a lifetime to divulge to the world some things that were kept secret from the American people by the FBOP. All I can say is that I got lucky that day.

Perhaps the CO did not carefully read every document recovered from the old man's locker. It was also comforting to know that many of these prison guards (COs) could not read or write very well, which could only work to my advantage in such risky situations. Perhaps the CO (correction officer and prison guards are synonymous terms) did not suspect any underhanded activity due to the inmate's old age and poor health condition. I continued to be lucky after this episode, perhaps because I started to take extraordinary precautions by devising techniques that made my activities difficult to detect both by guards and snitches (an informer in prison language) in prison from that moment on.

Walter told me that he had a severe form of sarcoidosis in his lungs and airways. He had been asking the doctor at the prison to recommend a transfer to Taft Prison Camp where it was hot and dry; the ocean moisture and cold temperature at Lompoc was making it very hard for him to breathe. He told me that living in a hot climate was one of the main treatments of his disease to help prevent progression to its severest and terminal form. This is a fact about sarcoidosis of the lungs that I recognized myself as a physician. The prison doctor had denied his BP-8s (the inmate's informal complaints to staff) and he was planning to file a tier level-2 formal complaint called a BP-9, which was meant to be directed to the attention of the prison warden. Walter had informed me that his case worker, DuBose, had scratched off her hours posted on her office door (which I verified myself to be true) and that he was frustrated in repeatedly making trips to her office to submit his BP-9 paperwork and finding her office door always locked.

Walter was old and very frail and could barely walk or talk, probably the slowest walking prisoner in the camp. On the other hand, DuBose, who was also my caseworker, weighed about 300 pounds and was all muscle and very intimidating to many, especially to the white-collar criminals. The rumor was that prisoners who were assigned to her better not ask any questions if they went to her office. A prisoner's question will not be answered nine out of ten times, and asking the same question three times would be grounds for the solitary confinement. In my limited experience with her, there was much truth to what prisoners said about her. I knew that I had to be very cautious about asking any questions at all, and if I did, I was better off limiting my questions to one or two and to be extremely polite and sound apologetic with every word I uttered to this living, breathing, female linebacker.

The day after I saw the old man, Walter, being escorted away from the camp, many prisoners told me that he was taken to the hole. As a general rule, there was no way for me to verify that personally. Violating prison policy—and anything a prisoner does that the prison guard or the prison staff does not like is a violation of policy, or a security threat or security matter—was grounds for you to be transferred to a solitary cell.

Many prisoners described solitary confinement, called the hole, also called SHU (Special Housing Unit) as essentially a room the size of a parking lot booth with very little light coming in. This little booth has a narrow see-through slit of a window well above the level of a person's head. There were prisoners who were taken away to a solitary cell and then eventually returned after serving one to six months in solitary confinement. I had the opportunity to interview them independently to verify facts about the SHU living conditions. They all told me that the one-hour daily release from the cell for exercise afforded to them by federal law was not accorded to them. I have reason to believe that to be true because the consistent reports about the SHU that were given to me were by prisoners who belonged to different prison gangs and some white-collar criminals who did not associate with one another. So they could not have conspired to deliberately give me false information. All reports from these prisoners were independent reports, not interconnected, and therefore likely very accurate.

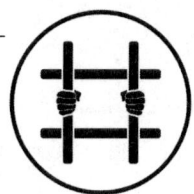

CHAPTER 2

# PLANNING AN UNDERCOVER OPERATION

THE EMOTIONAL COASTER OF WATCHING SICK PEOPLE unnecessarily suffer in prison led me from being a casual observer to a determined man. Further observations of some cases described in this section gave me the adrenal surge to launch a full-scale clandestine operation of my own with some help from others. Let's start with the prisoner who bunked on the opposing bunk, where we bumped heads throughout the night.

Actually, let's start with the real bunk first. The real bunk is that the prison system is obligated to provide medical care to all inmates, and that care must be the same standard of care that is considered acceptable in any community. Before proceeding, I hope each of you will stop and go online to take a look at a couple of links. The first describes their obligation and commitment.

Link: https://www.bop.gov/inmates/custody_
and_care/medical_care.jsp

Next, go to this page and take a look at the happy face of the inmate and the lovely smile of the prison caregiver.

Link: https://www.bop.gov/policy/progstat/6360_001.pdf

All of it is bunk, and I will prove that in the coming pages. Please keep both the words and the image emblazoned on your mind as you read through the experiences of each of the inmates interviewed.

Now back to my cellmate. I knew Benicio had been sick for a while but I did not know any of the details. On the morning of August 4, 2016, he showed me a BP-8, also known as an Inmate Request to Staff. According to Benicio, the document was typed by the correctional counselor Ms. Hawkins; responded to by the assistant Health Services administrator (AHSA) Ms. Marsha Pinnell; and co-signed by the unit manager (whose name I believe was Garrastazu), also nicknamed Shark by the prisoners. The BP-8 document typed by the prison counselor said the following:

> **INMATE'S COMPLAINT:** The above inmate is filing a BP-8 stating that he has been experiencing dizziness since July 23rd following treatment for pericarditis and effusion, a complication of valley fever that he contracted in February 2016. He states he also has Type II diabetes. As a result of the ongoing dizziness, he states he fell and injured his right knee on 7/27/16

Benicio informed me that the counselor did not include in her typed report his complaints of fever, chills, and body rash and that he was not allowed to write his own complaint. Then he showed me the extensive rash on his body. I thought that these lesions were just on his face until he took his shirt off to show me the rash was all over his corpus, neck, arms, and legs.

I read the second part of his BP-8:

**ACTION TAKEN** (prison officials' formal response to prisoner's complaint): Contact was made with AHSA Ms. Pinnell, who states: He will need to go to Sick Call for dizziness. The only Sick Call he had requested was for knee pain back at the end of June. If he fell on 7/27/16, he did not report that to the medical office. If he is not satisfied with the answer, he can file BP-9 for Administrative Remedy.

Benicio informed me that the prison response was full of lies because according to Benicio, he had put in several written Sick-Call requests and had gone to clinic everyday complaining of a fever and rash. I then read the third segment of this BP-8, entitled "Unit Manager: Comments and Assistance", which was signed by the unit manager with the following comment: Concur with the Counselor's conclusions and recommendations above.

I compared Benicio's BP-8 document with my own BP-8 in which I had filed a complaint for not receiving my medications and the prison doctor's disregard for my medical records and medical history. The prison's response to my BP-8 was written by the same counselor, responded to by the same AHSA, co-signed by the same unit manager, and included the same wording in the response that Benicio had received: "He did not report for Sick Call"; "He needs to go to Sick Call … If he does not like the answer, he can file BP-9 for Administrative Remedy"; "Concur with the Counselor's conclusions and recommendations." Similar to Benicio, I had also filed three Sick-Call requests, which the prison officials' response (Action Taken) did not acknowledge. How could two responses by the prison officials to two unique medical conditions of two unique prisoners with two unique medical histories be exactly the same? This looked suspicious, not to mention that the responses were strange—very unusual responses to very serious acute medical complaints. This was the starting point of my curiosity to find out what other prison documents signed by prison guards and officials might reveal to me if I looked deeper. I wanted to know if there was a pattern and not just an isolated coincidental finding that I accidentally ran into.

At 3:00 a.m. the next morning, Benicio's screams woke up the entire dorm. When he saw two correctional officers pass through the aisles with their flashlights on their 3:00 a.m. count, Benicio screamed that he had been spiking fever and chills in the middle of the night for three weeks now, that his body was full of blisters, and he needed an ambulance. We heard one of the COs tell him to calm down and wait for the clinic to open in the morning at 6:00 a.m. Benicio replied that he put in three Sick Calls in the last three weeks and they don't do nothing for him. "I need an ambulance," he yelled. "I need to go to the hospital." The CO replied, "There is nothing I can do for you. You have to wait for Sick Call when the clinic opens at 6:00 am in the morning."

"Well, I went to the clinic yesterday with Sick Call complaining of severe dizziness, fever and chills, they checked my sugar. I told them I had fever and chills, not sugar problem. I have blisters all over my body and have a fever. Please take my temperature. I have had valley fever before and I was hospitalized but no one has followed up on that. I think my valley fever is coming back. The PA [physician assistant] who checked my sugar at the clinic told me there is nothing else he could do for me. Please call an ambulance, I need ambulance." The guards ignored his pleas and left.

A prisoner with a smuggled thermometer took Benicio's temperature at 6:00 a.m. and it was 101.4°F. I closely examined his rash and suspected some viral infection, but the rash was extensive with lesions nearly covering his entire corpus and face. The lesions were also pustular (filled with pus). I told him I was not exactly sure what was going on. It could be a recurrence of valley fever with a superimposed bacterial infection, but most likely it was caused by a viral infection. I recommended that he go back to the clinic and tell the clinic staff about the fever and rash and have them swab the oozing pustules. I also told him that he might need urine and blood cultures and a chest X-ray to rule out recurrence of valley fever or septicemia. When Benicio returned from the clinic, he informed me that they gave him a tablet of Motrin and told him to follow up the next day.

Benicio followed up the next day with his complaints and the nurse told him that she would call the PA and then call Benicio out. The nurse asked the inmate to go back to his dorm and wait. He waited for the nurse's callout until 2:00 p.m. and then went back to the clinic, but it was already closed.

That evening, I wrote on a piece of paper "Prednisone 60 mg taper to 10 mg over 6 days" and gave it to Benicio and asked him to copy it in his own handwriting. I then told him to go to the clinic the next morning and say, "My sister is an RN for the last 30 years [I knew from my conversations with Benicio that he had a sister who was an RN] who spoke with the family practitioner she works for about my extensive body rash and the physician told her that I need this medicine for the rash to go away. Could you please get me this medication?" Benicio did exactly that the next morning and showed the nurse the piece of paper. The nurse at the window agreed with Benicio that he needed prednisone but then told him to come back the following day. Benicio was worried at this time that they would quarantine him (which is the same as solitary confinement in prison) if they thought he was contagious.

Benicio followed up the next day and the person at the window was a different nurse who told him she had no idea what the other nurse had told him the day before about coming back to the clinic and then told him the same thing: to come back tomorrow. That night Benicio had a higher fever and relentless chills; he went to the clinic once again the following morning. It was yet another person at the clinic window, a paramedic who gave him two tablets of Motrin and then told him that she would call the PA for him. She instructed him that if the PA did not contact him by 2:00 p.m. that day, he should go to the correctional counselor to report it. Benicio waited till 2:00 p.m. and then, not having heard anything from anyone at the Health Services, he went to the correctional counselor to complain about it. The counselor told Benicio to come back and see him if he did not hear from the clinic by 3:00 p.m. He did not hear anything from the clinic by 3:00 p.m. and immediately went back to the counselor's office, but the counselor was gone for the day.

At 3:45 p.m. everyone had to be back in the dorm to prepare for the daily 4:00 p.m. count. A speaker announcement was made, "Prepare for the Count," and repeated about fifteen times, as usual. As everyone stood straight up in front of their bunks and two COs started walking through the aisles doing their count and looking on both sides, we all heard a big thud. Benicio had fallen on the floor, hitting his head against the steel chair that was in the aisle at the demarcation line between my bunk and his bunk. The COs came running when they heard the noise. They called other people on their radios, and about 15 people from the three prisons on the prison complex (medium-security, low-security, and the two prison camps) showed up, including a paramedic, a nurse, the lieutenant, a unit manager, the AHSA, case workers, correctional counselors, and many guards. I knew better by now not to try to intercede, but before I realized I should not have opened my mouth, I advised a paramedic not to move the prisoner's neck because he could have broken it. I got lucky, however. They were so bewildered with not knowing what to do with the fallen prisoner that they probably did not hear my comments amidst this pandemonium in the dorm. I had never in my medical career seen a medical crew so lost with a patient who lost consciousness and fell, with a possible concussion to his head. They talked to one another on their radios trying to figure out what to do with the prisoner. They all came to check him out one by one, just looking at him but doing nothing, not even try to feel his pulse to see if he was alive.

Benicio spontaneously started responding in about 20 minutes. Now they knew that he was breathing and alive. It seemed like they had called the ambulance already and were waiting to transfer him to the hospital. Benicio got up with assistance and they took him to the prison clinic in a wheelchair, gave him Benadryl, and had a prisoner wheel him back to his bunk. They told him to wait in the dorm until he was taken to the hospital. He waited all evening and night until the next afternoon and no ambulance arrived. The next day they told him that they were waiting to take him to the hospital, which they eventually did much later in the afternoon. They brought him back to the dorm from the hospital within a few hours. I asked

Benicio what treatment he received at the hospital and if the hospital did blood work and an X-ray. I wondered why he was not admitted for his extensive rash and fever. He informed me that they gave him an injection at the hospital and told him that he was being discharged from the hospital and would receive ongoing treatment at the prison.

The prison clinic gave him two more "shots" in the week that followed; my guess is that by "shot," Benicio meant steroid shots for his rash. I discovered later he was receiving shots of Benadryl. His rash seemed to subside over the next two weeks but he continued to have a low-grade fever and chills every night. A month later he seemed to be completely recovering from the rash and the fever, but the large weeping lesions left behind permanent scars on his face and the front and back of his corpus. This reminded me of reading about the history of leprosy in the days when there was no cure; some people recovered from it but had terrible scars on their bodies.

As I watched Benicio recover, I became curious as to what was happening with the diabetic who was found in a coma some months prior. I remembered he was given only four units of regular insulin in the clinic for blood sugar levels of 488 after I had jolted him out of a diabetic coma. I visited his bunk and asked him how his diabetes was being managed by the prison clinic. He told me that the clinic finally made an appointment for him to see the prison physician Dr. Dhaliwal, who increased his prescribed insulin dose. The day after he saw Dhaliwal, he woke up and did his morning Accu-Chek (pinprick for sugar levels) as usual before going to the pill-call line for his insulin. The nurse at the window told him that she would give him 4 units of regular and 24 units of NPH (intermediate acting insulin). Being as well informed as he was about his diabetes (as most brittle diabetics are about insulin versus sugar levels), he informed the nurse that his morning sugar level before coming to clinic was 45 and that if she injected him with so much insulin, she would kill him. The nurse replied, "Don't blame me if you die; you are the one who wanted to get more insulin; this is what the physician prescribed and this is what you are going to get." He alleges that he begged the nurse not to give him so much insulin. He just wanted 2 units of regular, and no NPH but she denied him that option. He refused the insulin shot and left the clinic. According to the prisoner, this nurse was the same AHSA who made all the healthcare administrative decisions for the entire 3,000-inmate population in the three prisons of the Lompoc Federal Prison Complex.

Lompoc Federal Prison was considered a Level II medical facility of the FBOP, and it was very proud of this higher level of care, about which prison officials often bragged. I also learned from reading the prison manual that this medical facility had many "chronic care clinics" for many medical specialties. This made no sense to me because all prisoners, without exception, had been seen by only one general physician who was responsible for all 3,000 inmates. There were no specialty clinics noted anywhere by anyone. Most long-term inmates who had been at the camp for several years, including those who were very ill, informed me that during their entire incarceration period at the camp, which in some cases was as long as ten years, they had been seen by this one physician only once for Screening Intake at the time of their first arrival or transfer to the prison camp. And it was the same physician who treated the diabetic, who saw me and every other prisoner I spoke with: a foreign doctor from India with an MBBS and no clinical training in the United States. It was also the same physician who thought that I had told him a joke when I pleaded with him to review my medical records in his possession; it was the same physician who told me that I had to pay for my sins when I asked him to put me back on the medications that I was already taking before surrendering myself to the Bureau of Prisons (BOP). It was also the same physician who had told many other prisoners that they have to pay for their sins when they demanded their medications. Prisoners could not name another health provider on that prison complex other than this physician, a nurse AHSA, a paramedic, a PA, and a clinical director who was supposedly a physician or a PA but who did not see patients. Some even said that the only other physician in prison for 3,000 inmates was the clinical director who did not see patients because he did not have a medical license to practice. I had no way of verifying his licensure in prison, but I did read the government's literature on the BOP (that I received from another inmate) confirming that sometimes it hired unlicensed physicians as its clinical directors. Something was not adding up. Where were these specialized six chronic care clinics at this facility and the specialists associated with those clinics? No one seemed to know.

The same day that the AHSA, Marsha Pinnell, told the diabetic that she was going to give him 4 units of regular and 24 units of NPH for sugar levels of 45, I was scheduled for an X-ray at the medium security prison. It took them four hours to take X-rays on 12 inmates, which gave me the opportunity to sneak around and make close observations in the hallway inside the locked corridors on both sides. This medium-security prison clinic and all its exam rooms were next to the X-ray room on both sides of the hallway. I noted at least four rooms labeled "Exam Room" on the outside wall, but whenever the staff opened and closed the exam room doors to go in and out, I peeked to see that these exam rooms were actually fancy offices with leather chairs, a desk, computer and printer, book shelves and filing cabinets. There was nothing inside those "exam rooms" that looked like exam rooms equipped to examine patients. I also saw a prison official, a female, seated in front of a computer working in one of these so-called exam rooms.

Then I noted posters on the hallway walls that were placed by JACHO (Joint Accreditation Commission for Healthcare Organizations). They were similar to those seen in hospital corridors that remind healthcare staff of their legal obligations in terms of JACHO's requirements to qualify the healthcare institution for accreditation by the Joint Commission. The first poster read: "Do you know your patients' medications?" The second line read, "Reconciliation of medications is a requirement of the Joint Commission National Patient Safety Goal #8 (Requirement #8)." Then it listed four steps as 1, 2, 3, and 4 for the healthcare staff to ensure such reconciliation. I did not have enough time to write down the exact wording of the four steps as I was writing cautiously, looking both ways to see if any prison official walking by was watching me copy wording from these posters. It was hard enough to scramble for a pencil and paper to write this. Fortunately, one prisoner from the prison camp had a pencil and a piece of paper in his pocket that I was able to borrow. The gist of these four JACHO cautionary steps listed on the poster for the medical staff to obey was to prevent medication errors by following a set sequence of steps to ensure accuracy of dose and correct identification of the patient and the medication before administering it to a prisoner patient.

These observations of the healthcare at the prison catapulted my thoughts into a different mind-set. I wanted to know everything that I could. But I had a problem. If I wrote a bunch of stories I learned in prison, would people believe me? I devised a plan to dig out documentary evidence of this clandestine healthcare system in prison. It was not going to be without risk. I wanted to get third-party documentation from inside the prison, or documents that would speak for themselves, or perhaps prisoners' medical records if I could lay my hands on them without risking too much. Documentary evidence would help me be objective and minimize my own opinion. This meant that I had to find a way to work with chronically ill prisoners incarcerated for a very long time who knew things that no one else knew. Perhaps I could find someone among the prison staff. It would be worth a try, even though it would be dangerous to attempt or even think about. How was I going to pull it off? I had too many barriers in my way. For example, prisoners had been retaliated against whenever they got caught in the past for sharing personal medical information with other inmates. The punishment they had suffered was always solitary confinement. I was told that people had been thrown in a solitary cell for a piece of paper discovered in their lockers that belonged to someone else's medical records. Prison guards routinely searched inmates' lockers every day at random as well as on demand upon suspicion of any forbidden activity. The correction officers searched under prisoners' bed mattresses and in all nooks and corners. Those suspected of banned activities were searched a lot more frequently. And almost every day at least one person was escorted to the hole—it was a rare day that no one went to solitary confinement. Yet on other days, multiple people were noted to be escorted to solitary confinement. Sending people to the solitary confinement was a standard punishment for any and all violations. Just the idea of going into the hole was a terrifying thought for white-collar prisoners and for those who had not yet experienced it but only heard the horror stories of being there. A prisoner was not even allowed to put his hands in his pockets of his working uniform while at work or while roaming around the camp grounds after work hours or on the weekends. The clothing sold at the commissary was designed without pockets, nooks, crevices, or hiding spots, not to mention that sweat suits sold at the commissary were sold at five times the price in the civilian population, the equivalent of an average salary of a prisoner working full-time for five months.

The prison policy manual clearly stated that a prisoner could be sent into solitary confinement for up to 18 months for violating any such rules. Being caught copying a forbidden government document from the prison or copying the private information of other prisoners regardless of consent from the person sharing the information carried the harshest sanctions. I learned that someone had been thrown in solitary confinement for sharing medical records with other prisoners in an attempt to organize a healthcare class action lawsuit against the Federal Bureau of Prisons weeks prior to my arrival at the prison camp. Prisoners were terrified at the idea of sharing any information or even talking about it because they were never sure who was on their side and who was a snitch. So, trust was a huge issue in prison, especially with those who I did not know well enough yet.

One of my bigger problems was that I had a short-term imprisonment. How was I going to have enough time to warm up to prisoners and gain their trust to get them to share their private healthcare records or administrative documents or help me obtain these documents from the prison staff with regard to their own health administrative records? Befriending any of the already very hostile healthcare workers, on the other hand, would be almost impossible because healthcare workers, like the prison guards, were trained to say no to prisoners and refuse to engage in any friendly conversation with a prisoner. Many prisoners knew by now that I was a physician eager to help them with their medical problems the best way I could, but this kind gesture carried only so much weight. I could only tell them what needed to be done, what tests they needed, and what medications they needed, but I could not do anything for them nor could I write a prescription that they could bring to a pharmacy to fill. I only helped them with home-type remedies and healthy lifestyle habits such as weight loss and selective diets to reduce the risk of dying from worsening chronic and terminal medical conditions that they suffered.

The stakes were high for me and for those who took the risk to join me. For me personally, I simply did not want to leave the prison without this valuable inside information that seemed like a well-kept prison secret of the Bureau of Prisons. I knew that in the end, my efforts might not help, but at least I could live with a clear conscience of knowing that I tried everything I could to help leak this secretive information that could potentially lead to public awareness of what goes on in the United States in terms of human right violations and inhumane treatment of prisoners. In my opinion, this information that had been kept secret for so long is far worse than anyone out in the civilian population could conceive of.

I cannot share the full details as to how I pulled off this investigation with the help of prisoners and some nonprisoners. Just know that there are people in this world, including those working for the government, who follow the dictates of their conscience and try to do what is right because they are good-hearted, moral people. I made my moves cautiously, keeping in mind the safety and security of others involved. In the end, I managed to lay my hands on four kinds of documents that I have published in the companion book, *Prison*

*Papers.* This includes patient-related healthcare information and some medical records, but mostly administrative health records that are never seen, even in court cases; prison records that are designated by prison officials as "unreleasable portions" of health records; and sick prisoners' testimonies and affidavits under penalty of perjury and their prison diaries. I also managed to get an internal document of the BOP (DOJ), which was a dangerous step in my investigation. This is an official training manual that reflects the prison culture that lays emphasis on prison officials' training to always say no to inmates for everything, regardless of the prisoner's complaint or grievance; the government's rationale is that prisoners are liars, manipulators, and criminals who cannot be trusted for anything. And it does not matter if you are on the verge of death and asking for help, you are liar.

# SECTION II
# THE TRAIL OF TEARS

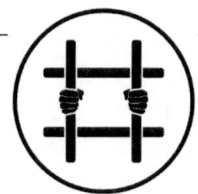

THERE IS NOTHING I CAN SAY TO FULLY JUSTIFY THE TITLE for this section. Trail of Tears refers to a dark event in U.S history with regard to Native Americans, not to mention the unspeakable suffering Native Americans endured at the hands of the settler colonials from Europe, one of the darkest chapters in the history of the human race since the evolution of our species. I would like to briefly explain what caused me to choose this title. One of the things I noted in prison was a disproportionately high numbers of American Indians just as there were very high number of incarcerated African Americans and Hispanics. But the actual event that triggered me to choose this title goes as follows: With my background as a scholar of the history of world religions and cultures, I was very keen in wanting to experience the religious ceremonies of all religious groups in prison. There were about twelve of them from Christians to Muslims, Shia and Sunni to Jews to Mormons, Nation of Islam, Jehovah's Witnesses, and Pagan worshippers and so on. One by one, I attended prayers and ceremonies of all of them with their prior permission. Now it was my turn to attend a ceremony of American Indians in their sweat lodge which I joined in twice. During my second attendance of the ceremony, I saw prison guard, McClinton, walk into their ceremony and destroy their sacred objects in and around the Tepee. He kicked around their sacred stones, sticks, symbols and artifacts. I can say with utmost confidence that this man would not have the guts to do this

49

to any other powerful religious group in prison, such as the Jews or the Muslims. He also kicked me out of the ceremony because he said I was not a Native American, therefore not allowed to participate. When I observed all this, the words, Trail of Tears, came to my mind and I thought to myself, "Trail of Tears continues to this day.", and decided to use this title at the spur of the moment. I could not bear the suffering that I saw prisoners endure at the hands of prison guards and officials, therefore I decided to give this Section the name, The Trail of Tears.

This section holds the stories of prisoners. Some of the stories are prisoners' testimonies and affidavits under oath written in their own words. Others are stories from their history as I put them together from their prison administrative and medical records. I verified the stories written by prisoners by thoroughly comparing them with their prison records to make sure that their stories were accurate and not exaggerations or understatements. Surprisingly, I did not find any exaggerations, but I did find some understatements. I wrote some stories on behalf of those who were unable to write their own or were not willing to write due to the fear of getting caught and then face retaliation. I knit together stories in chronological fashion. I will be redacting the actual names of the prisoners from the original documents that I intend to publish in the companion book, *Prison Papers*, while I have tried my best to spell out the names of the prison officials and guards involved in the stories to expose them publicly in this book, *Prison torture*, which you are holding in your hand. Each prisoner in each of the stories in *The Trail of Tears* is identified with a simple fictitious name.

I do want the American people to know that these prisoners have given me their full written authorization to share their names and their prison records as long as they are used in any form to expose the medical cruelty and the human rights violations in the Federal Bureau of Prisons including for purposes of revealing information to the congress for hearings, the president of the United States, civil rights activists and healthcare activist organizations, independent or governmental investigations, medical case reviews, documentaries, books, book reviews, audiovisual and print media exposure, and any potential class action lawsuits that may result from such exposure. [The exact wording of this consent is published at the end of the book.] The full identity and prisoners' personal data will be made available to prison reform activist organizations, civil rights activists, and public interest lawyers or anyone who is interested in prison reform. Every prisoner in this book whose story is presented was incarcerated due to a nonviolent crime of some sort including mental drug addiction or drug crime. Without expressing any undeserved sympathy for them, I can honestly say that some of these people are decent, compassionate human beings despite the fact that they committed crimes, in some cases minor crimes that landed them in prison. Some of these are not even crimes; they are just mental health issues that our government leaders consider as crimes with the infinite wisdom endowed on them by their God Almighty.

The most important thing to remember, to avoid misunderstanding, while reading these stories is that these stories do not just reflect the Lompoc Federal Prison, the site where the stories were put together. These stories reflect every federal prison in the United States because the prisoners whose stories are described herein have been transferred from one federal prison to another over the years, and they all describe identical medical cruelty practiced in federal prisons nearly everywhere in the United States. These prisoners' stories are firsthand experiences as they faced them in different federal prisons around the country. It is the same prison culture practiced everywhere with a rare exception of a prison healthcare employee who genuinely cares, who would like to help but is not allowed to. Prison healthcare employees who show sympathy will get in serious trouble or be booted out of the system.

So let us begin with the testimony of a 73-year-old prisoner Pete, whose story of bleeding from bladder cancer for five years truly broke my heart. His testimony is published exactly as he wrote it in his own words. I chose to publish his testimony first, not because this is a unique story, but because this prisoner articulated it better than many others.

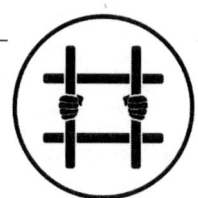

CHAPTER 3

# BLEEDING OF CANCER FOR FIVE YEARS: THE TESTIMONY OF PETE

I WAS ARRESTED ON FEBRUARY 8, 2003 AND WAS transferred to MDCLA [Metropolitan Detention Center in Los Angeles, a federal facility]. One week later, I saw an MD at the MDCLA medical clinic for the first time. Dr. Nicholas Arafiles took my weight and my blood pressure but did not do a physical exam. She put me back on some meds that I had been taking prior to my arrest. I was 56 years old at that time. The physician told me that she would be my primary physician and see me at the Chronic Care Clinic. She was curt with her answer and obnoxious in her manner. She also instructed me to report to Sick Call and inform medical staff of any urgent or emergency needs.

Three months later, I noted blood in my urine for the first time. Accordingly, I reported to the medical Sick Call. The medical staff ordered a blood and urine test but did not give me an appointment with the physician till six weeks later. When I finally saw Dr. Arafiles at the end of June, she told me that the urine test results were not available to discuss. I told her that I was starting to pass more blood in urine since the problem started. She gave me a urine sample canister and instructed me to go to bathroom and urinate in the cup and get it as full as possible. I noted that urine was dark and rusty color, clearly showing blood in it. She suggested to me that it was an isolated incident and probably would vanish. Then she said, "You know [Pete], I am not an expert in such conditions. I am not a urologist." I requested then she should refer me to a urologist. I offered to pay for the cost of visit with the said urologist. Dr. Arafiles said, "It will take a long time to refer you to a urologist and it would be complicated." Then she said, "I don't think you need to see a urologist. I promise you it will go away."

In early July (I do not remember the date), I reported a Sick Call to Dr. Arafiles when she was conducting sick calls in the housing unit. I complained of severe lower back and pelvic pain, something I had never experienced before. She got upset and stated, "You have no medical problems. It is all in your head. If you continue to approach me with these complaints, I will have you placed in the psych ward." I continued to complain of blood in my urine and my belief that complications of pain were associated with my request for a diagnosis and treatment. Dr. Arafiles continued to ignore my requests to see a urologist.

I requested that she, Dr. Arafiles, send me to White Memorial Hospital to be evaluated by a urologist and that I would be willing to pay the cost. In response, the medical staff did not send me to a psych ward but on August 6, 2003, they awakened me at 3:30 a.m. and ordered me to pack my belongings. I packed, and the guard escorted me to R&D (Receiving and Discharge) department at MDCLA. Two hours later, I was transported to San Bernardino County Jail. I arrived there at 11:00 a.m.

During the Medical Screening, Intake Process, a nurse called Ms. Canada took history from me verbally. I told her of all my health conditions including blood in the urine and I requested to be seen by a staff physician. The nurse said that she would make sure that I got the asthma medication that I needed before the next day. I continued to see blood in the urine with intermittent debilitating back and pelvic pain and painful urination.

I filed a series of written and verbal complaints to the medical staff and continued to ask for a treatment over a period of several months. I received a cursory and perfunctory physical and then was suddenly dismissed. No medical report of the physical [was] forwarded to me and no diagnostic test done, nor treatment given, nor a referral for urologist, something I had been requesting since May 2003 and now it was the month of August. I believe to this day that I was transferred from MDCLA to San Bernardino County jail and housed there under inhuman living conditions in a deliberate attempt to deprive me of medical treatment for my condition. This was a concerted effort to obfuscate my urgent medical needs.

On March 12, 2004, Mr. Scalisi. (my retained attorney) filed a motion with the court for Release of Bond in which he also set forth the medical complaints that I described to him. Honorable Judge John Walter assigned the motion to US Magistrate Judge Kenton Victor, who ordered me transferred back to MDCLA. Magistrate Kenton Victor also ordered MDCLA to examine my claimed conditions within 24 hours of my arrival back to MDCLA (unless, he said, the 24-hour period fell on the weekend and a physician was not on duty.) [The] magistrate ordered the warden of MDCLA to provide the court with a report of my medical exam results and a copy of it to my attorney. Court order was directed to the prison warden, Michael Benov, and Dr. Nicholas Arafiles. Both the prison warden and the physician ignored the court order.

It was March 24 when I arrived at MDCLA as per the magistrate's orders. A mid-level practitioner, Jaime Santiago, evaluated me medically in the Intake Screening Medical Exam, which is documented in the form called Medical Record–Chronological Record of Medical Care. The document shows that the condition, blood in the urine, existed but [there] is no mention of any diagnosis or treatment. The document bears a stamp of Dr. Arafiles, which clearly showed that Dr. Arafiles was aware of the hematuria (blood in the urine) but did not do anything about it. Thus, the warden and the physician did not adhere to the court order by Magistrate Kenton Victor.

My pain was becoming excruciating and debilitating. I did not know and was left in the dark as to the extent of how serious my medical condition truly was. I was now routinely passing blood in the urine. Blood in the urine was continuous during my stay at MDCLA and at San Bernardino County. I was never examined by a urologist for 5 years, which is evidenced through my medical records that are available today.

On March 26, 2004, I was transported to the Federal Courthouse in Los Angeles, California, for purpose of bond hearing. During the hearing, Judge Kenton told me that he never received the medical report from the prison warden, Michael Benov, at MDCLA, as per his court order of March 4, 2004. The judge said that he had called the MDCLA Health Services administrator who had informed him that I had arrived back at MDCLA from San Bernardino County on March 25, that MDCLA had not had the time to follow the court order from March 18. There was no exam nor any report from such an exam either then or anytime in the future.

Magistrate Judge Kenton further stated that the Health Services administrator had assured him (Judge Kenton) that the administrator would allocate Dr. Arafiles, my physician, prior to my move to San Bernardino to perform the said exam and prepare a report as I settled back at MDCLA. Medical records show that Dr. Arafiles made an entry on March 29 which was labeled CHRONIC CARE PULMONARY and COURT ORDERED. There is a notation made by Dr. Arafiles, based on my prior medical records. She neither interviewed or examined me for this notation. There is not even a mention of my complaint of blood in the urine. On the reverse side of the MD's note, mid-level practitioner, Santiago, made an entry that stated, "On 2/2004, a condition of hematuria (blood in the urine) existed," but no mention of any treatment or plan for treatment. Thus Dr. Arafiles violated [the] magistrate's order by failing to perform an exam on me. She failed again to refer me to a urologist even after the court order, thus the cancerous tumor (to be discovered later) was permitted to grow for a period of five years inside my bladder. Magistrate Kenton in his Criminal Minutes General Docket entry date of March 26 stated, "Plaintiff is obtaining inadequate medical treatment for his condition at San Bernardino and MDCLA facilities."

I prepared an Inmate Request to Staff, which is commonly known as Cop-Out or Form BP-8 in the federal prison system, on February 21, 2005, and addressed the request to the medical staff supervisor, otherwise known as the Clinical Director who is ultimately responsible for all clinical decisions. My complaint stated: "I am a 56-year-old who had the onset of blood in the urine approximately two years ago. Subsequently, I have had a recurrence of this problem periodically. I have no medical problem that could contribute to this problem. The most recent episode of blood in the urine was one week ago. I kindly request that a urologist evaluation be performed to evaluate the problem. Please ASAP! Thank you." I deposited the document in prison's mail system at MDCLA. I never received any written response, although BOP (Bureau of Prisons) policy requires such a response to all inmate requests via a Cop-Out that is received by any prison staff member. I was never scheduled to see a urologist.

Instead, I was subsequently transferred from MDCLA to yet another facility.

I can't truly describe all the psychological and mental suffering, in addition to the physical pain and suffering, in which I had to needlessly endure because of having an undiagnosed condition of bladder cancer, the tumor that caused me to pass blood through my urine for five years. I was not prepared to deal with such an extremely life-threatening health condition or bladder cancer since I had never been in prison before in my life. It was also embarrassing because everywhere I went in any kind of institutional setting to use the bathroom, someone was always present to observe the blood in my urine. The prison cells in MDCLA are designed to house two inmates and a door that could be closed during lockdown periods. Yet when the cell was locked down, I would hold off urinating until I no longer could bear [it] and only then would I break down to use the toilet. My roommate could see the blood in the toilet bowl and I felt humiliated.

In San Bernardino County Jail, the situation was even worse than MDCLA. Therein the housing units were 73-men open dormitory units, with the toilets and showers being open with full view of anyone within said housing units. There are no partitions between urinals, toilets, or the showers—they are completely exposed to anyone in the area. To urinate, I had to stand there releasing a stream of blood-saturated urine or was forced to sit down to urinate. This was necessary so that I would not be utterly humiliated by everyone watching me urinate blood into the toilet. Even female deputy sheriffs, who routinely worked in the housing units, were able to observe me urinating blood. I am a devout of Jewish faith, and a person from the Middle East who was born in Israel. Accordingly, I have a very strong religious and Middle-Eastern background and customs influence that mandate that Jewish men stand up to urinate and women sit down to do the same. I am still emotionally conflicted about the foregoing issues that I experienced at the hand of Dr. Arafiles and others employed by the FBOP (Federal Bureau of Prisons), ignoring my frequent and urgent pleas for medical help that was ignored with deliberate indifference.

I remained at MDCLA for fourteen (14) months until May 2005. My condition continued to get worse between my court appearance on March 26, 2004, and subsequent transfer. The pain grew consistently more intense and the duration of the pain lengthened in proportion to its intensity. Despite urgent pleas for medical help, protestations, and [my] literally begging to be seen by a urologist (and at my own expense), all requests were unceremoniously denied. The medical staff's stock treatment was issuing me Motrin, hardly a treatment for bladder cancer; nor was any type of relief treatment administered to release me of needless pain and suffering. Further, neither my counsel, the court that gave the order for an exam and a report, nor I, were ever given any type of medical report response to the magistrate judge's order of March 18, 2004.

I was transferred to TAFT Correctional Institute [TCI] in Taft in May 2005 as a result of being sentenced to serve federal prison time. In the custody of the FBOP, I promptly reported to the medical staff members during the Intake Screening that I had history of hematuria (blood in the urine) and concomitant symptoms of pain in the area. I was referred to a physician, Dr. Nduke Odeluga, on June 17, 2005. I reported my symptoms to the physician on my visit. I told him that I suffered from blood in the urine since early May 2003 in addition to lower back and pelvic pain. I also informed the physician that I had been reporting these symptoms to other medical department staff for the previous two years with no treatment forthcoming.

From the time I was transferred to TAFT, and remained therein until April 2006, my physical, emotional, and psychological health continued to decline further downward. This decline in health was spurred by the ever-increasing physical pain and inability to convince the medical department staff (and Dr. Nduke Odeluga) to diagnose my ill-health condition that was causing me so much needless pain and misery.

Dr. Odeluga at TCI saw me as a result of my report of blood in the urine and I reported symptoms to the physician specifically of blood in the urine, pelvic and lower back pain since early May 2003. I also reported to the physician that I had been reporting symptoms to the other medical staff for the past two years with absolutely no relief. During these discussions with Dr. Odeluga, [he] stated: "I don't know what to tell you concerning this issue. I am not an expert in this area. I need to discuss this matter with [the] prison's Health Services administrator to get approved to send you out to see a urologist." Again, there was no appointment made to be evaluated by a urologist. I was given Motrin as usual to mask the pain I was experiencing. The Motrin did not alleviate the pain. In November 2005, I was transferred back to MDCLA.

During my entire time at Taft, and the other institutions, I was not provided with the care and treatment that human decency and modern society demands. I was given perfunctory type of care. Again, after my transfer to MDCLA in November 2005, I was not provided any care or treatment for the underlying condition that caused me to pass blood in the urine, which also caused excruciating lower back and pelvic pain. I suffered like this for five years.

Back at MDCLA, I was evaluated by Dr. Sinavsky, because Dr. Arafiles was not available. I complained to Dr. Sinavsky that I had been passing blood in the urine and having lower back and pelvic pain. Dr. Sinavsky ordered blood and urine tests. These tests did not diagnose the cancerous tumor that was growing inside my bladder that was continuing to get worse. Dr. Sinavsky also showed deliberate indifference to my serious medical needs by not referring me to a urologist.

I was placed back into MDCLA sporadically for a period of five years between February 2003 and March 2008. During this period, I gave at least 6–8 urine tests. I clearly recall at least two of these urine samples were obviously bloody samples to anyone's eye. Yet none of the blood test results were found in the information I obtained when I received copies of my medical records when I was sent to Big Spring, Texas. It appears someone had sanitized the medical records to conceal the fact that blood was present in the urine samples. This fact of concealment has led me to believe that I was maliciously deprived of critically needed medical care treatment by a rogue medical staff that had factually and willfully acted with deliberate indifference. I needlessly endured the cruel and unusual punishment by the FBOP's agents and employees for five years.

In seeking resolution, I had submitted twelve Inmate Requests to Staff Members forms (Cop-Outs or BP-8s) to various medical department staff in various FBOP institutions and prison officials in good faith attempt to informally resolve my complaints. These complaints were specific to the need to be examined by a urological specialist who could perform the test and diagnose my critical health condition. I did not receive a single written response for any of the requests that I had sent to certain staff members and prison officials.

The BOP has specific policies that expect all staff members who receive inmate requests to respond by providing a written response to any request made by an Inmate. FBOP policy also requires that the staff make a good faith attempt to informally resolve all the inmate's complaints at the lowest possible level.

When I returned to Taft Federal Correctional Institute in January 2006, I again reported to Intake Screening medical staff members that I still had blood in my urine. I was scheduled to see Dr. Odeluga. When I saw Dr. Odeluga a week later, I told him once again of the same symptoms that I had before my departure from the institute the previous time. Dr. Odeluga replied, "When I see that it is necessary for you to see a urologist, I will make you an appointment." I said, "What do you mean when it is necessary? It has been three years already, what do you want me to do, fall out on the floor?" In response, Dr. Odeluga said, "If you don't leave right now and go back to your housing unit, I will call the guard, and he will place you in the SHU [solitary confinement]." I complied and departed the medical area for the fear of being punished for seeking medical attention.

I remained in TCI until May 26, 2006. From May 2005 to May 2006, Dr. Odeluga was my primary physician. He would give me only Motrin for lower back and pelvic pain. Through this one year at Taft, I provided two urine samples saturated with blood to the medical staff. And I gave two bloody samples to the nurse in the housing unit where I was confined. And I requested that the nurse deliver those bloody samples to Dr. Odeluga. Dr. Odeluga and I had a previous lengthy discussion about my ill health. Dr. Odeluga stated during the said discussion, "I am not too concerned about it. It is not urgent, because you are not passing blood constantly." The physician also said, "When you have a bloody urine sample, give it to the nurse." I did just that and gave two bloody urine samples in a two-week period. Dr. Odeluga still failed to send me to a urologist.

I was returned to MDCLA on May 26, 2006, and I stayed there till March 2008. During this two-year period, I was deprived of medical care and treatments to address my complaints of blood in the urine and lower back and pelvic pain. I was under the care of different physicians at MDCLA: Dr. Arafiles and Dr. Sinavsky. I could not convince either physician to properly treat me or to make an appointment for me to be examined by a urologist. I repeatedly asked and pleaded that they do these minimum requisite items for my health, and each one of them (Dr. Arafiles and Dr. Sinavsky) had overwhelming medical information and facts in their physical possession (in the form of my medical records) in addition to my verbal statements and complaints, but they refused to help. Any reasonable doctor would have known that I urgently needed to be examined by a specialist.

On December 26, 2006, I again prepared an Inmate Request to Staff Member form and addressed the said document to the Health Services director (clinical director). Within said Request Form/Cop-Out, I again apprised the clinical director of the blood in my urine and the fact that I was not being provided the proper medical treatment that was obviously needed. I was faced to endure pain and suffering for such a prolonged period of time. The continued pain and agony was indescribable, which contributed to the loss of sleep and constant urination from a diminished bladder capacity that a growing tumor was now occupying. I had to urinate frequently and, in addition to losing sleep from constant pain and suffering, I lost sleep from getting up every twenty minutes to an hour to empty my bladder that quickly filled with urine and blood.

In April 2007 (I do not remember the exact date), Dr. Arafiles called me in her office where she checked my blood pressure, weight, height and did asthma test (where I blow into a tube) and checked my heart and lungs. I got the impression that she was going through the motions and a litany of trivial medical procedures and conducting a perfunctory medical interview showing little concern for my well-being and that she wanted to have some type of check-in-the-box to show that she had seen me. Dr. Arafiles simply wanted to vouch my medical record that she clearly was doing something, which was nothing. It was obvious to me that Dr. Arafiles was not going to do anything to actually help me, and just needed something logged into my medical records to show that she "saw me."

Following these perfunctory procedures, Dr. Arafiles and I had lengthy discussion about my heart condition, asthma condition, and the hematuria (blood in urine). Dr. Arafiles ordered more blood and urine tests again. This interview with Dr. Arafiles was on April 26, 2007, which took place months after my December 2006 request form. It took an inordinate amount of time for me to be seen after my Inmate Request to Staff. This blood and urine test ordered by Dr. Arafiles was collected on April 26, 2007.

The blood test results did not diagnose the nature of my critical medical condition that was causing my hematuria and lower back and pelvic pain, in addition to the other ailments that I was experiencing practically all the time at this juncture. The actual cause, a huge cancerous tumor in my bladder, would not be discovered until a later point in time, when I would be sent to another facility that had me examined by a urologist, because she "wasn't an expert in such matters." This condition was saddled upon me unreasonably for a period of four years at this point. I was forced to suffer this prolonged excruciating and unnecessary pain, as well as other forms of suffering, due to the single reason that the FBOP medical staff doctors failed, refused, or neglected to provide medical care within an objective standard of reasonableness, and due to their actions and inactions, permanently injured me.

After enduring the foregoing problems and attitudes from Dr. Arafiles specifically, I requested to switch from the said Dr. Arafiles to Dr. Sinavsky at MDCLA. I was evaluated by Dr. Sinavsky in November 2007 (I am not certain of the exact date). During said evaluation, and initial discussion with the doctor, I described my symptoms, detailing the hematuria and lower back pain that had been afflicting me since 2003 in addition to feeling sick all the time. Dr. Sinavsky reviewed my medical records; I asked him to be examined by a urologist. To this request, Dr. Sinavsky stated, "I don't know what to tell you about the blood in the urine. I will order another set of blood and urine tests and we will go from there." I then stated, "Doctor, check the medical records, and you will see that I have had at least a dozen blood and urine tests done since May 2003. The blood and urine tests have not determined what is wrong with me and making me pass blood. I need to see a specialist, because it is obvious something serious is wrong with me internally. I request that you order that I be scheduled to see a urologist!" Dr. Sinavsky ignored my request. Following my initial session with Dr. Sinavsky in November 2007, I continued to experience the same symptoms that had been complained about since May 2003.

The medical department at MDCLA, and the physicians referenced herein, had me transferred out of MDCLA to yet another facility in March 2008, which they did without diagnosing or treating my ill-health condition. In March 2008, I was suddenly transferred from MDCLA back to

TCI. I was placed in a SHU, where I was confined to a very small room with another mate. Said occupants of the SHU were not allowed to leave the room, nor have the amount of regular inmate privileges that I would have normally had [had] I been placed within the general inmate population that I should have [been] placed within. I remained in the SHU at TCI for about two weeks, and then I was transferred to Oklahoma Federal Transfer Center, wherein I was placed in a general inmate population for about one week (with all my privileges). My destination on this transfer was Federal Correctional Institute (FCI), Big Spring, Texas. I arrived there in March 2008. I immediately reported my symptoms that I had been enduring for five years to the medical staff therein and requested to see a urologist.

Four months later I was finally examined by a urology specialist, Dr. Razzak Jabur—some five years after my initial complaint. The doctor performed a series of tests, including a blood and urine test. The urine was saturated with blood, which the said sample clearly showed. Dr. Jabur performed what he called /referred to as a scoping test. After said test, he had discovered a large tumor inside my bladder. This tumor was pressing against the left side of my bladder wall because, as he told me, "It has been allowed to grow for so long for such an extended period of time." He further ordered a CT scan STAT (immediately) but the CT scan was not performed by prison officials due to "being scheduled for immediate surgery by Dr. Jabur." The doctor performed surgery on July 25, 2008.

The said CT scan would have shown the exact location of the tumor in my bladder. This CT was very important to Dr. Jabur, so when he removed the tumor from inside the bladder, he would not damage the bladder itself. It was apparent to Dr. Jabur that the tumor needed to be removed without further delay. The tumor was so large that it was pressing against the bladder wall, and if it would be allowed to keep growing, it would have invaded (penetrated) the bladder wall, which would have necessitated Dr. Jabur removing the entire bladder.

Due to the urgency of the operation, Dr. Jabur could not have the benefit of the CT scan, which would have allowed him to determine if there were any other tumors in any other internal organs, like the kidney or the liver. According to the urology surgeon, there was a high probability that I had other tumors because the FBOP employee(s) had allowed said tumor to grow for so long and untreated. According to the surgeon, there was a 90% probability that the tumor was cancerous and it was also likely that the cancer had spread to other parts of the body, because it was ignored and not treated for a period of five years. Dr. Jabur did not understand why the prison and medical departments of all these different federal prison institutions had not sent me to be examined by a urologist five year prior. Dr. Jabur stated, "It's unbelievable that your condition went neglected for so long. If a person went to see an eye doctor and you told the doctor that you are passing blood in the urine, the doctor will tell you to go and see a urologist."

Dr. Jabur surgically removed the tumor from my bladder. He was amazed that I didn't lose my entire bladder, since the tumor was the size of a large fist, as he described it to me.

After the surgery, I went through medical treatments called BCG treatments. On pathology, I was diagnosed as having a high-grade carcinoma. This type of cancer, I was told, was associated with very high risk of spread ("movement of cancer cells from the tumor to other parts of the body," as the urologist described it to me).

Now I must endure a life of constant monitoring for any subsequent return of cancer. I am saddled with the fear of the cancer's return, mental anguish (from the past and what is going to happen in the future). Eight years later I am now at Lompoc Prison Camp in Santa Barbara County in California. For one year, I have been suffering from constant tremor in my left hand. An inmate physician has told me that it appears to be the beginning of Parkinson's disease, the "pill rolling motion" being the suggestion of early disease process. I have been asking for an appointment with a neurologist for several months now without any success. It seems that another nightmare has begun, while the old one is not yet over.

Before I (the author) tell you the next horror story, it is vital that I first review the four-tier Administrative Remedy (complaint) Process adopted by the Federal Bureau of Prison policy in a bit more detail. BP-8 is the first-level grievance that refers to the inmate submitting a written request to prison staff for an informal resolution, which the prison policy encourages to be filed electronically through an internal email system set up for the prisoners primarily for this purpose as well as to refill their medications (in preference to handwritten or typed complaints). The BP-9 refers to the second-tier level of seeking remedy, which is a complaint written directly to the prison warden.

If the issue remains unresolved, a prisoner may file BP-10 (third-tier level), which is an appeal to the regional director of the Bureau of Prisons in the region of the country where the federal inmate is incarcerated. The prisoner, however, is not allowed to write a BP-10 directly to the regional director. The complaint to the regional director must be first scrutinized by the warden and deemed appropriate for forwarding to the regional director. As a last resort, a prisoner may file a complaint to remedy the situation at the highest (fourth-tier level) by writing his complaint to the General Counsel, Washington, DC, Federal Bureau of Prisons. With a proper background about this system in mind, let me now tell you the story of Noah.

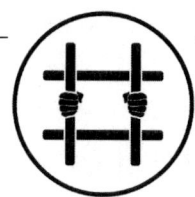

## CHAPTER 4

# ON THE BRINK OF DIALYSIS: THE STORY OF NOAH

NOAH IS A 36-YEAR-OLD MAN WHO HAS BEEN A TYPE I brittle diabetic since a very young age. This inmate's story is very simple, but also very disturbing. For two and a half years (from the date of his incarceration in June 2014 to October 2016, when I was released), he sought urgent medical attention for his failing kidneys, severe diabetes, and many other medical problems; he never received it. I am unable to tell you Noah's story in prison after October 2016 because I was released from the prison and lost touch with him and my sources. I can, however, give you a summary of his two and half years of pain and affliction to show you how prison authorities brutalized him.

Noah was on the verge of kidney failure when I first met him. After imploring the prison officials and the prison doctor for help for five months through verbal requests and Sick Calls and waiting at the clinic door for hours, Noah finally submitted his first written complaint to the Department of Justice, Federal Bureau of Prisons on December 3, 2014. In this official complaint, he explained that his medical complaints of kidney pains and swollen feet had not been addressed for five months and that the nurse at the clinic told him that the clinic didn't have any medical staff to see him.

In a written response to his written complaint, the prison officials advised him to "attend Sick Call for next available treatment," which the inmate did right away, but still no one attended to his medical ailments. On January 6, 2015, Noah wrote another complaint to the Federal Bureau of Prisons of the Department of Justice in which he explained that his legs had been swollen for six months due to kidney failure and now he was constantly urinating blood. He also described the difficulties of eating due to the lack of medications that he was supposed to be on as a result of the gastric bypass surgery that he had prior to his incarceration. He requested medications. In response, the correction counselor and the unit manager advised him to attend a Sick Call or else proceed with official administrative remedy process called BP-9 (which is a direct appeal to the prison warden). Accordingly, Noah again attended a Sick Call, and the only nurse present at the Sick-Call Clinic did not know what to do with him. Nothing was done.

Noah wrote a direct complaint to the prison warden (BP-9) on January 8, 2015, in which he explained that he had attended Sick Calls four times in one month and nothing was done for him. The prison warden in his official response to his complaint on January 21 listed all the medical illnesses and medical complaints of the prisoner, which he copied from the prisoner's written complaint, followed by the words, "but you don't request any specific relief." The warden claimed that his review of the inmate's medical chart showed that his medical problems were being addressed in several "chronic care clinics" in prison "for continuity and follow-up care." The warden claimed that the medical chart also showed that he had been "seen in Sick Calls on numerous occasions." The chart, according to the warden, also showed that the inmate had been prescribed medications for his hypertension and polyneuropathy and a follow-up appointment was already made with "a physician." The warden concluded his entire response by stating: "Accordingly, this response is provided for information purposes only. If you are not satisfied with this reply, you may submit an appeal on an appropriate form (BP-10) to the regional director within 30 days of the date of this response."

On February 13, Noah filed a Regional Administrative Remedy Appeal (BP-10) to the western region's director of the Bureau of Prisons. In his complaint, Noah stated that he needed medical attention and his medications and he was being ignored by the prison officials. In response, the inmate received a Remedy Appeal Rejection Notice on April 9 from the Penitentiary's Administrative Remedy Appeal Coordinator, an employee of the prison warden, explaining why his Regional Appeal could not be forwarded to the regional director of the Bureau of Prisons. The reason given was that Noah's appeal was "untimely." The rejection notice asked the prisoner to bring proof from the prison staff to demonstrate that his "untimely filing" (exceeding the 20-day deadline) was not his fault. Six days later, on April 15, Noah received the following notice from the Department of Justice, Federal Bureau of Prisons clinical director of the prison's Health Services department: "Your procedure/consult for radiology (kidney scan) has been disapproved."

Now ten months into Noah's incarceration, after the prison refused to forward his BP-10 request to the regional director of the western region of the Federal Bureau of Prisons, he was left with no choice but to start the remedy process (under prison policy) over again, starting with first-tier complaint level, a BP-8. On April 28, the inmate wrote a BP-8 to the prison staff in which he stated that his medical problems had gotten much worse and requested transfer to a Level III medical facility to which the prison staff responded, "Noah, Health Services Staff was contacted regarding your concerns."

On April 30, he submitted another first-tier Inmate Request to the Staff, Bureau of Prisons, and demanded a copy of all his medical records. He insisted that his medical records (based on which the prison warden had claimed in his response that the inmate was receiving appropriate medical care) and copies of all his Sick-Call slips be immediately released to his private county doctors located outside the prison: Drs. Snell and Martinez, who had also been requesting those records. The prison staff did not respond to Noah's request for release of his prison medical records.

On May 14, Noah submitted a written Sick-Call Request that stated: "The bottom of my feet has been hurting due to neuropathy and diabetic ulcers. I feel like I have nails pinching me. Also, my ears hurt, both left and right. My feet won't let me sleep. They wake me up due to pain."

In response to his request for this Sick Call and his persistent demand for the release of his medical records and copies of his Sick-Call slips to his private physicians, the prison's clinical director gave him a ray of hope on May 14, stating: "Your Radiology Consultation is Approved"—something Noah had been requesting for a long time to assess the deteriorating function of his kidneys. But there was no radiology consultation done after this "approval." Three and a half months later, on August 28, when the prisoner was starting to lose hope that this approved radiology test would actually occur, the clinical director of the prison sent him another ray of hope by once again sending him a similar notice as before that said, "Your Radiology Consult is Approved." Once again, there was no action taken after this second approval—that is, no test was performed; he didn't even receive a radiology consultation.

Noah was back to square one to start the Remedy Process all over again starting with the lowest tier level, BP-8. He could not have moved on from his BP-8 of April 30 to the next level appeal of BP-9 due to the missed deadlines imposed by the prison policy (all deadlines missed due to false hopes of these official "radiology consultation approvals"). On October 1, Noah commenced the remedy process again with another Request to the Staff (BP-8), which stated that he had broken skin and the blood was coming out of the broken skin on his arms and legs. He explained that he was at high risk for infection due to his diabetes but he had still not received any medications. He asked to be seen by a specialist. He again insisted that his medical records and written records of all his written Sick-Call requests be released to all parties involved, including his physicians outside the prison (a release for which he had already authorized the prison in writing many times).

Between January 1 and May 16, 2016, Noah submitted six emergency Sick-Call requests when his symptoms became intolerable, which included blood in urine, sleeplessness, tremendous itch on the skin, bleeding and pain on the soles of his feet, and legs swelling. He received no medical attention to any of these written Sick-Call requests he delivered to the healthcare workers at the prison clinic.

Having failed all options, Noah wrote a letter to the prison warden on May 24 in which he requested that he be given access to his own primary care doctor outside the prison by transferring him to a halfway house or placing him in home confinement. He waited for a response from the warden. Having received no timely response, he started submitting multiple Sick-Call requests, one after another. The Sick-Call Request form had a questionnaire that asked, "How long you have had this problem since being in prison?" to which he replied "2 years."

In another Request to the Staff, on June 21, Noah charged (and this time the request was typed out by a correctional counselor) that the prison had refused to issue him gabapentin, the only medication that worked for his neuropathy. On July 5, prison officials responded to his request stating: "Contact was made with AHSA (Assistant Health Services Administrator), Ms. Pinnell. She stated your matter was being looked into. If you are not satisfied with this response, you are advised to proceed with the Administrative Remedy process."

Between June 24 and July 8, Noah filed two more Sick-Call requests in which he emphasized that now it had been two years and two months since he reported these problems to the prison and nothing had been done. After going in full circle, having exhausted all means including administrative remedy efforts, appeals, letters to the warden, medical records requests, requests to staff, and innumerable Sick-Calls requests, he started the Administrative Remedy Process all over again—this time starting with BP-9 because all his BP-8 requests had been basically ignored. He filed a BP-9 on July 27 stating that he was still waiting for his medication, gabapentin, that was prescribed by his own physician outside the prison and then requested that he be given home confinement if the prison was unable to address his medical issues. The prison warden rejected Noah's request, stating, "You are appealing two different issues" and "You need to file them separately."

On July 29, Noah resubmitted the two Administrative Remedies (two separate requests for these "two different" issues) as required by the warden's Rejection Notice—one for not receiving his medications and the other, a request for transfer to a halfway house or to home confinement so he could receive medical care on his own. On the same date, July 29, Noah also put in an Emergency Sick Call to the warden that stated: "Problems with my skin, kidneys and feet, in need of treatment ASAP. And medications." He answered the Sick-Call questionnaire by stating that he now had this problem for well over two years and two months in prison. The only response Noah received from the prison was a receipt for his Administrative Remedy Request BP-9.

At this point, a low-ranking, kind-hearted employee at the prison clinic suggested to Noah that he write a direct and a personal letter to the prison warden outlining a timeline of his complaints ever since his incarceration to appeal to the warden's conscience. As a result of this advice, on August 4, Noah wrote a letter to the warden, copied the assistant warden, and attached a cover letter. This letter meticulously stated all the events of negligence of medical care, in a precise chronological fashion, with all events and episodes accurately described by him step by step, date by date. (His timeline story matches the chronology of events as manifest from his prison documents published in *Prison Papers* under his fictitious name, Noah with his actual name redacted.) This timeline letter to the warden summarized the history of prison violations and the medical cruelty the prisoner had been subjected to for more than two years and two months to that point.

On August 23, Noah filed a BP-10, an Administrative Remedy Appeal to the regional director of the Bureau of Prisons, the US Department of Justice. (A BP-10 is the next tier level remedy if a BP-9, Request to the Prison Warden, falters.) In this BP-10, he explained to the regional director that he submitted "specific complaints separately" to the warden as required by the warden's rejection notice, but he had not received any assistance in getting his medications and the critical medical care he so desperately needed. The prisoner included all of his correspondence with the prison warden and the supporting historical documentation.

Noah received a response from the assistant warden on August 29 in which the assistant warden said that he would not address Noah's issues because the prisoner had written the same letter to the warden. The assistant warden "encouraged" him to "patiently wait" for a response from the warden.

On September 8, Noah started another cycle of the Administrative Remedy Process beginning from the lowest tier level (BP-8, Inmate Request to Staff) in which he jogged the prison officials' memory that he had to be taken to the hospital for emergency due to the prison's negligence. He reminded them that he was admitted to the hospital for nonstop vomiting of blood on September 5. The attending physician at the hospital, Dr. Reimer, explained to Noah that his kidney function had deteriorated, and therefore his kidneys were in "critical condition." Dr. Reimer had recommended that Noah see a kidney specialist immediately and warned that the lack of care would immediately require dialysis. In his Inmate Request to Staff, Noah provided the prison officials the contact for Dr. Reimer, who he requested that the prison officials get in touch with for any questions. The prison officials ignored this complaint.

On September 20, the prison officials, in a written notice to the prisoner, refused to forward Noah's Regional Appeal to the regional director's office, which he had filed on August 23. (The prisoner's Request to the Regional Office must go through the prison warden; an inmate is not allowed to file it directly to the regional office.) The reason given for rejection was that the prisoner must first wait for a response from the warden. It said nothing as to when such a response would come, or if it were to come at all.

One thing I, the author, discovered during my investigation of several cases is that the prison officials always, without exception, conceal the fact from the prisoners that they are actually allowed (as per prison policy) to file for BP-10 if the prison warden defaults in not meeting the stipulated deadline for response. This part of the prisoner's legal right under Title 28 is deliberately removed from the prison policy in the prison manual, which is the only document the inmates are ever provided only once upon their initial arrival into the prison.

After this merry-go-around of the Administrative Remedy Appeal process twice, Noah wrote an extensive letter to Senator John Campbell from his hometown district in California in which he stated how he had failed to get any medical help from the prison. He made the senator aware of "obfuscation and delay tactics" that the prison was engaged in to deny him healthcare.

Finally, two months later, on September 26, the prison warden wrote a fill-in-the-blanks response. (There is an extensive discussion in "Reminiscent of War Crimes: Sisyphean Remedies" on the nature and character of these fill-in-the-blank responses from the warden in all medical cases of federal prison patients—a must read.) The warden's response stated that based on his review of Noah's medical records, all his medical problems were being taken care of including the fact that he had been given appointments with "a specialist, pending scheduling" and an appointment with "a medical officer, pending scheduling." Then the warden ended his response as usual, stating: "Accordingly, your request for Administrate Remedy is for Informational purposes only. If you are not satisfied with the reply, you may submit an appeal on the appropriate form (BP-10) to the regional director within 20 calendar days of the date of this response." Noah received this response from the prison warden on September 26, 2016.

I do not know if Noah had any luck in getting any medical care after this date because I was released from the prison and lost touch with him and all of the other inmates I was working with to gather their stories. In the last month of my time at this prison, I met with many prisoners who had written to their congressmen, senators, the surgeon general, and many high ups in the government over the years, even decades, in some cases providing clear evidence of prison abuse and violation of their basic civil rights. I only found one case when a politician responded to the prisoners' pleas for help: that of a rich celebrity inmate who got chemoradiation for his metastatic prostate cancer upon direct intervention by the congressman from his district due to tremendous pressure from his influential family. This speaks volumes about the establishment politics of our government representatives who work only for the wealthy that rule our country.

The next story is the story of a 53-year-old African American male suffering from a familial form of prostate cancer incidentally diagnosed in prison. The inmate has pleaded for help month after month and year after year with no signs of help in the future.

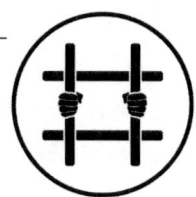

CHAPTER 5

# LIVING WITH PROSTATE CANCER: LIAM'S TESTIMONY

INMATE LIAM IS A 53-YEAR-OLD MAN WHO WAS FOUND TO have prostate cancer while in prison, a familial form of cancer that his father died of at the age of 54. He reluctantly and gradually shared with me some of his prison documents that corroborate his testimony, which I could not manage to get out of the prison, but I did manage to read them all and write this summary (see *Prison Papers* under this inmate's fictitious name, Liam). Liam was terrified of retaliation from prison officials if he shared his records with me or discussed his medical issues, as he put it. Finally, on August 29, 2016, he wrote the following testimony after a lot of persuasion.

I put in requests for Sick Calls for two months between August 2015 and October 2015. Finally, I was seen by Dr.

Girone who informed me that my PSA (prostate antigen) levels were very elevated, suggestive of cancer and that I needed to see a urologist within 30 days. I spoke with Ms. E. who does the scheduling. She informed me that I was on the list. I did not see urology till 4/21/16 nearly six months after my request. At that time, the urologist did a biopsy and the results showed that I had prostate cancer.

On August 20, 2016 [four months after the diagnosis and a year after the original Sick-Call requests], I was scheduled for a follow up with urology and I went, but the urologist could not explain the biopsy results to me because he said he had not received medical records of prostate biopsy results from the Health Services at the prison, so he could not tell me how serious my cancer was and what needed to be done. This appointment was a waste of time because he did not have a copy of my pathology report to discuss it.

As of today, August 29, I am still waiting to see the urologist to explain to me the biopsy results. Since April 29 of this year, for 4 months now, I have spoken to Mr. Gene Carrasca who oversees Health Systems Administration, prison warden Steve Langford, the Regional Medical Director, Dr. Pelton, correctional counselor Mr. Zepeda, and the Assistant Health Services Administrator, Ms. Pinnell with no results.

I reviewed the prison documents of Liam and noted the same type of prison abuse that I noted in Pete's testimony and Noah's story described earlier. A clear pattern of mental torture, deadly neglect, and medical cruelty of prisoners now started to clearly emerge in the course of my investigation. Liam's mother, Ms. A.J.J., was directly involved in his case and she spoke with Ms. R., the western regional director of Medical Services of the Federal Bureau of Prisons, on the phone and in writing. The prisoner did everything he possibly could in order to have his medical records released to his mother. The inmate also put in numerous emergency (911) Sick-Call requests to the prison clinic with no results. He was also approved to be approved and scheduled to be scheduled, to be seen by the urologist in this obfuscation game and was yet to be seen by a urologist for a follow-up on the day I left the prison months later. He also requested that he be transferred to the federal prison's Butner Medical Facility where cancer cases were treated, but his appeals bore no results. His documents show a never-ending series of requests and appeals to the prison staff that met with a dead end.

In my experience, there are two possible outcomes that prisoners with malignant cancer face. One outcome is no treatment at all, which means that they would eventually die in prison from the metastasis of malignant cancer, and the cause of the death will be kept a secret. No such death occurred during my own short stay at the camp but I heard of cases that are totally believable based on what I saw happening in front of my own eyes. If a prisoner is proactive, very persistent, and optimistic and knows how to write and barrage the prison officials with complaint after complaint, he stands a chance of much delayed sub-optimal treatment, which could still lead to his unnatural early death because the treatment was too late. I saw many cancer patients in prison who do not even bother to seek help because they have learned from other inmates that going to the prison clinic will be in vain. The day I left the prison to go into house arrest, Liam's life was still hanging in the balance despite his family's aggressive involvement at all levels of the bureaucracy of the Federal

Bureau of Prisons from local to regional levels to Washington DC. I will never know what the end point is going to be for any treatment for Liam's cancer.

Please allow me to make some general comments about the observations that I made while reviewing Liam's prison records as a professional physician trained to read medical records. I noted for the first time that any emails by prisoners written directly to any outside government authorities are not just blocked by the prison officials but also permanently deleted from the prison-controlled email system sixty days later. In my review of several hundred prisoner emails, I also noted that the electronic email requests for informal resolution of their grievances are rarely answered by prison officials. You have a better chance of winning a 100-million-dollar state lottery than to receive a response from the internal email system set up for prisoners' grievances. I noted only two examples where the prison staff had actually responded to a prisoner's electronic email queries. Liam was one of those people who received an email response from the staff.

BP-8s that are handwritten by inmates are a bit more likely to elicit response despite the fact that the prison officials and the prison policy emphasizes that prisoners file grievances through electronic requests to staff; however, all electronically filed BP-8s are ignored. There is a clear reason for this discrepancy. Prison officials have total control over the electronic requests. They can delete any evidence of an electronic request made at any time and wipe out the proof that a request was ever made, whereas they know that a prisoner is more likely to hold on to a photocopy of the written request that he made prior to submitting it. Therefore, ignoring all written requests would be a risky proposition for a potential lawsuit that might ensue in the future. This also explains why the BOP encourages filing complaints electronically, because it is easier for prison officials to get rid of them quickly by just pressing the Delete key. That is all it takes to provide medical care in the prison, DELETE.

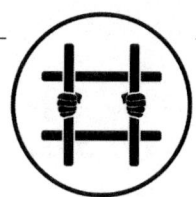

CHAPTER 6

# STROKE, HEART ATTACK, EPILEPSY, AND BLINDNESS: THE STORY OF MASON

THIS IS THE STORY OF A 61-YEAR-OLD INMATE, MASON. I asked him to write a testimony for me, but despite his willingness and strong desire to do it, he was unable to because of his terrible health condition. He had gone nearly blind in both eyes while in prison due to the denial of treatment. Mason's physicians had warned the prison officials before he self-surrendered to the prison on January 7, 2016, that he would soon go completely blind if he did not receive continued treatment for his eye condition, but he was ignored. He lost more than 90 percent of his vision with total blindness in one of his eyes.

Mason asked me to write his story based on his prison records that he helped me obtain from the prison authorities. He also gave me the documents that he had saved in his locker. His medical history was a part and parcel of his Presentence Report filed with the Bureau of Prisons by the Sentencing Court ahead of his surrender to the prison. This court document, however, was ignored by the prison doctors and the prison officials. I discovered that ignoring such court orders for appropriate medical placement of prisoners is a routine practice by the Department of Justice, Federal Bureau of Prisons. It violates these court orders, not frequently, but always. I knit together the following story for Mason based on my review of his prison health records published in *Prison Papers* under his fictitious name, Mason, with the actual name redacted, for those of you who would like to fact-check the following narrative.

Among Mason's medical records, the Straub Clinic and Hospital in Hawaii had submitted to the prison a letter prior to Mason's self-surrender that he had a history of detached retina, glaucoma, and atrophy of the optic nerve. The visual loss in his left eye was already irreversible; therefore, preserving the remaining vision in the other eye (right eye) was vital. Among other medical records and letters submitted by a professor of neurology from the University of Hawaii, John Burns School of Medicine, was the explanation that Mason had a diagnosis of localization-related (focal) partial epilepsy and epileptic syndrome with complex partial seizures with intractable epilepsy. The physician also submitted the names and doses of the medications that Mason must continue to receive to reduce the frequency of the unpredictable nature of his epileptic seizures.

Mason's prison records show that on January 16, nine days after his incarceration began, he experienced an absence seizure twice, which locked his fingers, ankles, and toes. After recovering from the seizures, the day after, the inmate brought this matter to the attention of the prison's nurse and the physician in a written Inmate Request to Staff (BP-8). The nurse ignored him, and the physician stated that the prison did not have the capability to manage his condition. Mason urged that if he did not receive his seizure medications, he would be hospitalized and could die. The correctional counselor Mr. Zepeda told him: "Give it time. You are in a prison and you cannot be on medical watch."

A week later, Mason submitted a written request to the prison authorities for the release of his medical records and a copy of the prison physician's medical note evaluation of his medical conditions. The week after, he made another written request (BP-8) for the release of his medical records in which he stated, "This is my second written request." He also explained that the food service was refusing to give him diabetic bread because they said that he did not carry a diabetic card to prove that he was on insulin. He requested a diabetic card.

A senior federal public defender from the District of Hawaii, Ms. Shanlyn A.S. Park, was informed about this through Mason's family and wrote a letter to the prison warden, Mr. Langford, on behalf of the inmate on January 27 in which she listed all the serious medical ailments from which Mason suffered such as seizures, stroke, hypertension, hyperlipidemia, diabetes, inequilibrium in walking due to stroke, invisible blindness, and major depression and then listed over a dozen medications that he was supposed to be on daily. Ms. Park informed the warden that she had learned from Mason's family about the medical cruelty in that the prisoner was not receiving his medications. The defender ended the letter to the prison warden by stating:

> As I am sure you are aware, a court may release a term of imprisonment if, after considering the factors set forth in 18

U.S.C. § 3553 (a), the court finds that "extraordinary and compelling reasons warrant such a reduction." And that "such a reduction is consistent with applicable policy statements issued by the Sentencing Commission." These reductions are available only "upon motion of Director of Bureau of Prisons," rather than "upon motion of the defendant as under 18 U.S.C. § 3582 (C) (2).

Given [Mason's] serious medical conditions, I would ask you to exercise your authority, pursuant to 18 USC § 3553 (A), and file a motion for compassionate release. If you are not willing to file such a motion, I respectfully request that BOP consider transferring [Mason] to a federal medical facility, as was recommended in his court Judgement, which is enclosed for your review.

The public defender attached a copy of this court order with Mason's letter to the warden of which the original was already in the possession of the warden, which he had apparently ignored as per prison's unwritten policy.

On January 17 and then again on January 28, Mason made electronic requests (BP-8s) to the camp manager, Mr. Garrastazu regarding his ongoing seizure episodes. He stated that his fingers curled into a locked position and one or both of his ankles and toes locked into an upward position. When the seizures subsided, he was then faced with trying to straighten out his hands and feet for hours. Mason also quoted the prison physician, Dr. Dhaliwal who told him that he (Mason) did not belong in prison and that he should be in home confinement under the care of his primary care doctor, neurologist, ophthalmologist, and other specialists. Mason also mentioned that his medical records had not been released despite several written requests made by him, records that he wanted to forward to his physicians back home. Mr. Garrastazu, the camp manager claimed that he took Mason's written request for release of medical records and stated that it would be forwarded to Health Services. But Mason never received a response from Health Services.

A month later, on February 20, Mason wrote a letter to the warden, Mr. Langford, in which he requested a Call-Out to discuss the medications that the prison had prescribed him in comparison to the numerous medications and doses that Dr. Holt, his primary care doctor, and Dr. Kore Liow, his neurologist, had prescribed to him. He complained that his medical issues had been ignored.

The prison warden, in his written response, stated that Mason had been put on the Call-Out with the clinical director, Dr. Lin. But since Dr. Lin was not available for two weeks, he should "report to Sick Call if he needed immediate attention" or "notify the healthcare staff." Mason wrote back to the warden: "Thank you. I will check the Call-Out List daily." He attended several Sick Calls after this point but no one paid any attention to his complaints. All Sick-Call requests were ignored.

Another month went by. Nothing was done. He was not put on the Call-Out list with Dr. Lin as he was promised nor did he ever hear from Health Services. On March 22, Mason submitted a BP-8 to the staff in which he stated, "This is my third electronic BP-8. I am out of my medications. No one ever responds." He stated that he was promised a diabetic card but he never received one. Instead, when he asked for the card, the food service told him, "we do not believe inmates; they are liars." He explained that he had reminded the health staff at the pill-line over and over again about his medications, and he was always told that he must fill his medications online electronically, using Trulincs, the prison's internal email system set up for prisoners. He kept making these online requests for medications but they were never given to him, no matter how many electronic requests he made.

During my investigation of many other cases in prison, I discovered that the food services does not have diabetic food nor diabetic cards. It is just a game that they play with the diabetic inmates and others who need a special diet for medical reasons. This is despite the fact that prison policy requires the prison to have special diets available for prisoners with certain medical conditions such as diabetes and Crohn's disease. In the case of inmate Kingsley, which is discussed later in this book, I discovered that the prison doctors and officials also had a universal and common practice of lying to the court that they were giving a special diet to all prisoners with special medical conditions.

Mason wrote another BP-8 to prison staff on March 25 in which he attached copies of his five previous inmate requests to Health Services. He traced a history of denial of his medications and stated that the prison had broken all its promises to have him called out to see Dr. Lin, to give him medications, a diabetic card, and so on.

Two weeks later, on April 5, the correctional counselor typed another complaint by Mason—his seventh Inmate Request in three months—in which she typed out his claim that he had made numerous attempts to get the Health Services to address his major-medical issues pertaining to having epileptic seizures and he was out of his major medications and was given no reason for the denial of medications. In response to his complaint, the counselor and the unit manager spoke with the healthcare staff and then advised Mason accordingly. They informed him that he must report to Sick Call as per Health Services if he cared to get his medications. They further advised him that according to the healthcare staff, he was "required to report to Sick Call in order to be medically assessed by a doctor concerning his medical issues." Mason informed the counselor that he had been going to Sick Calls and the pill-call line clinic day after day after day and nothing was done, but the counselor's answer was the same: "You must report to Sick Call."

The week after April 12, Mason filed the next level of remedy appeal to the warden (BP-9) in which he informed the warden that he had presented his medical problems to the medical staff on several occasions (and he attached eight previous written appeals) and yet he was still waiting for proper medical treatment with the proper doses of his seizure medications. He stated that he was out of his most important medications. He also complained about what the healthcare staff at the clinic had told him (a lower-level healthcare worker had told him the truth by a slip of his tongue) which was: "You may not see a neurologist because you're here only for two years of a short sentence."

I personally learned in my investigation that a prisoner did not have a chance to see a specialist in prison unless he was going to be in prison for a very long time, from 5 to 20 years, and that is only if it became ridiculously apparent to the prison officials through the inmate's emergency hospitalizations that the prisoner had a life-threatening condition that could and would kill him for sure, without a doubt. But if you are in prison only for a few years, your life-threatening condition will kill you because you would be on some kind of obscure waiting list that could take longer than your life expectancy in prison.

Having received no response from the prison warden to the letter that the office of the Federal Public Defender, District of

Hawaii, wrote to the Lompoc Prison warden on January 27, the defender, Ms. Park wrote her second letter to the Lompoc Prison warden on April 14—after waiting for four months for a response. This letter was sent to the prison scheduler, Ms. D.D., and a copy was sent to the warden, Mr. Langford. In this letter, the defender requested the prison to allow her to set up an attorney–client phone call with her client, Mason. The defender stated that she had been trying to set up this call with her client but the prison authorities had not been helpful, and therefore she was renewing her request in writing for an attorney–client phone meeting for the second time. She made suggestions for different hours of the day from Monday to Friday and then offered the prison to pick any time of convenience to make this attorney–client phone call possible. The public defender did not receive a response from the warden nor from the prison scheduler.

Meanwhile, Mason wrote an appeal to the prison warden on April 19 but did not receive a response in 20 days, as expected per prison policy. The prisoner filed another BP-8 on May 9 written to the healthcare administrator of the prison. It was entitled, "Sick Call – Urgent." In this letter to the health administrator, Mason informed him that he went to an emergency Sick Call and was told by Ms. Blitch, the nurse, to "come tomorrow because the Sick-Call schedule is full today." He explained that he was denied Sick Call even though he had visited Sick Call just after suffering a massive seizure in the chow hall where he had to be resuscitated with CPR and paddles followed by an ambulance taking him to the hospital. The fact that Mason had CPR and was resuscitated with defibrillators and then transported to Lompoc Valley Medical Center via ambulance did not qualify him for a Sick Call; he was shocked at this. He had gone to

STROKE, HEART ATTACK, EPILEPSY, AND BLINDNESS

the clinic because he was starting to see his vision going in and out in his right eye after this loss of consciousness along with starting to experience paralysis in the right side of his body, causing him to suspect another stroke. Mason warned the health administrator that he was already blind in his left eye and that if he lost all sight in his right eye as well, he would be completely blind. Those factors should have been good enough for the health staff at the Sick-Call Clinic to consider him sick enough to be seen by the nurse at the Sick Call. (Please note that I have dedicated an entire chapter to the topic of Sick Calls; see Chapter 20: The Sick-Call Scam.)

Having been barraged with requests from the public defender for a phone meeting with her client and now this hospitalization due to a potential stroke, seizure, or heart attack, the prison warden finally decided to write a response to Mason on May 18 to address his multiple appeals. In his response, the warden stated that based on his review of Mason's records, he was receiving all his medications, and he had been "approved to be seen by the neurologist" (subject to scheduling). When I reviewed this response written by the warden, it became clear to me that the warden had perjured himself based on the fact that the one and the only physician seeing patients in prison, Dr. Dhaliwal, had told Mason point blank multiple times that the facility was not equipped to provide him any care for his complicated medical problems, but the warden in his response made it look like Mason was being well taken care of in prison in multiple specialty clinics and receiving fabulous medical care. The warden contradicted everything that the prison physician had told Mason. The warden's response, as usual, ended with exactly the same words as in every single warden response in every single case I ever reviewed: "This response is for informational purposes only. If you don't like the response, go ahead and appeal to the regional director for Administrative Remedy BP-10."

After seven months of letters and phone calls from the Federal Public Defender of the District of Hawaii, the warden finally decided to write back to the public defender as well. When I reviewed this response, I noted this as another classic response (similar to the responses given to other inmates) written in a fill-in-the-blank format crafted by the warden's staff and based on manufactured medical records and a bogus history of having provided medical care to the inmate. I found this to be the case by reviewing and then comparing the warden's response with the actual medical history of Mason (There is an extensive discussion on this topic in Chapter 18, Manufacturing of Medical Records.) In their responses, the prison wardens at different federal prisons rely on medical records manufactured by the Health Services staff with the full approval and knowledge of the wardens. The medical records always show to an untrained eye that excellent care is being provided to all sick patients in the penitentiary. All are typical responses from all wardens of all prisons. Their response letters look like a product coming out of the same factory and the same machine, dressed and packaged in a similar style, written in legal language, but deprived of any truth whatsoever.

In his response to the public defender, the warden told her everything she wanted to hear to make the attorney–client meeting look redundant and unnecessary. He stated in his response written on July 11 that the public defender's client (Mason) was being "seen in Six Chronic Clinics" for "follow-up and continuity of care." (Recall Noah's story in which the warden made the same claim that Noah was being seen in these several specialty chronic care clinics at the prison.) Then the warden informed the public defender that all her "client's chronic medical conditions were at the treatment goals." In other words, prison healthcare staff was on top of it and that there was nothing for the public defender to worry about, because his client was receiving state of the art medical care.

Having read such a convincing letter from the prison warden, the public defender was speechless and was probably convinced that her client's medical conditions were being addressed properly at the prison. The public defender immediately wrote to Mason in prison:

Dear Mason

Enclosed is a July 11, 2016, letter I received from warden, Steve Langford, in response to our request for compassionate release or transfer to a medical facility. It appears your medical needs have been addressed; however, if you need further assistance in this regard, please contact me.

I hope you are doing better and have not had any further serious medical issues. Take care.

Sincerely

Shanlyn A. S. Park

Senior Litigator, Office of Public Defender/District of Hawaii

Mason received this letter from his public defender on July 29 and he immediately responded to the defender the very next day with a written letter, which stated:

The "Six Chronic Care Clinics" warden makes mention in his reply is erroneous. I have not seen any of these "clinics" anywhere. I have never seen any of the physicians in the "Six Clinics"—all we have here is a pill-line clinic run by a nurse. I have seen the facility doctor only ONCE ever since I became incarcerated on January 7, 2016. My prescriptions have not been refilled or adjusted nor have they discussed any adjustment of seizure medications with me. I had filed several BP-8s and BP-9s regarding my medical concerns and the replies have all stated that I am being treated accordingly and perfectly.

When I was taken to Lompoc Valley Medical Facility on April 24, 2016, after collapsing at the institution; resuscitated with paddles followed by CPR and then transported by ambulance, the BOP (Lompoc) has not done any follow up neuro-care NOR given or adjusted my Keppra (seizure medication) as instructed by Dr. Lenley Jackson, [the] doctor that treated me at Lompoc Valley Medical Facility.

On April 26, 2016, I was seen by a PA (Physician assistant), **Ms.** Turner, here at Lompoc. She was aware of my incident and hospitalization two days prior and the instructions from Dr. ALISTAIR, the hospital emergency physician; as of this date, July 31st, 2016, NO ADJUSTMENT nor a follow up with a neurologist has ever been done NOR to the prescribed medication, Keppra.

The reply he (warden) sent to you is a "STANDARD FORM LETTER" that they use and they just fill-in the blanks. Warden, Mr. Langford also makes mention in the bottom of his letter that Mason does not meet the requirements for compassionate release, NOR assignment to a Bureau of Prisons Medical Facility. I believe this is exactly what was ordered by the court at my sentence that I be assigned to a BOP medical facility.

Mason then urged the defender to immediately do the following for him: "Ms. Park, I would like you to set up an 'Emergency Attorney–Client Call' as I feel a verbal expression of my medical concerns needs to be addressed. Please consider my request so that we can discuss this in lengthy details."

The public defender realized that the warden had lied about her client being well taken care of in prison. She responded to her client immediately (dated August 5) promising Mason that she would set up an emergency attorney–client call but warned him that it might never happen based on her previous requests made to the warden for such phone calls, which had not materialized in the past despite many efforts that she had made.

The public defender immediately followed up with a second written request to the warden, dated August 12, for an attorney–client phone appointment with Mason. Her previous such written request made in April, four months prior, had been ignored by the warden. The defender's several attempts to reach the prison officials by phone calls and emails since the month of April had also been unsuccessful.

I was surprised to find out during my investigative research that many criminal defense trial attorneys, even after 30 years of working in the field, are not aware that the Department of Justice and Federal Bureau of Prisons do not allow attorney–client meetings. Prisoners are also not allowed to obtain a copy of any court documents that come through the prison that belong to a prisoner's court case. Attorneys cannot have a private phone conversation with their clients because it will be monitored like any other phone call or email conversation. Defense attorneys and their prisoner clients are not allowed to email each other. Some of these are blatant violations of the constitutional rights of prisoners. It makes it so much worse for those who are

innocent and still trying to prove their innocence because they are locked up without trials or due process of law. Defense attorneys are not allowed to call and speak with their clients in prison. Only short phone calls made by the prisoners are allowed, for which they don't have the money, and if they do, a 15-minute phone call costs the prisoner $3, which, in some cases, is the equivalent to one week of wages working full-time in prison calculated at 6 to 7 cents an hour, the common hourly rate for most prisoners. [in some prisons around the country, a prisoner's cost for a single phone call is as much as $20]. Prisoners are allowed no more than 300 minutes a month of total phone call time in a federal prison. When a prisoner calls his attorney, the call is recorded and monitored by the prison officials, so they will know all the details of a pending law suit, not to mention the fact that the prisoner now must be prepared for retaliation for making a lawsuit threat through such a phone call. If the prison officials know all the details of a pending legal action discussed between the prisoner and his attorney ahead of time, they could now fine-tune his medical records. (I will throw more light on this phenomenon in Chapter 18.)

Although the prisons have an unwritten policy that no access is given to any prisoner to discuss his case with his lawyer through attorney–client meetings, emails, or phone calls, the government prosecutors from the Department of Justice, are given instant access to prisoners on the phone or in person as and when needed, and as often as necessary. The prosecutors often call prisoners who are trying to sue the prison with the intent of threatening those prisoners and intimidating them into silence, dropping their lawsuits against the BOP, and/or compromising and settling with the Federal Bureau of Prisons at the government's terms or else face harsher time in prison or other consequences, such as further denial of medical care or other forms of retaliation.

As indicated earlier, the public defender in Mason's case sent a written request for attorney–client phone call with her client to several prison officials such as Ms. Diaz and counselor Zepeda with a copy of the request forwarded to the warden, giving them all possible options to arrange this phone call at the prison officials' convenience. I followed up on this in the following weeks and months and discovered that the prison officials once again ignored the public defender. Her attempts to communicate with the prison on behalf of her client for 10 months via writing, phone calls, and emails had been unsuccessful. An attorney may arrange to visit a prisoner in prison to discuss the case after a very cumbersome bureaucratic process, but not many prisoners can afford to pay attorneys to visit them in prison. It always boils down to who has money and how much. Wealthy clients will always find some justice if they ever go to prison, but in most cases, they don't go to prison in the first place. The criminal law is interpreted differently for the rich.

Two days before I left the prison, Mason was motivated enough to write me a brief testimony of his own despite his tremendous limitations due to health reasons; he was so motivated because he knew that I was about to leave the prison and he would never see me again. He wrote me a brief testimony of his trail of tears in his own words that I have published in *Prison Papers* under his fictitious name.

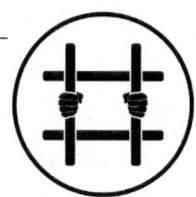

## CHAPTER 7

# IN A DIABETIC COMA: THE TESTIMONY OF JACOB

MY NAME IS JACOB. I AM 56 YEARS OLD. I AM AN inmate at Lompoc Prison for a sentence of 18 months. Before I came here, my lawyer told me that my health problems will be taken care of. I have celiac disease, gluten intolerance, and I am a type I brittle diabetic. I came here on 5/17/16. Three months later, in August, I still have not been given any sort of food option nor has any blood sugar been even remotely under control. When I first got here, I gave them my medical records from my doctor that stated I have celiac disease and need to test sugar many times a day and need a low glycemic index diet or I would become very ill and end up in the hospital. I had to check my sugar six to seven times a day to try to get it controlled before I came to the prison but the prison doctor did not want to hear it when I told him that.

On the outside, I was on insulin pump for 12 years, that was the only way to control my blood sugar. Here they try to control it with two shots a day. Can't be done. Most of my blood sugar numbers are between 300 and 500 (or higher undetected on the meter because the meter does not read above 500). Yet they are still giving me the two shots a day that does not give me enough insulin to control my sugar. If I am not high in the morning, I don't get a shot of insulin. I need it all the time, yet if my blood sugar is below 150, I don't get any till 5:00 p.m. or 7:00 p.m. On weekends, I get insulin after three meals. And it is usually been over 350 most of the day and around 500 or higher by 7:30 p.m. on weekends.

I am a brittle diabetic, which means my sugar levels go up fast and can come down fast even when given the right amount of insulin. I have had many low events below 30 to where I have been found in a coma and helped by other inmates to get sugar drink down me to bring me back from low events or comatose. Recently I was helped by a physician inmate in the camp because the Health Clinic here at the camp refused to help. I am very sick from extreme highs. I have filled several BP-8s (Inmate Requests to Staff) and BP-9s (Administrative Remedies to the warden) with no responses at this point for proper medical attention to prevent long-term problems. Lack of control from extreme sugar levels could damage vital organs, such as kidneys, liver, eyes, as I had been told by my primary care doctor on the outside.

One time I was told by the clinic here that I could have only two test strips per day and then handed only one at the medical pill-call line to test twice a day. Impossible to know what is going on; how to check and control my sugar without the test strips. This went on for a month. Now I get three strips a day but I have put in a BP-8 to ask for a minimum of five strips per day. DENIED. Also, they do not allow me glucose tablets for low events. I finally got ten tablets on 7/26/16 which I used with three low-sugar events in two days. Now I have been out of the tabs and have nothing for low events. My kidneys hurt so bad on 7/16/16 on a weekend, they gave me a double IV to flush the ketones from my blood.

I went from a hemoglobin A1c of 6.8 to 8. 2 in two months after arriving at the prison and now it is probably above 12, dangerously high and they refuse to test me. I have put in many Cop-Outs (Inmate Requests to Staff, BP-8s) for a medical meeting to control this. And I am told by paramedic Mr. A., "You will be fine, toughen up butter-cup."

The R.N. (Registered nurse) tells me, "You just have to let your body or system adjust to the food here." I filed BP-8 to get better health attention so I do not end up on dialysis or worse, but I have not had any help, just "denials" or "we will get back to you" or flat out refusals to any extra test strips or glucose tablets. The health service here is appalling in making my small jail sentence into a death sentence.

My BP-8 filed in June 2016 is still not answered till today (August 10, 2016). FBOP policy requires them to respond within 20 days. I am in a life-and-death situation. My gums have receded so bad from celiac disease that my jaw bone in the back is almost coming through."

Jacob gave me his notes from his prison diary. The handwritten originals were smuggled out of prison to be published as Prison Papers, but never made it to its destination.

Friday night my blood sugar was 440 at 8:00 p.m. from not receiving fast acting insulin. I went to OIC's (officer-in-charge) office, Mr. P. and asked if he could call a PA (physician assistant) or nurse to get a small shot of fast acting insulin so I would not be tortured all night or die. He said, "Not my job. If I did this for you, I would have to do it all the time for others, I won't do it unless you fall out or die." Then he said, I should have been at pill-call. I explained that I was but they refused to give me any long acting insulin. He responded, "not my problem."

8/1/16: Went into morning pill-call. My sugar was 55. Ms. Pinnell the R.N. (the assistant Health Services administrator) took up 10 fasting and 20 NPH. I told her I only wanted 5 and 10. She told me if I don't take what the doctor advised—it is my fault if I have problems. If I would have taken what he advised, I could not be here today to tell the story. This doctor is an arrogant quack.

8/12/16: Four days have gone by since I asked for a small amount of fast insulin at night to combat the dinner blood sugar. Still will not give me any. Approached OIC (Officer-in-charge) for high sugar—denied any help.

8/17/16: Eight days have now gone by since I received some glucose tablets. "Any day" they say.

8/17/16: Afternoon: Had meeting with the physician assistant, finally looking forward to addressing my health problems. She told me right away that she was there only to address my Cop-Out that I submitted in May, three months prior, which was for insulin dosage for better control. She then advised me that since I already had a meeting with Dr. Dhaliwal, she was not there to step on the doctor's feet, so I would have to place another Cop-Out (Inmate Request) for the next appointment with the doctor—It took me three months to get this appointment —now I will have to wait another three months to make another appointment. The main problem I came here today to discuss with the PA was not insulin but a chronic cough from yeast overgrowth up in my deep throat, swollen lymph glands in my neck, fatigue, aches, and receding gums. Yeast overgrowth is due to my uncontrolled sugar levels at night from eating candy and sodas for the low events, since they had denied me the sugar tablets. The R.N. did not even acknowledge any of my problems and complaints of my symptoms. She took my blood pressure and said, "Next" and kicked me out. Upon my request, she looked at my tongue and never said a word. My mouth is full of tremendous oral thrush, so much that I cannot even swallow food. You don't have to be a doctor to see that growth in my throat.

8/18/16: At pill-call, still no fast acting for my dinner. And the nurse said she still cannot fill my glucose tablets, it was filled on 8/10/16 and not up for another refill yet. Every low event takes up to 4 tablets and since the 10th, I have had 14 low events, two below 30. Well that would take over 50 glucose tablets. They only allowed me 10 for over a week. I think they are hoping I will fall out and die.

8/19/16: Went to PA Sick Call and told her that my lymph glands in my throat were swollen and very sore and I had a sore throat, she stated they were swollen and sore because I was touching them. Did not say anything about the sore throat and fever.

8/20/16: I had no diabetic log for the month of July because they only allowed me to have two test strips a day, given one at a time during morning and evening pill-calls.

Ms. Pinnell, the nurse who is also assistant health services administrator, advised of only two test strips.

Undated: I did not know for sure I was low until I near hit the dirt, so there was nothing I could do if I was high anyway so I never knew where I was: for a person who tested 10–12 times a day on the outside, I was really feeling like shit most of the time, always high except when I crashed, then they expect me to maintain some sort of normal with these large changes in my body without giving me the test strips.

Undated: I have been told many times they were going to throw me in the hole (solitary confinement) over what I knew was right but maybe I came off strong due to blood sugar imbalance.

Undated: My blood sugar levels in the last month:

3 times below 25

6 times below 35

15 times below 50

35 times above 300

11 times above 400

Three times over 500 (undetected on the glucometer)

Twice low (undetected) below 20

Undated: I am still without glucose tabs. My long-term health problems are adding up, and some starting to show, besides the damage this situation is doing to my organs and the life and death battle I go through daily not to fall off. My gums have now receded below the root line of some teeth and exposing parts of my jawbone and is very painful from high blood sugar. I ask before this situation kills me, or the long-term issues become irreversible, that I be sent to a facility that can deal with my health issues in a consistent and healthy manner. Not even once have we addressed the celiac disease and availability of food that doesn't poison my body yet.

Undated: Dr. Dhaliwal and I have met twice since I came here. He does not listen. And you can't understand his English when he talks. If he had control of my diabetes, I would be on dialysis or worse quickly. Don't think he has dealt with a brittle diabetic. Besides he does not seem to care for what I have to say. It seems like I am talking to myself.

Undated: The food is not edible here for me, not if I want to survive. They have not addressed my celiac disease and the need for my glucose tablets or the yeast overgrowth I am having in my mouth and throat. My glucose determination, stomach aches 24/7, headaches, joint aches, fatigue, bloating and foul gas and flu-like symptoms daily.

Undated: The three months here have felt like 3 years of daily torture. Between high blood sugar poison to me, for food and symptoms I am experiencing. Then they flush me with IV, then start the torture again.

The body will only take this so long before the mind will lose the will to survive. When this happens, game over!

Undated: One weekend I was over 500 at about 3:00 p.m. from no morning shot. Paramedic came down after call from OIC that I was in coma. They gave me a large dose of insulin then asked me to call OIC in one and half hours to have sugar tested again and to have the OIC radio up readings to him (the paramedic). When I went to the OIC, one and a half hour later and explained to him, he told me, "get the fuck out of my office. I don't want to be responsible. If the PA wants to know your readings, he can come down and do it himself. Get the fuck out."

Undated: My BP-8 and BP-9 Inmate Requests to Staff and for Administrative Remedies have not been answered. They say that there is no proof of any medical problems in my medical records, but here are copies of BP-8 and BP-9 and copies of all the stuff including letters from Seventh Day Adventist Hospital that they already have in my medical records, but they say I have no proof. It is like torture; poison me with food I cannot eat; kill my organs with terrible blood sugar control, then give me IVs to flush my blood, then torture me some more and then tell me, we will give you IV again if you want. And then tell me there is no proof that I have any medical problems.

Undated: BP-8 sent on June 1 asking for transfer to facility that can take care of me. I am still waiting for an answer on BP-9 that I sent out on June 20. Still no answer. It has been over three months. A BP-8 for more test strips and glucose tablets—I was told inmates get enough test strips to test two times a day.

Undated: My blood sugars change rapidly. That is why they call me a brittle diabetic. In my first two weeks, here, I was able to test 3–4 times a day and guess the rest. Now I don't know for sure until I hit the dirt from a low or feel like the flu from a high blood sugar. With the small amount of testing I could do in the first two weeks I recorded:

6 times below 35

15 times below 50

5 times over 300

11 times over 400

3 times too high for the meter to record

2 times too low for the meter to record

2 times found in coma

Undated: Other health concerns in just last three months of torture. Receding gums below the roots of my teeth and bleeding.

Neuropathy in feet and bladder. Stomach aches 24 hours a day due to untreated celiac disease, gluten overload. Yeast overgrowth in my mouth and deep throat from high blood sugar, unable to swallow food. Every joint and muscle hurts. My legs and feet cramp at night. Nerves causing shakiness in my hands and legs. Emotional turmoil from chemical imbalance. Headaches. Swollen lymph glands and tenderness. Depression/cry a lot/shot nerves.

I would like to describe Jacob's brief story, which I put together based on some of his prison records that were sent out of prison but I have had a hard time locating. Seventh Day Adventist Hospital wrote a letter on October 9, 2015, to the prison officials, which was a part of Jacob's medical records. The letter stated, "To Whom it May Concern," in which the physician described to the prison officials Jacob's diabetes and celiac disease. He stated that the patient's sugar often fluctuated between 30 and 360 during the day. Dr. SAMUEL, Jacob's private physician, warned that Jacob would have to be hospitalized if he did not get a gluten-free diet for his celiac disease and insulin pump to control his unpredictable very high and low sugar levels. It is clear from Jacob's prison records that nine months after this letter from the Adventist Hospital, he was still begging for basic care.

He wrote an Inmate Request to Staff the following year on June 27, 2016 (the year after the official submission of his medical records), in which he explained that he had gone as low as 21 in his sugar levels within 24 hours and asked for sugar tablets. He complained of painful kidneys, low back pain, intestinal pain due to a gluten-loaded diet in the chow hall, and painful feet due to neuropathy. He warned that he was afraid he would not come out of coma one of these days and requested an insulin pump. In response, they denied him sugar tablets.

He wrote another complaint on July 12 in which he requested a minimum of five glucose test strips, even though his doctors had him test up to twelve times a day (he was being given only two per day). To this complaint, Ms. Pinnell, the AHSA, responded by stating: "Inmates are given enough strips to test two times a day. There is no documentation supporting your claimed medical issues." She ended her response by saying, "If you are not satisfied with my response, you are advised to proceed with the Administrative Remedy Process." The unit manager supported her response. The unit manager's approval of the healthcare staff's decisions is an automatic thing in all federal prisons, as I noted from reviewing prisoners' medical records from various federal prisons. I did not see one exception in nearly a thousand prison responses that I reviewed on behalf of many prisoners.

I lost touch with Jacob after October 25, 2016, so I do not know his fate. Upon my advice, he managed to smuggle one of his glucometers out of the prison, which had electronic recordings of sugar levels as high as 500 and as low as 20. Jacob had lost tremendous weight. He was about 6 feet tall and weighed 120 pounds—a sign of failing kidneys due to unmanaged diabetic nephropathy, which would likely lead to the need for dialysis very soon followed by death. I only hope that he will stay alive till he finishes his relatively short sentence.

The prison provides a 3,000-kilocalories, almost all carbohydrate diet to brittle diabetics that would theoretically require more than 1,000 units of fast-acting insulin before meals, which only means one thing: either the diet will kill these diabetics or the insulin (if it were given in correctly calculated doses). Either way, they must die a slow death. There is no special diet for anyone in prison with the exception of Kosher food for observant Jews due to the Jewish lobbying for the Jewish white-collar criminals. Prison is a death trap for diabetics. They must die a slow death in prison if they have a long-term sentence or, if they come out of prison alive because of a short sentence, they always require dialysis after their release, which is also an initial stage of slow death because dialysis works only for so long before the kidneys give in.

The worst news out of all this is that the Federal Bureau of Prisons lies to the American public in stating that the "federal prison provides special diet to those with medical conditions when medically indicated." The BOP advertises itself that way to the world and everywhere in its official publications, including large sign boards on the walls of their prison clinics. Most horribly, prison officials lie to the courts and judges that prisoners with special dietary needs are being given a special diet in prison, and they falsify medical records accordingly to prove the veracity of their claims to the court. I caught many such legal cases in real time, such as the case of Kingsley (see Chapter 15). In litigated cases, the prison officials frequently use the argument with courts that there is no proof that the plaintiff had a claimed medical condition, and therefore no treatment was warranted, while concealing the actual medical records of the prisoner from the court system and revealing only forged medical records that show prisoner in great health. This is consistent with prisoners' allegations that they are often told when they demand medical attention, "your medical records have no proof that you have this medical condition."

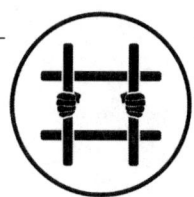

CHAPTER 8

# THE MAN WHO LOST HIS FOOT: THE TESTIMONY OF ELIJAH

THE NEXT TWO STORIES—THAT OF ELIJAH AND JOSEPH— are prime examples of a prison culture that loves to punish far and beyond the punishment already levied by the courts.

Elijah, a 68-year-old man, lost his foot for only one reason: prison officials see the use of medical cruelty as additional punishment and a necessary measure as part of their well-defined duties in prison culture. Elijah had already served 20 years of a 25-year prison sentence at the time I met him. He was one of the kindest people I met in prison, a true gentleman. Following is his story in his words, testimony that is corroborated by his medical records and Administrative Remedy requests, letters, and pleas, which are published in *Prison Papers*.

117

The following testimony is corroborated by my medical records:

Injured left foot in 2010–2011 (see my prison medical records for exact dates) while walking on the tract. My left foot started to swell; it swelled up so much that it caused blisters all over the foot.

After going to the infirmary, I was put on oral antibiotics, which did not work. I was then taken across the street to the medium security prison and put in a hospital room and was given IV antibiotics to try to bring the swelling down. That was unsuccessful also. Finally, I asked for an X-ray to be taken, which should have been done immediately (see medical records for the date of the X-ray).

The X-ray was read by Dr. O'Brian who has a private practice and is/was under contract with [Federal Bureau of Prisons, El Reno]. He said that I had dislocated four bones in place while healing.

Surgery was performed on 11/2/11. Three screws were installed to hold the bones in place while healing.

After surgery, it appeared to me that the four bones were not relocated before putting the screws in to stabilize the bones for healing.

This can easily be confirmed by visually examining my left foot; it is now deformed.

Dr. O'Brian saw me immediately after the surgery and told me that he had put three screws in my foot, and that they would have to be removed because of my diabetes.

After surgery, I was taken back to my unit (in El Reno Prison Camp). Approximately 30 days after surgery, Dr. Smith seen me at the orthopedic clinic at the medium security prison where he ordered an X-ray to be taken and after reading X-ray he said my foot was healing fine. He did not comment on the deformity of my foot.

February 4, 2011, at the next orthopedic clinic (which is held about every 30 days but in this case, it was almost 7 weeks. At that time, Dr. O'Brian told Ms. Grismer (Dr. O'Brian's nurse) that the screws would have to come out. She asked if it was an emergency, and Dr. O'Brian said, "No, but they would have to come out. She asked: "Within 30 days?" He replied, "Yes, thirty days."

It was two months later when I was taken back to the hospital for the removal of screws by Dr. O'Brian His nurse came to see me immediately after surgery and told me that Dr. O'Brian had broken off the head of the middle screw while trying to remove it. The screw had stayed in way too long, she said.

NOTE: The screw in the right side of my foot had rubbed a hole through the skin; you could actually see the head of the screw protruding through the skin. I showed the protruding screw to Ms. Cherry at the medical clinic, she then called her superior, Ms. Razc, the Physician Assistant, then told me that she had gotten herself chewed out for her effort. I also had (while on a visit) showed the hole and the head of the screw to a visitation officer and my daughter and son-in-law at the same time.

At the next orthopedic clinic, I was seen by Dr. O'Brian's assistant. I was upset and complaining about the deformity of my foot; I told him that I felt like I was butchered. That

I had been in construction my whole life and never would I or did I fix a busted floor joist without first straightening it and then reinforce it to keep it in place. I asked why the bones were not relocated before installing the screws? The conversation was a little heated on my part, and Ms. Grismer who was facing me swiveled around away from me and said, "I feel your anger."

Both Dr. O'Brian and his assistant both said that my foot would eventually have to be amputated. That was the excuse they gave me for not relocating the bones before he installed the screws.

Every day my foot swells up during the day and goes down at night.

On August 10, 2011, there was an MRI done and in the radiologist's report it states, "attempt to repair a fractured navicular." [Please see the entire report.]

As of May 2013, I have been in the hospital in and out with problems with regard to my foot. One Dr. explained to me that because of the deformity of my foot, it causes the toes to rub together which in turn causes ulcers between my toes, which get infected, which causes me to end up in the hospital repeatedly. I am constantly being shipped/transferred from my family to Fort Worth Medical Center October 2011 through May 2013.

The following is a brief story of Elijah based on my review of his medical and administrative records of seven years from the beginning of 2010 and to near the end of 2016 studied from the perspective of an experienced surgeon and a physician. I was not able to access his records prior to 2010. Elijah's records reveal a lot more than what he states in his previous testimony. His records are published in *Prison Papers* under the name Elijah with the actual name redacted.

Elijah's oldest prison healthcare record that became available to me showed that he filed a Request to the Staff on November 11, 2010, in which he explained to Ms. Grismer, the healthcare administrator at Federal Correction Institute (FCI), El Reno, Oklahoma, that one of his screws was working its way out after his "foot surgery." He stated that he had been to several Sick Calls and had shown the screw sticking out of his foot with ulcers and infection to several people in the health clinic including Ms. Razc, Dr. Zevin, and Dr. O'Brian He received a written response to his written complaint by Ms. Grismer who stated, "You have been placed as priority for Dr. O'Brian to see in-house consult."

After waiting for two more months for post-surgical removal of screws, Elijah finally wrote a complaint on March 10, 2011, to Ms. Grismer in which he reminded her of his conversations with her in the surgical clinic: "Ms. Grismer, it has been nearly two months since Dr. O'Brian said that the screws in my foot must come out. Our conversation during my last visit with you and him (the Dr.) was: Dr O'Brian: 'Screws must come out.' Ms. Grismer: 'Is it an emergency?' Dr: 'No, but they have to come out.' Ms. Grismer: 'Within 30 days?' Dr: 'Yes, within 30 days.'" This complaint was followed by Elijah's request to the healthcare administrator to release his medical records to his family. He stated: "Pardon the interruption. Ms. Grismer, I am requesting the following people have any and all access to my medical records: 1. E.K. (mother); 2. S.E. (daughter); 3. KYE (sister); 4. D.H. (sister); 5. R.H. (family attorney). Please send me the necessary form to authorize release of my medical records to these individuals. Thank you." Elijah never received a response from Ms. Grismer to his request for release of medical records to him and his family.

Fast forward to August 2011, almost six months later. I noted a radiologist report of Elijah's foot from Saint Anthony Hospital in Oklahoma. The MRI report on August 10 by the radiologist Phillip Stratemeir, MD, stated that the distortion of the left foot with disruption of the cuneiform was "stress related." The radiologist found a staple in the navicular bone and then stated that it was an attempt to repair a fractured navicular. The radiologist also noted a distortion of the second metatarsal. This was the radiologist's polite way of saying that the prison surgeon drove nails into the bones without straightening out the broken bones. It has been my own experience as a surgeon that radiologists are generally cautious about exposing surgeons' mistakes (or their colleagues' mistakes) except when there was a serious wrongdoing or a criminal act. Even then, radiologists do not honestly expose the surgeon's wrongdoing because they are colleagues after all, and have to work together, so they must cover for each other's mistakes. This was one such example. Such criminal malpractice is relatively rare in the outside world but very common in prison.

In an email to Ms. Razc, the physician's assistant, Elijah inquired through an email two weeks later on August 25 as to the result of the MRI test. In an email response, Ms. Razc minimized the results of the report, telling Elijah that it was stress related because there was no inflammation. The bottom of her email response to him stated the following: "The above message is intended for official use and may contain sensitive information. If this message contains sensitive information, it should be properly delivered, labeled, stored and disposed of according to FBOP policy."

Ms. Razc offered Elijah a copy of the report if he visited her at the clinic only on certain days and times. This is consistent with what I discovered and observed in prison—that is, there are some lower-level healthcare employees with qualms of conscience in that, although they follow the orders of their superiors, they love to expose the prison's criminal activity when they have an opportunity to do so without getting caught. Such employees, unfortunately, never last; they end up being fired and stripped of their government employee benefits for divulging confidential information (reports that the FBOP calls "unreleasable portions of medical records," that is, ones that expose criminal activity because it puts the prison at liability), or in majority of the cases, they end up quitting because they cannot bear to watch such inhuman treatment of prisoners in front of them day after day. Such employees are very few and far between, and they often get into trouble for giving prisoners forbidden verbal or written medical healthcare information. Such employees are a serious problem for the Department of Justice because their "unauthorized" release of "nonreleasable information" leads to lawsuits by leaving a piece of evidence in the hands of the enemy. It is hard to understand why any portions, whatsoever, of a person's medical records are "unreleasable portions."

Most of Elijah's medical records between 2011 and 2014 are also missing. However, he managed to get copies of all his Administrative Remedy records from 2015 onward, which I used to put the following story together in a chronological fashion. These documents suggest that Elijah was rapidly losing his vision in early 2016. Later in 2015, he had been attending Sick Calls to draw attention to his rapid loss of vision in both eyes at the age of 68. This is clear from a document that I found that was written by him sometime in January

2016. Elijah addressed this letter to the clinical director of the prison, Mr. Lin, in which he refers to his 2015 Sick-Call requests. It states:

Approximately 60 days ago, I submitted a Sick-Call slip stating, "I was in urgent need of seeing an optometrist … that I am rapidly losing my vision." I also gave Mr. Garrastazu. (camp manager) a copy and he faxed it to Dr. Lin, the clinical director. Since that time, my condition has deteriorated. I now cannot see anything with my left eye.

In title 28 of USC, Congress saddled the Bureau of Prisons with the obligation (not the option) to provide adequate medical care compared to medical care one would receive outside. Program statement §10.32 states a prisoner has the "Right to be free from affliction of cruel and unusual punishment as guaranteed by the Eighth Amendment. Violation of Eighth Amendment rights have been found where there is an intentional denial of needed medical care, or when a prison official's conduct indicates deliberate indifference to medical care of prisoners."

It is my opinion that not being able to see properly, when the vision can be corrected is a violation of my Eighth Amendment right to adequate medical care. I would no doubt under Medicare benefits receive the treatment needed to correct my vision.

I am asking for the treatment /procedure(s) needed to restore my eyesight to be approved and performed in expeditious manner before I go irreversibly blind.

On April 22, he wrote another BP-8, a Request to the Staff that read:

I am in urgent need of seeing an optometrist. Last Friday, PA Turner was kind enough to talk to the optometrist and I was supposed to be on the Call-Out today to see him. Didn't happen! My family is ready to contact whoever is necessary to complain about the seemingly deliberate indifference to my medical issues. Can you advise me who to have them call? I cannot see with my left eye now and don't want to go blind.

As you can see in Elijah's testimony, he is asking the prison officials, "Can you advise me who to have them [my family] call?" It is like hen in a henhouse asking the fox in charge of the henhouse for advice regarding who to call to complain against the fox. Elijah is very aware of this but he feels helpless and does not know what else to say.

On April 29, a correctional counselor typed out another BP-8 Request to the Staff on behalf of Elijah in which she stated that he was going blind in his left eye and was requesting removal of his cataracts. The medical staff responded: "Inmate must sign up for a Sick Call." By responding in this fashion, the medical staff ignored the fact that Elijah had gone to the same medical staff and signed for innumerable Sick Calls and he was completely ignored by the staff at Sick Calls. When he protested that he had been to the Sick Calls countless times, they told him the same thing: "Attend Sick Call."

A month later, on May 6, Elijah appealed to the warden in an Administrative Remedy Request BP-9 in which he referred to his previous Sick-Call requests to the clinical director and his various attempts to get an appointment with the optometrist for many months. He named unit manager, Mr. Garrastazu, and the physician assistant, Mr. Turner, to whom he had spoken with and written several requests. The warden responded on May 9 to Elijah's request stating that his case was referred to utilization review, and the warden's response was "for informational purposes only" and that if Elijah disagreed, he "may proceed with regional appeal within 20 days."

Elijah wrote a letter to Garrrastazu on June 2 in which he stated that he had "a fast-acting species of cataracts as per the optometrist examination report" and now he was starting to stumble over objects despite being careful, and he did not recognize any faces. He requested a consult with an ophthalmologist. He attached copies of his previous Administrative Remedy appeals. Elijah received a response from the administrative remedy coordinator of the prison that stated, "Additional time is necessary to respond to your Administrative Remedy. We are extending the time to Respond as provided in the Administrative Remedy Program Statement of the Federal Bureau of Prisons."

Seeing no help coming forth from the prison officials, Elijah wrote a letter directly addressed to the optometrist on July 1—the one who had told him that he must see an ophthalmologist within 30 days due to the "fast developing type of cataracts" that he had. He urged the optometrist to do anything he could to expedite the restoration of his vision. The prison officials are supposed to honor any plea for any urgent action recommended by a doctor or a specialist contracted with the prison, but the federal prison officials often say that these outside doctors cannot tell the prison what to do (as you will see many prison officials quoted as saying in this book). The optometrist ignored Elijah's letter. My understanding from my investigation is that the optometrist did not respond, not because he did not want to help, but rather because he knew that him telling the prison officials what to do not only would be fruitless but also may have repercussions for the renewal of his contract with the prison.

Elijah wrote a letter to Surgeon General, Vivek Murthy urging him to help. In this letter he stated, "I am very fearful of the retaliation for submitting this letter to your office but am more fearful of going blind." He explained that the prison officials (and he named them all), including the warden, clinical director, and physician assistants, had ignored his requests to see an eye doctor and asked for the surgeon general's intervention.

You will see many sick inmates writing letters to senators, congressmen, the surgeon general, and other officials in the government, but their efforts are always in vain. Prisoners never receive a response from these outsiders for reasons that are clear. Politicians have no political gain from helping a prisoner who is locked up and has no voice. I find it sad because these same politicians will jump on the bandwagon and are all over the television when they want to look good over trivial controversial matters—ones that increase their visibility in the media—but they would not move a muscle even if they know that horrific crimes are being committed against prisoners and their basic human rights are being violated by the Federal Bureau of Prisons. There are no dividends in it for them.

Having not heard from the surgeon general, Elijah wrote letters to senators, Barbara Boxer and Feinstein, in which he traced his long history of medical cruelty by the denial of his Sick Calls, appeals, and requests for administrative remedies, including the fact that five years prior he lost his toes due to serious mismanagement and that now his foot will have to be amputated, and it was all preventable. Then he explained similar refusals five years later of not allowing him to see an ophthalmologist for being nearly blind. You guessed it. All these letters to politicians fell on deaf ears; he never received a reply from them.

I promised Elijah that when I got out of prison, I would contact these senators and try to find out why they thought it was not important enough for them to respond to the letter of a prisoner who was being treated as a subhuman in prison. If I were to take a guess, I am willing to bet that Elijah will continue to be denied surgery for his blindness for years to come even though I cannot verify that because I am no longer in prison and have lost touch with him and lost access to all my sources. All I can tell you is that Elijah continued to file more requests to prison staff and remedy appeals in the months of August, September, and October 2016 to no avail. The originals of his written appeals are published in *Prison Papers* under his fictitious name with the actual name redacted.

Before I conclude Elijah's case, I want to discuss an actual court case of foot injury in prison to compare it with Elijah's foot injury treatment during his incarceration. This comparison, in my opinion, will help you, the reader, fathom the seriousness of medical cruelty that goes on in our federal prisons.

An article in the *Arkansas Democrat-Gazette* (October 29, 2010) entitled "A Lawsuit That Was Avoidable" explains the case of Jose Luis Gonzalez, an inmate who, while serving a drug-trafficking sentence at a federal prison, suffered an injury to his left ankle and leg. According to journalist Linda Satter, Mr. Gonzalez made numerous requests to the prison health staff emphasizing the possibility that he had a possible fracture. He visited Sick Call four times, only to be told to "return the next morning" and that he "could not be treated until next week and that he must make an appointment." He had to wait for almost four weeks for an X-ray only to have his X-ray "mixed with another inmate and X-ray his chest instead." A second X-ray, which was rescheduled for the following week, showed that his fibula and ankle were fractured.

He was taken to Saint Francis Hospital where surgery was performed requiring two screws to be placed in his ankle.

Similar to the many other stories you have or will read in this book, Mr. Gonzalez was given discharge orders that prison officials did not follow when he returned to the prison. The prison's physician, Dr. Prince, withheld a narcotic prescription for pain and confined Mr. Gonzalez to a holding cell. For several days he was only given pain medication twice a day and was not monitored by the prison health staff. He was not even given assistance when he needed to go to the bathroom. His cast was removed before his ankle was healed and he was given a walking boot, which limited his day-to-day activities. Soon after he was transferred to another prison.

After five years of litigation, US District Judge, Susan Weber Wright ordered that Mr. Gonzalez receive "$10,000 a day for pain and suffering and mental anguish for the 28 days until he received treatment" and another "$528,000 for the permanent injury he will suffer for the rest of his life." To determine the amount awarded to Mr. Gonzalez, Judge Wright included "the testimony of a doctor for the plaintiff who said ankle fractures are 'on the top end of the pain scale' ... and that the traumatic injury would have been 'clear to a general practitioner such as Prince [the prison physician].'" According to Dr. Prince's testimony, however, "she didn't think Gonzalez was in pain." But how was she to truly know this when it was reported that Dr. Prince would not allow a Spanish-speaking medical staff member "serve as an interpreter during the visit." When Dr. Prince was asked if she "made any efforts to have Gonzalez's requests translated," she replied, "I asked him to get it interpreted for me. That I think is part of his responsibility for communicating with the medical staff." It was also noted that Dr. Prince left out information in the radiology requests and other medical notes. In Judge Wright's order, she noted that "he was not provided with a wheelchair or crutches, nor was he provided pain medication other than Motrin." She also stated that "the failure to treat Gonzalez's fracture in the four weeks before the X-ray being taken 'is nothing less than a gross negligence.'"

This article is *déjà vu* of all the stories in this book that you have read and are yet to read. Every sentence in the article should sound familiar, particularly to Elijah's case. Although Mr. Gonzalez's case is very similar to Elijah, it is not as serious, compared to Elizah's case. Mr. Gonzalez was awarded almost $1 million in damages for pain and suffering that he endured at the hands of the Federal Bureau of Prisons for denying him foot care after injury, but at least he underwent surgery that saved his foot, unlike Elijah, who now must lose his foot.

This real-life example of a lawsuit provides corroborative evidence of the style of prison torture and abuse highlighted everywhere in all of the cases mentioned in this book, without exception. This public record of a court case shows FBOP's practice of falsifying medical records; omitting diagnoses; using delay tactics and the prison's Sick-Call Scam; being deliberately indifferent; using unusual and cruel punishment; withholding life-saving medications; giving prisoners the bureaucratic run-around; locking up sick prisoners in the solitary cells for being aggressive when demanding care for their medical conditions in violation of their basic human, constitutional, civil, and legal rights; and depriving them of the benefit of basic human decency that has been long regarded as part of the enlightened culture in the West.

Little does the reporter, plaintiff lawyer, and judge in this reported case know that there is no sick prisoner in the federal prison today with a case that is "avoidable." This report makes it sound like this case may be an aberration—that it could have been avoided. They don't know that there are no exceptions in the Federal Bureau of Prisons; there is only the rule. It is just that 99 percent of such prisoners will never have the opportunity to sue the government. Most prisoners will meet their mental, emotional, spiritual, financial, and in some cases physical demise before they have a chance to sue the government. It will be too late for them, for most of them, for almost all of them. In this case, however, Mr. Gonzalez was one of the lucky ones to find justice. As Mr. Gonzalez's attorney, Milton DeJesus explained, the government waited to admit liability, "because the government attorneys didn't think until then that he would really pursue the case to trial."

I would like to add that this reported court case is an example of a rather minor case of a prison's healthcare abuse compared with the horror stories that I have yet to describe in this book. If the federal and state court systems were to provide a fair compensation to all the sick prisoners (using this case as a yardstick), the dollar amount would add up to hundreds of billions of dollars—or perhaps trillions—but the secrets of the prison systems successfully manage to stop 99 percent of prisoners' lawsuits even before thoughts of suing the government cross their minds. If this relatively minor case deserved almost a $1 million compensation in the court's opinion, then each case described in this book deserves between $10 and $100 million of compensation for reasons that are self-evident based on the stories described. There are estimated tens of thousands of very sick inmates in our federal prisons out of a total federal prison population of 250,000. And there are hundreds of thousands of prisoners in similar circumstances if you include state prison populations where healthcare has not improved despite the daring act of the US Court of Appeals for the Ninth Circuit in 2009 in which a panel of judges released 40,000 inmates because the state of California failed to provide healthcare even to the sickest of the inmates.

Let us now move onto the testimony of someone who did not just lose his foot, but lost his leg. All he needed was some antibiotics for a small blister infection on the sole of his foot. But apparently the higher ups in our federal government think that it is ok to punish a prisoner by withholding an antibiotic. They would rather have a prisoner lose his leg than receive even the bare minimum medical attention that one might need in a timely fashion to avoid a huge disaster, including death in many cases.

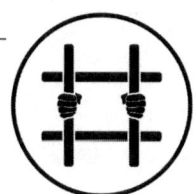

CHAPTER 9

# THE MAN WHO LOST HIS LOWER LIMB: THE TESTIMONY OF JOSEPH

FOLLOWING IS THE TESTIMONY OF A 64-YEAR-OLD MAN, Joseph, who first lost his toes and then lost his entire right leg. All he needed was one week worth of antibiotics in a reasonable time to get rid of a small blister. The Department of Justice, the Federal Bureau of Prisons, refused to give him the antibiotics because its healthcare employees were "too busy." Busy with what? Busy with the time-consuming task of refusing healthcare to all inmates in prison. Saying no to everyone apparently takes a lot of work, because prisoners resist and they want medical care; it keeps the prison doctors, nurses, and health officials extremely busy fighting back. Here is Joseph's testimony:

133

Federal Prison Camp, La Tuna, Arizona: A blister developed on the bottom of my right foot. I first noted it on 10/9/11. The blister was due to wearing facility-supplied work-boots. The blister became infected with MRSA [Methicillin Resistant Staphylococcus Aureus], a life-threatening, highly contagious infection. Dr. Altenburg [prison physician] was aware of the fact that I was to be given a soft shoe pass because of diabetic neuropathy and needed diabetic work-boots. And in fact, stated I no longer needed diabetic work-boots. Dr. Altenburg and the medical staff was aware of the infection and that I was an insulin-dependent diabetic. Medical staff PA, Mr. Hawkes, swabbed the infected area from my foot on 10/12/11 and sent the specimen to an outside laboratory for diagnosis and ordered antibiotics. The lab identified the infection as MRSA and labeled it as "severe infection." Dr. Altenburg and the medical staff, having received the lab report, knew the seriousness of the infection, but failed to provide proper treatment and respond to the medical situation. In fact, I was told for several days that the pharmacist was "too busy" to fill my prescription for oral antibiotics. Many days later, I received the oral antibiotics.

Standard of care for my condition would have required hospitalization and IV antibiotics. Dr. Altenburg, being the physician of the facility, was well aware of my medical situation, having prescribed the oral antibiotics, failed to properly treat my condition, thus allowing the infection to progress to a point that amputation was the only treatment available to cure the infection. My leg was amputated on 11/3/11. To this day, 10 months later, I am still in wheel chair with no known time frame as to when I will receive a prosthetic limb. My suffering continues. I have requested help from Dr. Altenburg, medical staff, case manager, counselor, camp administrator, and the prison warden with no results. My basic rights as a human being identified by the Eighth Amendment of the US Constitution have been violated and ignored. I have been under Dr. Altenburg's care from June 2010 when I arrived here at the prison, first at the FCI (Federal Corrections Institute) and currently at the FPC (Federal Penitentiary Complex) since May 2011. All medical care has been under the direction and supervision of Dr. Altenburg. Medical records will support all my claims.

Joseph handed me the following affidavit written by an emergency room (ER) doctor, Dr. Thomas, MD, also an inmate at the prison at La Tuna, Arizona, in 2011. Dr. Thomas was a board-certified ER physician for 30 years. He examined Joseph from time to time in the Arizona Federal Prison. His affidavit, which he wrote before his release from the federal prison, throws more light on Joseph's story from the viewpoint of a physician. (The original affidavit can be found in *Prison Papers* published under the physician's fictitious name with his actual name redacted.)

## Affidavit of Dr. Thomas MD

At the request of Joseph, I am writing this affidavit. My name is Dr. Thomas. I am currently an inmate at La Tuna Federal Prison Camp in Arizona. I have known Joseph since I was transferred to the camp in July of 2011. Before being incarcerated, I worked as a full-time emergency physician for over 31 years in emergency departments in Southeastern

New Mexico. I am a 1978 graduate of the University of New Mexico School of Medicine and am licensed in the State of New Mexico, Medical License # [given] and am Board Certified in Emergency Medicine.

Joseph who is type II insulin-dependent diabetic for the last 15 years, approached me on October 10, 2011, and wanted me to look at an area on the plantar surface of his right foot. He stated that he had developed a blister due to his boots, but was unsure exactly when because of his current neuropathy and diminished sensation. He was worried both because of the ulcer that was developing and due to prior amputation of toes on the same foot last year for the same reason.

The ulcer was in the mid-posterior plantar surface in front of the heel. The ulcer had a diameter of approximately 2.0 cm with a depth of 0.5 cm with a necrotic base, and he had already developed tenderness and erythema around the ulcer with swelling of the foot. I told him that he needed to go to the clinic and be seen as soon as possible. But, from my experience, having seen many diabetic foot ulcers similar to this, that if he came into the emergency room, he would be X-rayed, cultured, have lab work done and be admitted and placed on IV antibiotics for a limb-threatening infection. I told him at that time that being a diabetic he needed to be aggressively treated or he would wind up losing his leg. Joseph subsequently heeded my admonition and the following morning presented to the clinic and was seen by the nurse who instructed him to return the following day to see the physician's assistant. The following day, a culture of the ulcer was obtained and an antibiotic (Bactrim DS) was prescribed, but was not given.

I continued to check on Joseph's progress on a daily basis over the next two weeks and observed progressive swelling, warmth, and redness of the foot, as the ulcer enlarged, began to deepen, and developed a foul-smelling discharge. I kept asking if they had begun his antibiotics yet, to which he replied "no," and I continued to tell him he was going to lose his leg and that he needed to be hospitalized and placed on IV antibiotics due to the cellulitis and possible osteomyelitis.

He was finally given the first dose of Bactrim on October 16, 2011, and was told the culture had come back with heavy growth of MRSA. Over the next 10 days he was faithful in taking his medication at the pill-line clinic, but each day the swelling, redness, warmth, and tenderness progressed above the ankle until it involved the entire lower right leg below the knee, and the ulcer had tunneled deeper and continued to produce a purulent discharge. Towards the end of this time he began to complain of chills, body aches, and fever. Throughout this time, I encouraged him to continue to press for hospitalization and IV antibiotics, which he claims he had mentioned numerous times to the medical staff and he was turned down.

Finally, on October 26, 2011, Joseph was removed from the camp for emergency admission to Sierra East Medical Center and began on Vancomycin, Zosyn, and Clindamycin in light of the positive culture for MRSA which was done at La Tuna. X-rays were done on October 27. They revealed gas in the soft tissue consistent with gangrene of the foot. A

CT scan of the foot the same day revealed significant erosive destructive changes throughout the tarsometatarsal joints and probable overlying osteomyelitis with subcutaneous gas around the tarsal bones and base of the metatarsals, and there were irregular margins and diffuse erosive changes, highly suggestive of osteomyelitis.

Due to the extensive progression of the disease process while at La Tuna, Joseph required a lifesaving BKA (below the knee amputation) despite receiving aggressive antibiotics over the first eight days of hospitalization. The BKA was done on November 3, 2011, and he was transferred to El Paso, LTAC (Long-Term Ambulatory Care) Hospital until being released back to LA Tuna prison on November 29, 2011.

It is my experience in dealing with diabetic foot ulcers that they are caused by multiple factors associated with peripheral neuropathy, excessive planus pressure, repetitive trauma, peripheral vascular disease, and wound healing disturbances. All of these factors probably played a part in the onset of Joseph's disease process. Many of these are unavoidable in prison due to diet, poor management of diabetic patients, requirement to wear work-boots and walking as the only means of transportation.

Diagnosis and treatment in regard to standard of care is another issue altogether in prison. The inmate had no choice in seeking healthcare but must rely solely upon the medical staff to assume full responsibility for the health needs of each inmate if, and when doctor or nurse choose to hold clinic. Then the inmate must accept the diagnosis and care which is provided without any chance of a second opinion or alternative treatment short of filing BP-8, BP-9, and BP-10 (Administrative Remedies), series of requesting remedies. The only alternative the inmate has is to repeatedly return to the clinic window in hopes that the worsening condition will spur a higher level of care.

The standard of care outside of the FBOP for diabetic foot ulcers with limb-threatening infection requires immediate hospitalization, IV antibiotics, and surgical debridement as soon as any one of these characteristics are noted—a greater than 2.00 cm of cellulitis, a deep ulcer, odor or purulent drainage, fever, ischemic changes, lymphangitis, or edema. All of these were present in Joseph's instant case. Once these are noted, empiric IV antibiotics must be initiated especially if MRSA is ever suspected; and deep cultures from the base of the ulcer or tissue specimens are obtained along with blood cultures and diagnostic imaging with X-rays, CT, or MRI of the foot. Other than an X-ray, which was never done, none of these can be done at La Tuna. Finally, depending upon the findings, surgical debridement with resection of all necrotic bone and soft tissue along with exploration and drainage of deep abscesses must be accomplished, unless worst case scenario, a complete amputation needs to be done for those who are beyond even these aggressive interventions. In Joseph's case, he did not receive medical attention even after an official laboratory confirmation that he was infected with heavy growth of MRSA, a life-threatening infection for anyone, diabetic or not.

It is my opinion in this case that had Joseph been treated for his diabetic foot ulcer more aggressively and in a more timely manner according to the standard of care, that he would have retained his limb, or at least had a much higher likelihood of doing so. Instead, due to grossly sub-optimal delayed treatment, Joseph has suffered irreparable harm.

—Signed by Dr. Thomas on 5/2/12

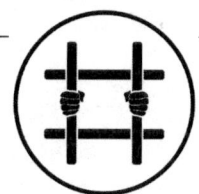

CHAPTER 10

# TORMENT IN HELLFIRE: LIVING WITH SUICIDAL ITCH FOR ONE YEAR

KYLO IS A 63-YEAR-OLD INMATE AND EX-GANG MEMBER. When I met with him in prison, he already had a history of being in and out of federal and state prisons for 40 years with not much respite. He was bold and his language was quite rough. He told me that he did not care about retaliation from the Bureau of Prisons; he had congestive heart failure for which they had not treated him for a long time. He was going to die in prison anyway, so he was "going to tell them the way it is." He said he had been put in solitary confinement for months at a time for demanding medical treatment and now he did not care anymore. He stated that he had given up on any hopes of getting medical care.

141

Kylo was obese and could barely walk. He walked with a cane and had to stop or sit down every few yards because he was out of breath. He informed me that he had congestive heart failure and COPD and had a previous heart attack. I did not have to be a physician to see that he was seriously ill. He was thrilled to know that I was a physician who always wanted to give him tips now and then as to how he could minimize the consequences of his ill health in the absence of medical care, so he became a fan of sort, but he could *never* finish a sentence without using the word *f**k* somewhere in it. He was angry that he would die in prison not so much because of his long sentence, but because of the lack of medical care for his congestive heart that was killing him. He told me that he had been in state and federal prisons since his late teens, locked up intermittently but frequently for almost 40 years. He said he could not care less if the guards found out that he shared confidential information with me and put him back in the SHU for another six months.

Kylo informed me that he was transferred to Lompoc penitentiary in California from Florence prison in Colorado. He described a story of a scabies breakout in Florence prison that lasted more than a year. More than 100 inmates in prison got infected; many of them became suicidal from constant itching, yet the prison refused to treat them. Kylo was one of those who itched for a year and felt like he was going to die. At first, I thought that Kylo might be exaggerating, as some prisoners do. But later, some other prisoners who had also been transferred from Florence prison, for example Kye and a third prisoner whose name I do not recall, confirmed the same story to me, thus giving me the confidence that the story was likely true or at least true for the most part. I wanted to verify this story nonetheless. I had no doubt that this story was true after I saw sick prisoners being treated as sub-humans in my own prison. What I witnessed was that sick domesticated animals and pets get much better care out in the civilian population than humans in American prisons.

I asked Kylo if he could provide any official documentation or medical records that would corroborate his story. He gave me tons of documents of his written and verbal complaints that he filed with the prison officials with regard to him and other inmates not receiving treatment for scabies. He brought me documentation in an erratic fashion on an ongoing basis as he found it; this included a lot of communications with regard to the scabies outbreak at Florence prison. He told me that the prison nurses, the doctor, and the guards retaliated against him for bringing the scabies issue to the attention of the authorities in a town hall meeting held at the prison. The prison officials discontinued his heart and pain medications and his privilege of seeing the prison doctor in response to his aggressive approach for seeking medical care.

I liked Kylo's fearlessness and guts. It was a dangerous form of fearlessness with a ringtone of truthfulness in it. He did not care if he got caught in his transactions with me, which would get me in serious trouble as well. Two other inmates who had been transferred from Florence, including Kye, claimed they had similar documentation about the scabies breakout in Florence, but they explained that they were too afraid to share any of that with me because of fear of retaliation from the prison officials. For example, when I asked Kye if he would mind sharing any documentation with me in regard to his appeals for seeking medical treatment for his scabies infection, he replied, "Make no mistake, it is a matter of time before they find out what you are doing and I guarantee you will find yourself in the hole." I backed off immediately and never spoke to him about this matter again. But he unilaterally kept warning me because he knew I was trying to gather information from many prisoners.

The documents Kylo managed to glean for me included many of his handwritten appeals, with poor English. His style of writing in his complaints to the FBOP reflected his fearlessness; sometimes he used a bit of a rough language but the contents of those complaints are verifiably true according to his prison records that I reviewed. Following is the story that I stitched together by sifting through tons of disorganized paperwork, spending countless hours to find a chronological story. (The originals of Kylo's prison records are published in *Prison Papers* under his fictitious name with the real name and identity redacted.)

The earliest prison document that I was able to dig out from Kylo's disorganized pile was dated November 17, 2014, which was a complaint that he wrote to the Federal Correctional Complex in Florence, Colorado, about itching on different parts of his body due to scabies. In his complaint he stated that the prison health staff was telling him to "come back tomorrow," "come back another day," or "come next week," or "don't worry about it," and "it is not contagious." He also explained that the prison authorities had retaliated against him by withholding his pain medications and discontinuing him from seeing the prison doctor for filing multiple complaints against prison officials on behalf of himself and all other prisoners suffering from scabies and for denying them treatment. He also stated that all his Sick Calls had been a waste of time because after signing up for the paperwork for Sick Calls, an actual appointment was never made for him to be seen at the clinic. He specifically mentioned Dr. Santini and the physician assistant Mr. Cordova. He referred to various Administrative Remedies he had filed in the past with no help coming forth. He requested adequate treatment or transfer to another facility where he could be treated for scabies.

Kylo never received a response to this letter from prison authorities. So he wrote another Administrative Appeal using a BP-9 to appeal to the warden of the prison complex in Florence Penitentiary, Colorado, on December 8. In his appeal, he explained that the judge at his sentencing had ordered that he (Kylo) be sent to a Federal Medical Center due to his congestive heart failure, hypertension, asthma, COPD (chronic obstructive pulmonary disease), blindness in right eye and loss of peripheral vision, and chronic sciatic nerve caused by retrolisthesis of L4 and L5 vertebrae. He requested that he be accordingly transferred to such medical facility, which was equipped to take care of his medical problems. He stated that he was suffering and that the current facility was not addressing his medical problems.

The health department of the prison responded to his first complaint about scabies dated November 17 while ignoring complaints about his other medical problems. The response came on December 12, stating, "The camp prisoners have been treated for this matter," referring to the scabies breakout.

The response to his second complaint about his medical problems came from the Department of Justice, Federal Bureau of Prisons, several days later. The response stated: Administrative Remedy Rejection Notice: a) You must resubmit your complaint on proper form within 5 days of this Rejection notice, b) your allegations on your BP-8 do not match your allegations on BP-9 remedy appeal.

Kylo wrote another complaint to the prison staff on December 24 in which it becomes clear for the first time that Kylo was transferred to Florence, Colorado, from Pahrump, Nevada prison, and he was in

Taft California prior to that. In this complaint, the prisoner traced his history of being transferred from place to place and promised an MRI of his back but was still waiting for that MRI after several months. He explained that when he informed Dr. Santini and the physician assistant, Mr. Cordova, of this history of back pain and false promises made to him to do a much-needed MRI for his lower back on numerous Sick Calls that he attended, they finally gave him a cane to walk with as his final treatment plan. He requested an MRI and an appointment with an orthopedic surgeon.

The correctional counselor gave Kylo a handwritten response on December 31 in which the counselor wrote, "Your issues regarding medical have been forwarded to the appropriate department for further review."

The following year in 2015, on January 6, Kylo submitted another BP-9 Administrative Remedy Request to the prison warden in which he accused the prison officials of having a bogus Level II Medical Care Facility and pointed out the absurdity of addressing his medical issues just on prison paperwork, such as "steps to resolve," but no steps were ever taken to resolve anything at all. He again requested transfer to a medical facility that was capable of providing medical help.

On January 28, the warden rejected Kylo's appeal by writing back to him: "You raise more than one issue, related issue or appeal more than one incident report. You must file a separate request/appeal for each unrelated issue or incident report you want addressed. You may resubmit your request in Proper form within five (5) days of the date of this Rejection Notice."

On March 23, Kylo filed another appeal to the warden in which he complained that the prison doctor, Dr. Santini, had promised him an MRI for L4 and L5 retrolisthesis, back in July 2014, nine months prior and it was not done. He also accused Dr. Santini and Mr. Cordova of treating the prison population's scabies with athlete foot cream for toenails while prisoners continued to suffer from horrific itch and infected the entire prison population. He again demanded medical transfer to another prison where he could be treated.

Dr. Santini and Mr. Cordova responded to this appeal to the warden by saying that Kylo had been scheduled for an MRI, and they also promised to review his case on March 27. Dr. Santini did see him on March 27, on the day of this scheduled appointment (somewhat unusual, because in my experience, almost all promises for medical appointments in prison are bogus and exist only on paper). No wonder this appointment turned out to be a trap. The prison officials wanted to create a basis to deny his repeated requests for a transfer to a medical facility by generating new medical notes to downgrade his care level. These updated medical records would show that Kylo was "healthy and did not warrant any such transfer." So he was denied transfer on this "medical notes visit" and also informed that his care level would be reduced to Care Level II as opposed to what the court had ordered, which was Care Level III.

On March 31, four days after this doctor's visit, Kylo filed an angry Administrative Remedy Request to the warden in which he stated that Dr. Santini denied his request for transfer to a medical facility despite his medical files showing that he had congestive heart failure, COPD, high blood pressure, asthma, bouts of pancreatitis, eye problems, and retrolisthesis of L4 and L5. He stated that he was in great pain when he walked due to his heart. He pointed out that anyone with three major medical problems as per law qualified for a Level III medical facility as the court had ordered in his case. He also explained that the MRI promised to him nearly a year prior was still not done. Then he requested that he would rather be transferred to a higher-level medical facility where he would get some medical attention, even if it meant that the prison raised his custody level (that is, a higher security prison with less privileges). He stated, "Raise my custody level and send me wherever I can be away from games and deliberate indifference towards my medical needs." Kylo would rather relinquish his privileges of freedom in prison camp and go to the high-security lockup if he could only get urgent medical care or any care at all.

Kylo waited for two months and there was no response from the prison warden. He filed an Administrative Remedy appeal to the regional director of the Bureau of Prisons (BP-10) on May 18 in which he stated, "This BP-10 is filed pursuant to CFR Title 28 sub-section 542.18 which requires 'inmate' to file next step when no response is forthcoming within the designated time by BOP policy." (Most prisoners are not familiar with the law, so the prison officials take full advantage of prisoners' rights under Title 28 by keeping them in the dark about this law.) In this appeal, he reiterated all his medical problems, described the history of his illness in prison, complained about the "deliberate indifference and cruel punishment" by Dr. Santini and PA, Dr. Cordova, and requested an immediate transfer to a medical facility where someone would address his medical conditions.

The prison warden refused to forward his Regional Appeal to the regional director through a notice he sent to Kylo via the prison's administrative remedy coordinator on May 22. He gave the following reasons for refusal to forward his regional appeal: (1) "You did not provide a copy of your institutional Administrative

Remedy Request BP-9 form or a copy of the BP-9 Response from the warden," and (2) "You must wait for the institutional response and then file your appeal." The coordinator, in her Rejection Notice, said nothing about Kylo's entitlement under Title 28 to appeal to the regional director if the prison warden failed to respond within 20 days. But Kylo was smart enough to know ahead of time that his BP-10 would be blocked from being forwarded because the prison officials always kept hush-hush about prisoners' rights to regional appeals under Title 28 (that is, if the prison warden failed to answer a complaint within a specified period). So Kylo made a copy of his BP-10 appeal and sent it directly to the North Central Regional Director's Office of the Bureau of Prisons by certified mail, bypassing the prison warden. He thought that the regional office would at least take notice of his legal right to appeal to the regional director under Title 28 if the prison warden did not respond as per specified deadline for an institutional response.

A response came from the North Central Regional Office two and a half months later on July 31, again breaking the stipulated deadline requirements for response. This response clearly shows that the regional offices of the Federal Bureau of Prisons (six in the United States overseeing 122 federal prison penitentiaries around the country) work hand in hand behind the scenes with individual prison complexes to violate the BOP policy and prisoners' legal rights under Title 28. One would expect better treatment as one goes up in the hierarchy in the government, but this corruption is pervasive at all levels of the Bureau of Prisons of the Department of Justice. Instead of agreeing with Kylo that a Title 28 violation had occurred at the level of the prison warden, the response from the regional office stated: "We concur with the manner in which the warden addressed your concern. You have consistently been provided timely and appropriate medical care in accordance with program Statute 6031004 (Patient Care and National Drug Formulary)."

What jumps out distinctly from this paperwork that Kylo received from the BOP's regional office is that the regional office clearly tampered with this prison Administrative Remedy record by making an attempt to falsify information about the receipt of his regional appeal. There are two bright red stamps on the paperwork returned to him: one says his regional appeal was "Received May 21, 2015," and right underneath, there is another stamp that states, "Received July 27, 2015." Clearly the regional office is trying to cover up and falsify documentation in an attempt to go along with the prison warden, but some sloppy office clerk at the regional office poorly trained to falsify documentation is not using his/her falsification skills carefully and is therefore caught red-handed in this paperwork. The BOP will have no defense against this in the court of law. (Please see this particular document with two stamps along with all of Kylo's documents in *Prison Papers* published under his fictitious name.)

Paul M. Laird, the regional director of the North Central Regional Office of the BOP then tells the prisoner: "If you are dissatisfied with the response, you may appeal to the Office of General Counsel, Federal Bureau of Prisons, 320, First Street, NW, Washington D.C. 20534. Your appeal must be received in the office of the General Counsel within 30 days from the date of this response." I believe that the Bureau of Prisons does not have much to lose at this time; they have already falsified Kylo's medical records at all levels of the FBOP's bureaucracy to their full satisfaction. The prison warden also knows that they have means to sabotage Kylo's attempts to file with Washington, DC, in exactly the same way they did with the regional office. This is just one among many devices the prison wardens use to make sure the inmates miss deadlines for further appeals at higher levels. It is a piece of cake for them to make it happen; they are in charge and in absolute control. (Chapter 19 is devoted to the fraudulent schemes employed by prison officials, where you will learn a lot more about how these schemes work.)

Thanks to these schemes, Kylo is now back to starting his requests to the staff and the warden again in the hope that someday someone might listen. He attended many Sick Calls for several months to follow. His medical condition became worse and worse. I saw him barely able to walk more than ten steps at a time without being out of breath due to his worsening congestive failure. Attending these "nonexistent Sick Calls" and a "nonexistent clinic," as he puts it, did not help him at all.

After wasting away for an additional eight months, Kylo once again mustered the strength to start writing his appeals. He appealed to the warden in 2016, the following year on March 3 in which he stated, "Due to my serious chronic medical problems, the court made a presentence report (PSR) in Jan of 2014" (see this presentence report In *Prison Papers* under his name.) Again, he traced his complete medical history in which the physician and the PA at the prison falsely promised that his medical problems would be taken care of when he arrived at the prison on June 1, 2014 and explained to them that he was designated by the court to be incarcerated at a Care Level III medical center. Once again, he brought up the fact that the prison officials in Florence, Colorado, told prisoners itching from scabies for six months, "Don't worry, it is not scabies. It is just due to the Colorado's barometric pressure." He brought up all his grievances that an MRI promised for two years was never done, an ophthalmology consult for loss of peripheral vision was denied, and he was denied transfer to a medical center for care. He again said, "I have been classified as Care Level III by the judge at sentencing, as I have more than three chronic medical problems, criteria for Level III Care." He listed his ten chronic medical conditions: (1) congestive heart failure, (2) hepatitis C, (3) severe back problems causing extreme pain and walking difficulties due to retrolisthesis, (4) asthma, (5) COPD, (6) high blood pressure, (7) glaucoma/cataracts causing progressive loss of vision, (8) pancreatitis, (9) loss of equilibrium and hearing loss, and (10) severe burning pain sensation radiating in his chest due to congestive heart failure, which was incapacitating him. Finally, he discussed a Dr. Alfred who had forged medical records by writing a physical exam and evaluation in the medical chart without ever seeing Kylo in order to reduce his care level to Level II to dodge the court's official designation of Care Level III for him. He also complained that the prison continues to purposely give him Neurontin for pain even though he had been told in the outside ER that his excruciating kidney pain was due to the side effect of Neurontin because of his already compromised kidney function, a renal impairment that was a contraindication for the use of Neurontin.

The prison health staff immediately reacted to Kylo's complaint within days (dated March 7) in which they defended themselves against Kylo's allegation: "Dr. Alfred has seen you and reviewed your health problems and treated you accordingly. Per policy, you have been downgraded to Care Level II which makes you ineligible for transfer to a medical center."

One thing I learned through poring over thousands of prison documents of several prisoners is that when prison officials have falsified records and want to cover it up when challenged by the inmate, they respond very quickly with the creation of new paper trail to keep legal defense current and up to par just in case. Otherwise, the prison health staff may not bother to respond to an inmate's complaint for months. I thoroughly searched all the prison records of Kylo that I could access but did not find evidence anywhere that he was ever seen by this man called Dr. Alfred. Any claim of such existing medical documentation by Dr. Alfred was therefore a false claim by prison officials, which was also consistent with Kylo's claim that he had never been seen by anyone named Dr. Alfred, who supposedly "examined him" to determine that his care level be reduced to Level II because Kylo was now allegedly "healthy" and "exercising daily" as noted in his chart entry by a mid-level practitioner, Mr. Camacho.

On March 10, Kylo wrote the following complaint (BP-9) to the warden: "The official medical records (attached hereto) contradict your response. NO BOP Health Services Clinical encounter is recorded with Dr. Alfred. Dr. Alfred diagnosed severe medical issues in absentia in order to reduce my level of care to Level II in order to deny me adequate placement for medical care for two years." Kylo also attached all records with his BP-9 submission. In addition, he explained that he was unable to walk or stand without overpowering pain; he had respiratory issues, burning pain in his chest, and persistent nightly pain in his left arm, and had lost his peripheral vision in his right eye. He again requested appropriate placement for adequate medical care STAT.

One and a half months later, on April 16, the prison warden of Florence prison rejected his appeal with a notice served through his Administrative Remedy Coordinator. The rejection reasons given are as follows:

Rejection Reason #1: You may only submit one continued page (equivalent of one letter-size (8.5 x 11) paper. Text only on one side. The text must be legible.

Rejection Reason #2: You may resubmit your request in proper form within 5 days of the date of this rejection notice.

This was followed by the coordinator's remarks: "All your extra paperwork can be presented to the staff members when they discuss your issues with you."

Kylo was now back in the hands of the staff to review his extra paperwork, the same staff that was already threatening to throw him in the hole. Imagine the same staff reviewing this extra paperwork!

More than three months later, on July 26, Kylo wrote the following to the prison staff: "On February 2, 2014, the Sentencing Court reviewed a myriad of chronic debilitating health problems that had caused me to be hospitalized prior to my incarceration, and recommended I be designated to Rochester Medical Facility in April of 2014." He further stated: "I filed an appeal on March 17, 2016. The response was 'I had been seen by Dr. Alfred who in absentia gave me a physical exam and downgraded my care level designation to Care Level II. I needed to go from Level III to Level IV with deteriorating health condition, not in the reverse direction down to level II." Another three months passed and he received another rejection letter from the prison warden that said, "For the reasons listed below the Regional Appeal is being rejected and returned to you. Reject Reason # 1: Concur with the rationale of the regional office and /or institution."

In October 2016, just before I left the prison, Kylo wrote the following BP-11 to the Washington, DC, General Counsel's Office of the Federal Bureau of Prisons—the highest-level appeal. He sent it directly to the General Counsel's Office, bypassing the prison warden. When I asked him why he sent it directly, he said "The prison warden would reject it if I submitted it to him; he is not going to forward it." "But it would not be accepted by Washington DC either if it came directly from you," I informed him. He agreed, replying, "I have been trying to get to Washington, DC, level for years, but they keep spinning me around. It will never reach Washington, DC, if I gave it to the warden." I reviewed his BP-11. It was addressed to General Counsel, Washington, DC. Among other things, his complaint stated, "I was downgraded from Care Level III to II in March of 2016 without a physical exam by a physician who never saw me. I was never seen by Dr. Alfred (never met him). As stated in report dated March 7, 2016, I was downgraded from care level III to level II with a physical exam in absentia at Florence by this physician that I have never seen." Kylo also explained that prison officials forged his medical records but actually did not do what the records stated was done for him. For example, he explained, "A script was allegedly written by a PA, Fernando but never filled." He described a litany of medical conditions that he was suffering from that were not being addressed in prison. He also complained that the prison had continued to impose Neurontin on him even though he was urinating blood from it and he had been forbidden from using that medication by an outside doctor due to his history of kidney impairment for which Neurontin was contraindicated.

I, the author have no doubt that the BP-11 did not help Kylo either, but I will never know because I am no longer there. I have published an entire set of Kylo's prison documents, specifically those that show that prison officials conspired to manufacture false medical

155

records on Kylo to downgrade him to Care Level II, not just falsifying but also violating court orders. (See a note by a provider, Camacho R., an MLP [mid-level practitioner] published in *Prison Papers* under inmate's fictitious name. Also see published related documents that show Kylo was designated by the court as Care Level III to be sent to Rochester Minnesota Medical Facility for "unstably complex chronic care.")

A few days before leaving the camp, I asked Kylo if he could give me any evidence of court documents that would show that the judge at his sentencing designated him for a Level III medical facility. He gave me a document dated June 11, 2015. I reviewed this document, which was from the Department of Justice website, that designated Kylo for Level III care (which referred to unstably complex chronic care). He told me that after a review of his medical file in Honolulu, the prosecutor and sentencing judge agreed to recommend him for Rochester Minnesota Medical Center to treat his health conditions along with the back surgery that he needed. He said that he had filed numerous appeals to be transferred to any Care Level III facility as per the judge's order ever since he came to prison, but they continued to falsify his medical records to show that he was healthy enough not to need transfer or medical care.

Because of Kylo's long history of being in state and federal prisons for 40 years, I asked him to write a testimonial describing his experience as it specifically related to the healthcare system in different prisons since his first imprisonment in the Ronald Reagan era. He wrote the following testimony of his experience about the healthcare system in federal and state prisons in his own words and handed it to me a few weeks before my departure from the prison. I immediately mailed out a copy of it to a secure address like all other documents just in case my work ever got confiscated and I got thrown into the SHU. Following is the testimony of Kylo's experience with the healthcare system in federal and state prisons in his own words.

September 1980, I began a journey into the State Prison System in California and into a deadly medical care system that provided the worst medical care. Prisoners were dying for lack of care. And lots of negligence. Thank God, I did not need much medical attention as I was young in 1980s. I was in and out and was incarcerated at Folsom, Chino, Soledad, Solano, and Corcoran state prisons. There I seen many die for medical neglect. Around 2001, I was at Lancaster State Prison, where I saw first memo regarding a federal judge ordering the state prisons in CA to fix and correct medical care problems. The honorable Thelton Henderson (Senior Judge, San Francisco) gave state prisons 4 years to fix the problems. The medical care got worse during those years due to overcrowding, so nothing was done.

The neglect coupled with arrogance, incompetence and deliberate medical indifference came to an end due to the Honorable Henderson's appointment of a federal regulator of all the 32 state prisons in CA. I personally benefitted from the positive changes that started in 2005 with the federal overseer actually hiring competent medical healthcare providers. As proof, I needed life-saving liver treatment and a surgery on my left hand. And I got the medical care I needed. As I sat in the SHU from 2008 to 2012, while there and then, in 2008 the appointed overseer recommended a decrease in prisoners to meet the demands of the state budget. So, the

Honorable Henderson got with the other federal judges and formed a panel to order the state prison system to release 40,000 prisoners from camps and low-level custody prisons. CDC (California Department of Corrections) fought back to refuse the order and refuse to release anyone. The case went to the Supreme Court and judges sent people to Chino State Prison where they found prisoners living in gyms converted into prisons, extreme crowding had gyms and offices full of double bunks, causing unsafe and unethical situations for prisoners living next to each other with not enough supplies for hygiene nor enough toilets nor showers etc. Supreme court of the nation ruled against the most powerful lobby in the state ordering CDC & R to release the 40,000 prisoners to keep a cap of how many prisoners it can possibly have to be able to provide adequate medical care to avoid violations of constitutional 8th Amendment that prohibits cruel and unusual punishment in a variety of medical deliberate indifferences.

The last three and half years for me in the federal system are déjà vu experience of those dark days in state prison. Same or worse neglect; same system of delay, neglect and playing games.

I really don't know if the Federal Judge Henderson can do anything to help fix the federal prisons' nonexistent medical system. But I again see and hear about many prisoners dying. And many acts of medical deliberate indifference along with retaliation against those who complain.

A couple of weeks later, on October 11, 2016, Kylo wrote me yet another statement, similar but a bit different. The handwritten version is published in *Prison Papers* under his coded initials.

10/11/16: Sworn Testimony of Kylo

(Inmate's Register # ...)

36 years ago, I was in the California state prison (Registration #C...) and for over 30 years I saw the worst medical care ever, seen those people die over a tooth abscess. Even had a Celli commit suicide. The State Prison Medical was about denial and delay of treatment coupled with arrogance, disrespect and negligence, incompetence and deliberate medical indifference for all sick prisoners. All this until mid-2000 when the Honorable Judge Thelton Henderson (senior federal judge, San Francisco) took control of State Prison Medical.

On May 2013, I was indicted by a federal grand jury and had just been hospitalized in Honolulu for two months. And after three and half years waiting for adequate medical care and writing numerous worthless appeals, I wonder why I am even bothering to put on paper what I have seen and heard about "medical care" in the Bureau of Prisons. If someone was to ask the director of medical care as to how many prisoners die every month of preventable natural causes and add to it the deaths of people on probation within six months after release, the numbers will be probably in thousands. I have heard and seen examples of it. While at Florence, Colorado, I seen inmate S. from Modesto waste away while asking for medical care. S. was shitting in his pants and medical staff, Physician Assistant, Mr. C. and Dr. S. just made jokes about it "faking it." S. is dead and that is a fact. Was there while E. died for lack of care. Was there when A. was sent to the hole and committed suicide there. Rumor has it they cremated him before the family could do anything to find out why he took his life. My good friend M. (El Paso) died 60 days after he left Florence; he also asked for treatment and died a few weeks later while on probation. Others died but I heard about others. My neighbor tells me about a perfectly healthy young man who kept going to Sick Call complaining about pain (in Texarkana). He was told "nothing was wrong"; he woke up dead and still one morning. My friend C. (in Culver City) died here at hospital after he was finally diagnosed. He was only 35 and left a 12-year-old daughter.

Robert at Duluth Minnesota seen more deaths in Florence for he was there and I am positively sure he counts several more deaths where he is at, for the medical care at the FBOP is nonexistent. Takes years to get a much-needed surgery. I have been waiting for 40 months to get my medical issues addressed and all I have to show is neglect, denials and delays along with several transfers if I continue to insist on asking for medical help. At Florence, Colorado, I waited two and half years to get to see a neurologist who sent me to a neuro-surgeon who recommended lumbar epidurals for my spine, and when I went back to him, he told me that the Florence prison had not paid him for the epidural procedure and he did nothing for me because he said he was not getting paid.

I saw David die in Texarkana Federal camp. I saw a healthy young man from Low (low security) die soon after they finally took him to the hospital after waiting for months and months. I saw J.M. commit suicide. I saw A. commit suicide at Florence Camp. They cremated him before his mother had a chance to see him and then gave the mother some money. I learnt M.C. from Florence Camp died 60 days after he left prison because he received no care in prison. I saw S. die of brain cancer in 2001 (he was shitting in his pants), but they would not let him see the doctor. I saw E. die. Kye here at the Camp knows more about him because he was his close friend. I saw the baseball player die of MRSA infection in five months because they would not give him antibiotics. Robert at Duluth, Minnesota, knows many young healthy people die who did not have to die. Robert had deformed feet and they refused to give him orthopedic shoes for years.

I never thought I would experience anything worse than what I saw at the CA state prison in the 2000s. And that was due to overcrowding. This one is not. This one is worse because in state prison, at least I was able to get surgery done in five years after the state prison reform by Honorable Judge Thelton. Here at the federal prison they take you to the hospital only if they know for sure that you will die if they didn't. I am dying here for the last three and half years in the federal prison system of congestive heart failure and many other life-threatening conditions and I know I will die here in the near future without medical care. I also know that C. two bunks from me will die of a massive seizure one of these days. He has been having seizures twice a week now but they don't care. They defibrillated him and don't even bother to bring him to the hospital to see what is going on with so many seizures. They know that hospital will find out what kind of care they are giving him here. I know that their paddles (defibrillators) will not bring him back one of these days. His seizures are becoming more intense and prolonged.

They refuse to give him his medication.

I am 63 years now and I have tried everything; I have exhausted every appeal and administrative remedy. I never thought I would experience anything worse than California State Prison System, for what I have seen and experienced at the Federal Prison is not just overcrowding that was just as bad, but here they transfer prisoners on years of waiting list for a medical test, so now we must start all over again every time we are transferred, and if you dare appeal and file BP-8-9-10-11, the retaliation by medical is a systematic uniform program. Comparing that with State Prison (prior to federal take-over of 2005), this is way worse. At least the state system made us wait for years to get surgery but did not transfer us from place to place to make us get in line all over again. Here in Lompoc Federal Camp, the situation is quite bad. I have been here since May, six months already, and had a serious pain in my arms with breathing problems, chest pains and a sense of disorientation (probably my congestive heart failure). Seen a doctor once who ordered me various EKGs until he got the reading he wanted, a Percocet for pain and forgot about me since then even though the chest pain persists.

I filed a BP-9 and he responded, "I was treated for shoulder pain." And he was giving me Motrin? The BP-9 I submitted included hospital records from Hawaii and California that indicate I had cardiac problems. So, he responds with "shoulder pain" for pain radiating to my arm which I was told by my physician in Hawaii could be a new pending heart attack. I asked the sentencing judge to help me with my serious medical problems, she recommended me to a medical facility in Rochester, Minnesota, in hopes that I could survive the ten years' sentence. Three and half years later, I can barely walk with help from cane. I now have a level 9/10 pain in my lower extremities. Every day I get nothing for pain, not Motrin, not anything. I was on gabapentin for two years but I finally had to refuse because my kidneys were hurting from its side effects and I was pissing blood. So, I stopped taking it and they tried to put me on zombie meds which I refused as well. I am neither crazy nor depressed. Just pissed that these people show no empathy for the sick. Right by my bunk, there are two people who collapse about once a week for lack of proper medications. Doctors know, they just don't care and I sure hope they don't end up dead one of these days during loss of their consciousness.

I hope and pray someone, someday soon does something to fix the systematic denial of adequate medical care. And I sure hope a good god allows me to get out not in a body bag but alive. As far as appeals etc. I have no more faith in due process nor procedure after filing so many appeals requesting adequate medical care or transfer to a medical hospital prison.

I was Level III for a year at the camp. When camp administrator found out, medical gave me a physical exam in absentia and downgraded my care to Care Level II and transferred me here to get rid of me, so I would have to start all over again.

Under penalty of perjury I declare all the above to be true recollection as far as I can remember.

Kylo Signed

I asked Kylo to specifically provide me the medical notes that indicate or suggest that he was seen by Dr. Alfred who downgraded him to Care Level II based on his evaluation. Kylo dug out the following notes, which, he explained, an empathetic healthcare worker slipped into his hands, a worker who knew that these medical notes were forged.

The first one of these notes is Kylo's Intake Screening at the time of his transfer to Lompoc Prison Camp.

2/16/16:   U.S. DEPARTMENT OF JUSTICE

BUREAU OF PRISONS

HEALTH SERVICES DEPARTMENT

MEDICAL DUTY STATUS

Confined to Living Quarters except meal lines, pill line and treatment

Other: Double mattress for medical purposes

Limitations: All sports

Other: Orthopedic Shoes

CANE 6/9/14

Start Date 6/9/14

Exp. Date 6/13/14

Restriction – Not Medically Cleared

Comments: Care Level III X-ray of lower back showed retrolisthesis of L4-L5

Signed on 2/16/16 Camancho. R. MLP (mid-level practitioner)

Kylo informed me that the mid-level practitioner who wrote the above intake medical note is the same "care provider" who later

164

forged a note suggesting that he had been seen by Dr. Alfred who downgraded him to Care Level II care. When he reviewed his medical records that were released to him, no such note by Dr. Alfred existed. The medical notes that I reviewed are consistent with Kylo's narration that he was never seen or medically evaluated by anyone who went by the name of Dr. Alfred.

A few days later, the mid-level practitioner forged a new note in order to put an end to Kylo's endless complaints about the court's designation of him as Care Level III. The note states the following:

BUREAU OF PRISONS

HEALTH SERVICES

CLINICAL ENCOUNTER – ADMINISTRATIVE NOTE

Provider Camacho R. MLP

Per physician: Dr. Alfred. (Reg Care level status – was changed
    from CL3 to CL2)

61-year-old white Hispanic male's BOP records since 6/2013
    seen in Emergency Department 6/13 HON, treated and
    released, no hospitalization reports noted.

Arrived FLP 6/14

Has consulted pain management for spine/radicular pain.

Last CCC 12/15 reported that he uses a cane and albuterol,
    but exercises regularly

Labs in 3/16 next CCC 6/16 (6 months)

Asthma: did not find that he has history of intubation,
    hospitalization or request frequent clinical intervention
    (one visit 2/16 for acute bronchitis)

CHF (congestive heart failure) must meet NYHA class III,
    since he exercises regularly, I doubt he meets criteria.

HTN (hypertension: blood pressure)

Glaucoma:

Chronic low back pain/neuropathy: consult report for steroid injections.

I find nothing that warrants Care level III, may be CL2, since he is scheduled every six months. Care level II requires clinical follow up 1–6 months (episodically less often) or > 70-year-old care Level I requires follow up no more than q 6 months (with occasional acute care episodes). I suggest medical hold until rehab/pain management consult completed.

Completed by Camacho R. MLP on 2/19/2016

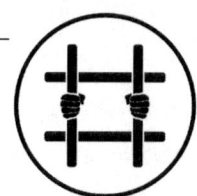

## CHAPTER 11

# FROM A NINE-FOOT HOLE TO "THE HOLE": THE TESTIMONY OF A 77-YEAR-OLD INMATE

THE FOLLOWING IS THE TESTIMONY OF A 77-YEAR-OLD, very sick and frail inmate, Walter, who fell into a nine-foot hole at work while on the job at the prison's horticulture farm. He asked for medical care owing to tremendous pain he was experiencing caused by microfractures. He was sent to the solitary cell for persistently demanding medical attention. In addition to his job-related accident, he already suffered from a case of severe sarcoidosis, heart attack, triple bypass, cardiac stents, vertigo, and nystagmus. Walter was incarcerated for two years from November 23, 2015, to November 23, 2017.

## VT Horticulture, Lompoc USP
## (United States Penitentiary)
## Inmate Testimony

I was injured on the job on 3/19/16 at VT Horticulture at the Lompoc Farm while working in the pm (12:00–2:00 shift). We were moving potted plants from the shaded platform to the east side of the green house building. I fell backwards into an open, uncovered, unmarked concrete pit which can best be described as a type of window well. There is a 4" curb around the pit (easy to trip against and unmarked or protected as a hazard.) The pit is about 4–5 feet long, 3–4 feet wide and 4–5 feet deep. Falling backwards, I hit my head against the concrete wall first and then hit the bottom with my full weight (185 lbs.) on my back against the concrete bottom. I am 77 years old, 5' 10" tall, the hole is 4–5 feet deep; the ambulance paramedics estimated the fall at 9 feet deep. Two fellow prisoners pulled me out of the hole. I was dazed from my head hitting the wall side as I fell to the bottom. The wind was knocked out of me. As I got up to walk around, someone said I was pale. I replied, "I think I am ok" (not knowing the full extent of the impact). Mr. Marshal, the horticulture CO (corrections officer) said I 'd better go up to the medical office to get checked out. As I walked up the hill to the medical, pain in my back started to increase and became more noticeable. No one was at medical as usual, so I went to the CO's office and explained to Mr. Zepeda, the correctional counselor, that I was injured at horticulture and was told to report to medical, but no one was there. Mr. KC. Tebbs was there in the room and noticed

I was in pain. Mr. Zepeda called down to Mr. Marshal and confirmed the incident that he had been there. By that time the pain was getting intense and it was hard for me to breathe. I felt like I had broken something, back or ribs or both. Mr. Zepeda had two inmates help me walk back to the medical. He had called the PA (physician assistant) on duty at the Medium Facility (medium security) to come over to our Medical Clinic. The PA whose name is Anderson, a black male, did a quick evaluation and had me lay down on the gurney. By the time, I was having more severe pain, 6/10 [pain is measured on a scale of 10, with 10 being the worst], I was getting rhythmic contractions and spasms in the muscles in my back at approximately T4–T8 area where the impact was. I couldn't inhale without setting off the spasms. This was about one hour past injury. The PA became concerned and called MD who recommended that I be transported to ER at Lompoc Valley Medical Center. The ambulance came within the next hour—it was still light, probably 5–6 pm. This ride was very painful with every road bump causing painful muscle spasms increasing in intensity. At the ER, I was initially seen by the RN who advised that I would be seen by the MD soon. Shortly thereafter a male Hispanic came in and asked a few questions and felt my neck and head. I said that is not where I was injured, it is my mid-back T4–8. He had not introduced himself and I thought he was a trainee or a PA. I probably wasn't too cordial to him because I didn't know who he was or what his role was. Later, he came back and ordered a CT and digital films. By that time, the pain was hitting a 10/10 with each intense muscle spasm. He ordered diazepam 5 mg or 10 mg. It did not do anything for me. I asked for soma (that is what I prescribe for my patients for muscle relaxation). He said they did not have that available. By that time, he knew I was an OMFS (oral and maxillofacial surgeon) and was familiar with what was going on and he changed his demeanor and was more communicative. It turns out he was the ER-MD.

The CT results came back and he said there was no major fracture evident (major? – what about minor? it felt he was not disclosing everything). I recognized that CT was low resolution and wouldn't show disc ruptures or dislocation, or costo-chondral separations and I asked for an MRI. He said he had to get first authorization from the prison. I complained of numbness in my feet and ankles now. The authorization took an hour. By that time, I was having regular spasms that caused me to writhe and move on the gurney and the feet numbness was more pronounced. The ER Dr. said I would have to hold still for the MRI and I said then give me something for the pain. It was apparent he didn't like me telling him the obvious, but he came back with Dilaudid which worked well enough to complete the MRI, which took 60–90 minutes. Later he came back with the radiologist reporting that there were no fractures, no disc ruptures or dislocations, or costochondral separations. I was surprised— given the pain level. I asked for an overnight admission for pain control but he said he couldn't get that cleared through the BOP (Bureau of Prisons), "not on the budget."

It was now 9 or 10 pm. I had not eaten or drunk anything since the injury (9 hrs.). A meal had been ordered for me but had been eaten by one of the staff. I asked for something to eat to take with me if I had to go back to the prison. I was given a turkey sandwich in a plastic box expired the day before. The BOP guard assigned to me put me in his car with a wheelchair and we drove back to the prison camp. I needed help getting to my bunk via wheelchair, the pain continued through the night—no sleep and no pain meds (our pharmacy was closed they told me). The next morning the PA brought me a wheelchair and a prescription for Percocet for a.m. and p.m. to be picked up daily at the pill-line. I was given two weeks' recovery time off work before I would have to go back to work. I had no follow up for injury by the Camp MD. I was tapered off Percocet to just a.m. use after the first week, then put on Tylenol in a.m. only during the second week. I got severely constipated from the narcotic and asked for a laxative or a stool softener. The PA said, "Use a spoon." FBOP limited my ER care. I have asked for copies of my medical records, OSHA report, on the Job Injury Report, Workman Comp's Report, Safety Officer's Report and all hospital records. Three weeks later, I was told I had to submit a written request for the release of all these reports, which I did right away but never got a response from BOP.

It is now 6 weeks' post injury and I have not seen any improvement in the numbness (anesthesia) in my feet and ankles. Deep tendon reflexes are absent as per an inmate physician's exam on me. There is complete anesthesia in both feet with sharp shooting pains in my left foot middle toes. I went back to Sick Call and spoke with PA, Ms. Jessica Turner to report these signs and symptoms. I also reported a constant vertigo and imbalance over the past two weeks. It is positional—changing from elevated to recumbent and vice versa caused severe vertigo for 3–5 minutes. The room spins to the right and I cannot maintain balance. The same thing occurred when I lay down. Also, if I turn my head quickly to the right or left, I lose my balance and fall. There is nausea and I cannot tell if there is nystagmus. I am concerned there is a stato-conia dislocation (traumatic habgizithine concussion from fall injury.) Also, I am concerned there is a residual or permanent damage to the spinal nerves (sympathetic and/or parasympathetic functions—impotence is also a factor). I asked for an orthopedic spine specialist consultation to review CT, MRI and digitals to explain the symptoms. PA Ms. Turner said she would arrange this plus a neurology consult for the paresthesia/anesthesia issues. She said she will set up a consultation with Dr. Girone who is visiting here from Regional Medical this week to resolve medical issues that have arisen from Dr. Dhaliwal, the prison doctor's actions. I will ask him (the regional medical doctor) these questions then. Also, I am having flare up of my pulmonary sarcoidosis and need a current evaluation by a pulmonary medical specialist. I am having the white thick phlegm discharge in the mornings with rhonchi (lung sounds). It is not purulent but very thick—it appears to be lymphatic exudate from the Hilar lymphadenopathy that was documented by the UCSF (University of California San Francisco) pulmonary specialist 20 years ago. It has been in remission lately but flares up with stress. I was told previously that if it recurs, to have it reevaluated. A biopsy was recommended then but not done due to the danger and risk from proximity to the great vessels (aorta and vena cava). There may be a need to go on steroid therapy to prevent spread to major organ systems. Sarcoidosis is a granulomatous (noncaseating) autoimmune disease that forms in the pulmonary and respiratory tree. I also asked PA Ms. Turner for monthly labs to monitor my borderline renal and diabetic status. I have only had a lab series once in the five months being here, whereas I had them monthly prior. And I don't know when the next one would be for comparison with previous labs to monitor progression of disease. Or will there be one ever again?

Also, I am concerned about having lost 25 lbs. since being here. I have nightmares and I wake up screaming which disturbs everyone else in the dorm. I submitted a written request from the medical staff after my injury and now again a week ago, for a copy of: my medical records, CT and MRI scan radiological report with a DVD copy of the scan, all the test results, hospital record including ER doctor's report, all BOP medical records of my recent injury at work—Safety officer's report, OSHA report, Workmen Comp's Report. So far there is no response.

Dr. Girone from the Regional Medical has come and gone without me being seen as was promised by PA Turner. I was supposed to see him on a Call-Out last Thursday, but it did not happen.

Last Monday, I started having epistaxis episodes (nose bleeds) of the right nares and on several times during the day. The next day, on Tuesday, bleeding was constant starting at 3:00 a.m. to 10:00 a.m. (for six and half hours continuously).

I went to the Sick Call at 7:00 a.m. hoping to see Dr. Girone. PA Turner said he was only at the Medium Facility that day but that Dr. Dhaliwal was here. He told me to wait. After three hours of waiting, he finally saw me (apparently not concerned about active nose bleeding still going on right in front of him). I saw him at 10:00 a.m. and I reiterated all the problems I had and my requests for a consult with Dr. Girone from the Regional Medical since issues were not being addressed. Dr. Dhaliwal's English is so poor, I could hardly understand what he was saying. He said, "you are bleeding—stop your prescription for aspirin." He said nothing about my prescription for clopidogrel (called Plavix, a much more potent blood thinner for my 5-vessel cardiac stent pass). He asked me to stand up to do an otoscopic exam (ear). He turned my head sharply to the side to look in my ear. This sideways motion triggered a severe vertigo episode (Epley maneuver) and I went down on the floor. Why is he not familiar with that maneuver known to cause vertigo, something a medical student learns first day in his class? Is he a real doctor? Where did he go to school? This is supposed to be very basic knowledge for all physicians. Dhaliwal seemed shaken and flustered by this when he saw me on the floor. He went to the computer and supposedly "renewed" my medications. He then wandered off track and started asking me about why I was in prison camp and what was my offense. Totally off the subject. Then he went into the story of a relative of his who went to jail for nine years for IRS problems.

I reiterated my need to see Dr. Girone in order to approve the consultations I had requested since nothing was being done to date. I again asked for orthopedic spinal consult, neurology consult, pulmonary medical consult, ENT consult. He noted that PA Turner had mentioned them. He said I would see Dr. Girone on Thursday.

Finally, I received an "Injury Report from the Safety Dept." It was entitled: "Clinical Encounter." It described PA processing me to go to the ER for evaluation. There was nothing in this "report", blank. Nothing was given to me, no injury report, no safety report. No hospital records given, no OSHA, no Workers' Comp, nothing that I requested was given to me.

I asked this 77-year-old frail man, who could barely walk, to give me a list of his medical problems for which he believed the BOP denied him medical attention. He gave me the following list just two days before he was segregated (solitary confinement) for demanding attention to his medical problems. He had five vessel cardiac stents 18 months prior to incarceration and was on 75 mg of Plavix a day. He had pulmonary sarcoidosis, which was diagnosed 20 years ago, and was maintaining remission by constant management of pulmonary inflammation through hot/dry climate. He had hypertension (high blood pressure), which was controlled with Toprol 50 mg daily. He had diabetes and was on metformin 1,000 mg a day. He had low renal function (kidney function) and BUN and creatinine (indicators of kidney function on blood work) were abnormal. He had bilateral eye cataracts. The BOP optometrist recommended lens replacements because he had 2/50 vision, which is below the commercial driver's license (CDL) requirements, but the FBOP ignored the recommendations of its own optometrist. He had peripheral neuropathy with paresthesia in both feet and no deep tendon reflexes since his work injury at the Bureau of Prisons, Lompoc Horticultural farm. An ear, nose, and throat specialist (ENT) consult confirmed vertigo and nystagmus, and statoconic dislocation from labyrinthic concussion. He had requested an MRI with contrast and surgery to correct the vertigo. He also asked for a pulmonary consult for sarcoidosis, transfer to a hot/dry climate, and a neurology consult for anesthesia and absent deep tendon reflexes.

Walter wrote the following testimony for me in terms of the denial of care for his medical problems.

> In six months since my injury at work for FBOP, no treatment to define the vertigo, no MRI or consultation as recommended by the ENT. Administrative relief has been denied for treatment for vertigo. Transfer to hot dry climate (to Taft) to reduce inflammation to lungs from the cold wet climate of Lompoc denied. Recent episodes of epistaxis (nose bleeds), having phlegm production, declining renal (kidney) function (reflected by BUN and Creatinine levels); recent new appearance of gouty arthritis in right foot; uric acid blood levels ordered upon request but never actually done; renal (kidney) damage from sarcoidosis; denied BP-8, 9, 10, 11 administrative remedies for second chance early release to rehabilitate for reentry as an alternative. Need cataract surgery, vertigo surgery. Need professional license renewal to resume surgery career, CDL, CPR ACLS, anesthesia recertification, 50 hours of CME. Without these I am disabled and unable to work.

> Intentional delay and withholding diagnosis and treatment which is abysmally below any standard of care anywhere in the world; intentional deliberate medical indifference.

Negligent infliction of emotional distress. Violating my 8th Amendment rights through cruel and unusual punishment. Dr. Dhaliwal, the Lompoc Sick-Call doctor is incompetent, fails to recognize seriousness of sarcoidosis, says "It must stabilize before I can treat it." How does a medical condition stabilize without treating it? It is like saying to someone who is having heart attack or stroke: "I cannot treat it till your stroke stabilizes first." Intentional delay by his inaction or by restraint by BOP policy. Dr. Dhaliwal does not know Epley maneuver, something that a medical student learns on first day in medical school. What medical school did this prison doctor go to?

I have been making appeals for transfer to a hot/dry climate for sarcoidosis, have been appealing for cataract and vertigo surgery; no results thus far.

To the best of my knowledge, Walter was still in the solitary cell (the hole) two months later when I left the prison. I have no idea what had become of him. I was hoping that he would be returned to the prison camp before my departure so I could learn about his experience in the higher security prison and the hole where he was locked up. I looked for him every day till the morning of my departure but he was never released back to the prison camp during the rest of my stay. Walter's administrative records are published in *Prison Papers* under his fictitious name with his actual identity redacted.

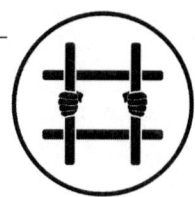

## CHAPTER 12

# A BROKEN HIP IS JUST THE TIP OF THE ICEBERG: THE STORY OF ARTHUR

THIS IS THE STORY OF A 62-YEAR-OLD INMATE ARTHUR, who had been in prison for two years. He was transferred from Terminal Island Level III Medical Facility. He had a history of a broken hip, two heart attacks, a stroke, diabetes, and hypertension. This story is an excellent example of the fact that the Level III medical facilities in the federal prison system do not necessarily have any better medical care than Level II. The inmates at Level II facilities beg and fight for transfer to Level III. They do not know that the grass looks greener on the other side. For example, Arthur waited to get an MRI of his broken hip for two years at Terminal

Island, a Level III facility where he was initially locked up. Just when it seemed an MRI was about to be done after years of waiting, he was transferred to the Level II facility in Lompoc Prison, where he had to start the remedy appeal process all over again. Transferring inmates who have medical needs to other facilities without transferring their medical records with them is a potent device the prison officials use to deny medical care. (How this device is used is described at length in Chapter 20.)

Arthur had trouble writing. He always needed someone's help in writing his complaints. He did not have anyone helping him at Terminal Island before his transfer to Lompoc. Therefore, he had incomplete and poor records of his complaints at Terminal Island, but he was able to do a better job at writing his complaints after his transfer to the Lompoc Prison Camp with some help from me and others. Arthur was one of the 95 percent of sick prisoners who do not keep a paper trail of their "medical care" in prison simply because they are unable to do so. They do not have the money, resources, or the education to do so. In other words, they are screwed if they ever want to assert their rights or sue the Bureau of Prisons because they have absolutely no evidence to prove what they are complaining about. The BOP has created a very harsh environment for anyone, even with someone with a good head on his shoulders, to be able to keep track of any records, for many reasons; it is simply very hard to do so for any average prisoner under such a harsh and prohibitive environment. This is why I have very few documents on Arthur that I published in *Prison Papers* under his name, Arthur.

Arthur wrote an Inmate Request to Staff at Lompoc Federal Correctional Complex on September 6, 2016, in which he stated that he was assigned by the court to Terminal Island because he was a cardiac patient with diabetes and hypertension. He had already suffered two heart attacks and a stroke that affected the left side of his face and caused blindness in his left eye. In addition, he had been permanently disabled due to a broken hip caused by work accidents in 2008, which had placed him on work restrictions. He explained that an orthopedic surgeon at Terminal Island had ordered an MRI on his hip in May 2015, over one and half years prior, but it was never performed. In March 2016, an MRI was again ordered by another orthopedic surgeon due to an emergency situation. The surgeon also recommended surgery, but instead of doing that MRI, they transferred him to Lompoc in July 2016. An MRI was still not performed after transfer to Lompoc six months later—now a total two years of waiting since the first request was made by the orthopedic surgeon who recommended an MRI to be followed by immediate surgery.

Arthur explained that his condition had worsened in the last 18 months and now he was in chronic pain in his hip and knee 24 hours a day, seven days a week, and he could not walk. He asked for an immediate consult with an orthopedic surgeon for emergency medical care, an MRI, and long-awaited surgery. The correctional counselor and the unit manager responded with the following: "Medical Department Staff advised that you were seen by the orthopedic doctor. An X-ray was done and you were prescribed pain medication. If you are still having medical issues with your knee and hip, you need to go back to Sick Call so you can be referred back to the orthopedic doctor for further medical evaluation." The prison healthcare workers had been playing this game of sending Arthur back to Sick Calls for further referral to an orthopedic surgeon once every year and he knew this game well. Therefore, he was very angry and upset.

A week later, on September 13, he replied to the staff in a BP-8 Request in which he stated:

> This is in response to your "Action Taken" for my BP-8 request. I was recommended an MRI followed by immediate surgery 18 months ago, by an orthopedic surgeon. He was certain that I needed surgery based on my gait and the seriousness of my condition based on his physical exam. I do not understand why I need to line up all over again in Sick Calls; this might take two additional years to get an MRI. My condition has much worsened, not gotten better. I can barely walk. Please I ask you to do the right thing to send me to an MRI followed by immediate evaluation by an orthopedic surgeon for a surgery that has been long awaited.

The prison staff and the warden were a bit shocked to read this. They did not expect an inmate to pull the rug from under them in this fashion. They did not know, of course, that the author of this language in Arthur's request was me, the author of this book. I had crafted this BP-8 request for Arthur to leave no way out for the prison officials. So within 24 hours, a nurse at the clinic, allegedly the healthcare administrator of the prison, called Arthur and asked him to sign a document that said, "I withdraw this remedy request." The nurse in the clinic promised him that his medical problems would be taken care of if he withdrew his BP-8 Remedy request. But he refused to sign it. He had learned enough by now to know how this game was played, and he strictly followed my instructions not to allow the clinic to spin him around this time.

During my last month at the Lompoc prison, Arthur was having signs and symptoms of a new heart attack with chest pain radiating into his right shoulder. He started putting in Sick-Call requests daily but he had not yet been seen by anyone with regard to his complaint till the day I left. So I do not know his fate.

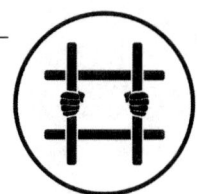

CHAPTER 13

# HELP WILL COME IF YOU COULD PROVE YOU'LL DIE: AFFIDAVIT OF A 62-YEAR-OLD INMATE

**S**AMUEL'S STORY IS BEYOND WORDS. THE TITLE OF THIS chapter reflects exactly what happened to him. He was in the clutches of death every time he got any medical attention at all. You do not wish on your arch enemies what he endured in front of my own eyes day after day, week after week, month after month. Following is an affidavit he wrote to make it public knowledge, and he added, "If I could only get some medical help or get a lawyer interested in representing my case while I am still in prison!" These are his words.

My name is Samuel. I am a 62-year-old man currently serving a 96 months' sentence (a total of 8 years) that started in February 2014 at LA Tuna Federal Prison Camp located in Texas. Upon my surrendering into custody, I brought along with me my prescribed medications which included a year's worth of supply of Advair for my chronic asthma. However, upon my incarceration at La Tuna FBOP, all my medications including the one with one-year supply of Advair was confiscated from me and disregarded. Then I was prescribed Asmanex by the BOP Medical Staff to be used in place of Advair which was a BOP's "nonformulary" medication according to FBOP Medical Staff at La Tuna Federal Prison Camp.

After initially taking Asmanex in March 2014, I immediately began itching throughout my entire body the next day. I reported those symptoms to the La Tuna FBOP Medical Staff immediately when I presented to Sick Call and I was told by the nurse on duty to continue taking the Asmanex until I see the doctor assigned within the next three weeks. Approximately three weeks later I was seen by Dr. Michael Lin who stated that "it isn't the Asmanex causing your itching." He continued my prescription of Asmanex. Approximately two months after taking Asmanex, I began breaking out with itchy and inflamed rashes all over my body.

As such, I again presented to Sick-Call and it took two more months (total 4 months) before I was scheduled to see a doctor again. Therefore, I stopped taking the Asmanex and the rash and itch went away but my breathing became extremely difficult and laboring due to lack of asthma medication. I explained all the symptoms to Dr. Lin at our medical

Sick-Call. In response, he stated to me, "If you do not take Asmanex, you will suffocate and die." He then informed me that he could not prescribe Advair because it was "nonformulary drug, not on the BOP list of approved drugs." As such, I was left with no other choice but to take Asmanex to help me breath but deal with rashes and constant itch. "It is not the Asmanex that is causing your rashes," again stated Dr. Lin who then prescribed Clobetasol cream and prednisone tablets for my rash.

Neither of the medications worked for my rash and the prescribed Asmanex only exacerbated my itching and inflamed rashes all over my body. After over a year of being on the medication (Asmanex) prescribed to me by the FBOP Medical Staff at La Tuna, specifically Dr. Lin, I suffered major complications from the medication and was admitted into Providence Memorial Hospital at 201 N. Oregon St. El Paso, TX on February 15, 2015, and I remained hospitalized for 9 days after being diagnosed with "Steven-Johnson Syndrome" and "Toxic Epidermal Necrolysis" caused by prolonged use of Asmanex, to which I was allergic to, as noted in my hospital medical records as per the treating medical staff at Providence Memorial Hospital.

During my stay at Providence Memorial Hospital, I was prescribed Advair. After being discharged from Providence Memorial Hospital and returned to La Tuna Prison camp for aftercare treatment, instructions were provided to the La Tuna FBOP Medical Staff 'Not to Substitute' my prescribed Advair with Asmanex which caused me to be diagnosed with Steven-Johnson Syndrome. The hospital doctor clearly wrote in big and bold capital letters on his prescription slip given to BOP. I continued to present myself to Sick Call at La Tuna FBOP Camp requesting the prescribed Advair, but the medical staff refused to prescribe me Advair and continued providing me with Asmanex instead and [I] was again admitted to Providence Memorial Hospital on May 25, 2015, where I stayed hospitalized and got treated for Steven-Johnson Syndrome and prescribed Advair until my release from the hospital to an acute long-term care hospital where I was kept till June 19, 2015, before being released from this ALTC hospital one month later. Upon my release from the hospital, I was prescribed and supplied with a week's worth supply of Advair to take back with me to La Tuna FBOP. After my supply of Advair ran out, I was not prescribed anything else other than prednisone until I was scheduled to see a FBOP regional medical director on June 25, 2015, at which time I was prescribed Advair by the regional director after he reviewed warnings given by the hospital doctor. It was one [and] a half years later when I finally got this medication.

As a result of my prolonged use of Asmanex being prescribed by FBOP Medical Staff at La Tuna and specifically Dr. Lin, I was diagnosed with Steven-Johnson Syndrome of which there is no cure to date. Now, I continue to suffer daily/nightly with symptoms, including excruciating itching and pain, as a result of this disease, of which I have to live with for the remainder of my life. Not only does the Stevens-Johnson Syndrome disease affect me physically, but it also affects and impacts my mental health as I was recently diagnosed with chronic depression and anxiety as result of constant pain and excruciating itch all over my body which is now anticipated for the rest of my natural life.

I transferred from La Tuna FBOP Camp in Texas to Taft Prison Camp in California in mid-November 2015. I stayed at Taft Prison Camp for approximately one month and had to be relocated due the complications of my disease, Steven-Johnson Syndrome. I have recently been relocated to my current FBOP facility at Lompoc Prison Camp in California as of December 29, 2015. I am now here at the Lompoc Prison Camp and by co-incidence, I am under the care of the same medical doctor Dr. Lin who is now transferred here to Lompoc and is the FCC's clinical director, promoted to this higher position by the Federal Bureau of Prisons. This is the same doctor who caused me to be infected with Steven-Johnson Syndrome disease which shall remain with me for the remainder of my life. Since being here at Lompoc camp, I have had two episodes and flair ups as a direct result of Steven-Johnson Syndrome disease for which Dr. Lin has provided me with antibiotics and prednisone.

The above statement is my declaration which serves as an affidavit and is supported and documented by medical records from the hospital and emails within my possession that are available upon request.

Respectfully submitted
Inmate Samuel
Registration # given
Lompoc, West Farm Road, USP
(United States Penitentiary)

I asked Samuel to request his medical records from the BOP, but there was no cooperation from the FBOP for the release of his medical records—not a surprise. However, I managed to obtain his records from the hospitals where he was hospitalized for months at a time. I reviewed those records. Following is a brief summary of what the records show as viewed by a seasoned physician.

Samuel was admitted to the ER of Providence Memorial Hospital for shortness of breath and generalized extensive rash and skin breakdowns on February 2, 2015; his first hospitalization after one year of incarceration. The emergency room physician's medical notes show that upon arrival, Samuel had hypoxemia due to exacerbation of a long-standing history of bronchial asthma. The note stated in bold letters that the symptoms were caused by an allergy to Asmanex, which led to multiple skin breakdowns all over his body, neck, and mid thighs bilaterally and caused severe shortness of breath with hypoxia (oxygen deprivation.) The ER physician's assessment was "severe allergic reaction to Asmanex," triggering hypoxemia and bronchial asthma in a patient with prior history of hypertension and congenital heart abnormalities such as dextrocardiac congenital abnormalities with situs inversus. The physician immediately ordered to discontinue Asmanex and start the patient on Advair, give him IV steroids STAT, and perform pulmonary evaluation with DVT prophylaxis. Samuel's EKG upon arrival showed a right bundle branch block of his heart.

Samuel's discharge from the hospital on February 23 showed the following assessment by the discharging MD: The inmate was discharged with a diagnosis of severe allergic reaction secondary to Asmanex that led to Stevens-Johnson Syndrome and extensive blistering lesions on both the skin and mucosa and respiratory failure due to acute exacerbation of asthma caused by Asmanex. Upon his discharge from the hospital, the discharging attending physician wrote the following prescription for Samuel, to be filled at the prison pharmacy. The prescription dated February 17, 2015, states:

ADVAIR ONLY: BRAND MEDICALLY NECESSARY
DO NOT SUBSTITUTE
ADVAIR: 250/50 - 60 dose DPI
Sig: i puff bid (twice a day)

Nine days passed since Samuel's discharge from the hospital and return to the prison, and the prison officials did not fill his prescription. He wrote an appeal to the prison officials on February 28 stating that he nearly died in the hospital if it were not for the divine intervention and the hospital nurse on duty Ms. Pierce. He begged for his medication. He wrote another Inmate Request to Staff for this medication on March 2 but the staff did not respond. There was no response from the medical director or medical staff after a second request. Weeks after making multiple requests and emphasizing that any substitute for Advair as per the hospital physician would rehospitalize him or kill him. He finally heard back from the medical staff in which Ms. Avila. stated: "I was notified today by the pharmacy that the Advair was not approved. You will need to be prescribed the same substitute, Asmanex, from our formulary. Watch for a Call-Out."

Samuel wrote another urgent Request to Staff on March 5 reminding the staff that the hospital's prescription said in bold letters, "PLEASE DO NOT SUBSTITUTE; ADVAIR ONLY AND BRAND NECESSARY." He asked, "Why going contrary to the doctor's instructions? I have complained for one year that I was allergic to the substitute until I almost died."

Nearly three additional months elapsed and Samuel was now on the brink of death. He wrote the following statement to the staff and the warden on May 24 in which he described his experience with the prison clinic that morning: "I returned to the pill-line and reported my rapidly deteriorating health condition." He explained to the nurse that he was dying and could not breathe and the nurse, Ms. Blitch threatened him: "You will be thrown into the hole if you don't leave right now." According to Samuel, he was "becoming more afraid to die in prison camp, talk less dying in the hole." He was unable to sleep that night and cried from the pain throughout the night while the entire dorm heard him weep.

The following morning Samuel collapsed and was taken back to the hospital via ambulance. I reviewed his hospital doctor's notes obtained from his second hospitalization at Providence Memorial Hospital on May 25. Dr. William C. Janss's history and physical states that Samuel from La Tuna prison returned for admission with Steven-Johnson Syndrome, a rash covering most of his body and mucous membranes, his mouth, hands, and the soles of his feet. The doctor noted that the patient was recently hospitalized for weeks due to the same reasons, that is, life-threatening reaction to Asmanex, which the prison was advised not to use again. The hospital decided to admit Samuel for stabilization with a plan to eventually transfer him to an acute long-term care hospital. It took Providence Hospital more than two weeks to stabilize his condition before transferring him to El Paso Long-Term Care Hospital on June 7.

I reviewed the doctor's progress notes from the long-term acute care hospital. The notes show that Samuel was still full of multiple dermatitis, including blisters, vesicles, and bullae on most of his trunk and upper arms, the nasal mucosa, anterior nares as well as oral buccal palatal mucosa with odynophagia upon his arrival at the acute care hospital, despite two weeks of efforts and treatment at the Providence Hospital to stabilize him prior to transfer. It appears from the doctor's notes that Samuel was not yet out of danger. The admitting doctor at the long-term acute care hospital described Samuel's weeping ulcers due to recurrent Steven-Johnson Syndrome and the patient experiencing tremendous pain as a result. This explained to me what Samuel meant by "I am dying" when he went to see the nurse at the pill-call line just before his collapse and hospitalization. Apparently, he was begging the nurse for help to which the nurse responded, "If you don't leave right now, I will send you to the hole."

Samuel stayed at this hospital for an additional month where he was evaluated by infectious disease, psychiatry, and other specialties and ultimately discharged back to his detention facility on June 19. His discharge summary from the hospital describes his history of being given Asmanex despite multiple warnings.

I was able to obtain some prison medical records written after these three hospital admissions (two admissions at the Providence Hospital followed by a transfer to El Paso Long-Term Care Hospital). One of the prison medical notes that I reviewed was written by the regional director of the Bureau of Prisons, Russell Kenneth MD, which stated:

> Has been hospitalized 2 times over the last 12 months. The last time he was hospitalized was for approximately one month, the first time for 9 days. He has a long history of allergic reaction to substitute inhaler (Asmanex) and last time here developed TEN(?)requiring approximately one-month hospitalization (including LTAC, Long-Term Acute Care Hospitalization). With his significant history of good response

without side effects to Advair and albuterol would request continuance of these secondary to the following:

1. Hospitalization has been expensive and with his history of utilizing any failed medication, or medications, that have not beneficial (proven harmful,) would likely cause more hospitalizations including increasing morbidity and possible mortality (death).

2. His most hospitalization was directly related to utilization of a medication alternative to his previously documented proven medical treatment.

It is obvious from the medical notes of the regional medical director of the Bureau of Prisons that he, along with all other institutional prison officials, was aware all along that Samuel suffered tremendous harm from the substitute imposed on him and withholding Advair, his life-saving medication. They knew he was severely allergic to Asmanex which nearly brought him to the brink of death. It is also apparent that the final decision to put him on Advair was not so much to save his life but because "hospitalizations have been too expensive" for the Bureau of Prisons and leaving him on the substitute would cost more. The only logical corollary one can draw from this note is that it would have been ok for the BOP to let Samuel die if the BOP had not been exposed by the outside hospitals through their own medical records, putting the FBOP in a defenseless position. By the same token, one can conclude that had it not been for the outside institutions, the FBOP had no intentions of providing Samuel with the appropriate treatment for his condition.

After over a year and a half of this physical and mental torture and inhuman treatment, the prison doctor finally gave him Advair, but soon started giving him a hard time when refilling his Advair, which is business as usual for all inmates seeking the refills of their medications. I have no idea what happened to Samuel after I lost touch with him in October 2016.

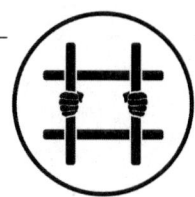

## CHAPTER 14

# THE HUSH-HUSH BUSINESS OF A BROKEN SPINAL INJURY: TESTIMONY OF GREY

GREY WROTE THE FOLLOWING TESTIMONY ON OCTOBER 1, 2016, and gave me permission to publish it. He is another case of work injury (recall Walter) in which no work injury or Workers' Comp reports exist. The work injury was kept hush-hush till Grey accidentally found out the result of his X-ray, which explained why he was having such crippling, unbearable pain. No treatment or surgery was offered to him other than a limited amount of pain medication. He was never informed about the X-ray report.

In November 2015, I hurt my back at work when a forklift operator knocked over a pallet of bread and I tried to save it. About two hours later, I could not stand up or walk and that lasted for about a week. After two weeks, I was able to take off my back brace and stand up straight with difficulty and pain. Now I just managed to stand up straight and remove the back brace when the doctor said to me, "You are in pain and it is causing your incontinence?" I said, "yes." He then said, "You are ready to go to work." I thought he was joking, so I asked him if he was joking and he said, "You are ready to go to work. I see no reason to continue you laying on lower bunk chrono." ("Chrono" is a medical designation in prison lingo for a lower bunk for the disabled.)

After telling the nurse, Ms. Blitch what Dr. Dhaliwal had said, she just gave me lay in and lower bunk chrono. No one examined me or even check my blood pressure, not the doctor, not the nurse. From the time I hurt my back in November 2015 till today September 26, 2016, almost a year, I have not been given one Call-Out to see the doctor concerning my back pain. Every time I have seen medical staff, it has been because I walked in on them, no matter the fact that I have been putting in a minimum of two Sick-Call requests per week since November of last year, now almost a year. Sick-Call request should result in a Call-Out but it never has.

Around the end of July or beginning of August 2016, I managed to see Dr. Pelton, the regional medical director because I heard that he was in and I crashed into his office without permission taking a huge risk of being thrown into the SHU for doing that.

I explained to him about my back and how I had just gotten out of the hospital where I had been taken for emergency because of a hemoglobin count of 6.0 and for colonoscopy for possible colonic bleeding. I explained how they (the medical staff) had not given me my medication after getting out of the hospital. Then I explained about how I have been in consistent pain for the last several months.

Dr. Pelton explained my X-ray and said, "no wonder you are in so much pain, your L-4 vertebra is crushed." Then he said that I qualify for pain medication and he gave me Tylenol #3, two tabs in the morning and two at night. Taking Tylenol #3 helped a little bit but I asked Dr. Dhaliwal to give me something stronger. I was taking Tylenol #3 and extra strength Tylenol 400 mg a day at that time. Dhaliwal prescribed morphine 30 mg a.m. and 30 mg p.m. That seemed to help for about a week but then it would not allow my body to rest.

Dhaliwal also prescribed Cymbalta. When I asked him what the side effects were, he told me, "It will make you sleepy." I had horrible side effects from Cymbalta and as I could not sleep, tightness in my chest, discolored lips, itchy skin, couldn't eat and could not urinate. So, I stopped its use.

On September 23, I went to pill line in the morning and told Ms. Deepka that I was in extreme pain and have been for two days. She told me, "Sign up for a Sick-Call for Monday morning." I told her that I had been signing for Sick-Calls for long time and she repeated, "Sign up for Sick-Call." Later that night around 6:30 p.m. I sent a friend to get the CO (corrections officer). My friend informed the CO that I told him that I was in "too much pain to go to medical and need my pain pills to be brought to him." The CO [Harris] said [to his friend], "The Medical won't be giving him his pills and the lieutenant says that he will put Grey in 'seg' (segregation/isolation/solitary confinement) if he can't make it to the pill-line."

When the CO, Mr. Harris, saw me, he told me, "Medical will not bring you pills and the lieutenant says that if it is a problem, then he will put you in 'seg', so you will be closer to your pills." At 7:15 p.m., Mr. Harris (CO) yelled at me because I had not gone down to get my pills and ordered me to go to the pill-line before the nurse left. Through assistance, I made it to the pill-line and told Ms. Deepka, "I am in extreme pain and I need something more to help me deal with it." She asked if I had the same pain that I had been complaining about earlier. I told her "yes, I have not had any relief for three days." She told me that she would take care of me. She said, "Go back to your bunk and I will call Dr. Dhaliwal and then come to you." In excruciating pain, I was almost back to the dorm 15 minutes later, when I watched Ms. Deepka drive away.

At 8:20 p.m., I asked Mr. Harris for the name of the lieutenant that made me go through that pain. He replied, "No one made you do anything. I told you medical will not bring you pills and if it is a medical emergency, then the lieutenant will move you closer to medical so you can get your pills" [referring to what he previously noted as segregation, i.e., solitary confinement]. I told Mr. Harris that is not what he said and again asked for a name and Mr. Harris refused to tell me the name of the lieutenant.

Two days later on September 26, at about 6:45 a.m., I had a friend tell the CO that because of pain I could not make it to the pill line. The CO never did anything and never came to see me or call medical. My friend then went to medical and told Ms. Blitch that [I was] in pain and can't make it to the pill-line. Ms. Blitch replied, "I don't make house calls, if he wants his medication, then he has to come to pill-line."

At 9:25 a.m., I spoke with CO, McClinton and told him that because of pain I was not able to make it to the pill line, that I needed my pain pills because otherwise I will be in greater pain and recounted the events from last night and this morning. His only reply was, "I can't help you. Maybe you should file your paperwork."

Around 10:15 a.m., I wrote a note to Ms. Hawkins, my Correctional Counselor, saying I needed help. I am in too much pain to get to the clinic and I needed nurse to come to me because I could not walk. There was no response.

Here I am now laying crippled with excruciating pain in bed with broken spine. And I am told that MRI and surgery may take years. And they won't stop giving me NSAID for pain even though I have told them that the bleeding in my colon was caused by Motrin (NSAID) which hospitalized me with hemoglobin of 6 [blood count = 6: normal blood count is 13–15] in the first place. I have Crohn's disease for which they have never treated me." (See Grey's handwritten testimony which is published in *Prison Papers*.)

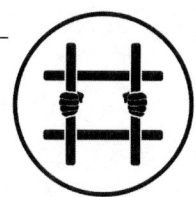

CHAPTER 15

# JOB'S DISEASE: A BIBLICAL CURSE AND PUNISHMENT WELL DESERVED

KINGSLEY IS A 58-YEAR-OLD PHYSICIAN, AN INMATE WHO is allegedly incarcerated for some kind of IRS tax evasion case. His case is still pending in the appeal courts; meanwhile he is incarcerated for four years. He suffers from a rare autoimmune disease called Job's disease. This is an extremely rare but devastating disease, so much so that there are only a few lines of reference to it in the *Harrison's Principles of Internal Medicine.*

Kingsley's case bears resemblance with Kylo and many others in the sense that the sentencing court and the probation department clearly stated in their presentencing reports that Kingsley be sent to a higher-level care because an ordinary prison setting was not equipped to address his rare medical condition. Kingsley was thrown into a Care Level II facility once the Bureau of Prisons took over his custody from the court system. The moment he was taken into custody, the falsification of his medical records began, a practice which is second nature to the medical staff that runs healthcare in federal prisons. I saw his medical records being fabricated right in front of me like a reality show, which I will describe in this story. But first, Kingsley's testimony in his own words.

To begin to explain how such a disparity between expressed intent and manifest institutional performance can exist, let me indulge in "Mein Kompf" (My struggle). I was sentenced to 41 months in the federal system at the beginning of summer 2016. Aside from appealing my own conviction, my greatest concern leading up to sentencing was to ensure that my medical needs would be understood and effectively addressed in custody. My medical predicament was a rare condition called "Job's Disease." It was aptly named after the Biblical character who had been mercilessly tortured by Satan. Job's disease is a particular type of autoimmune disease where the immune system misfires and attacks various innocent parts of the body. Its victims experience ever present torment from skin lesions and inflammatory tumors, along with a laundry list of other internal cruelties. If left unchecked, it offers the additional long-term prospects of destabilizing into cancer. While treatment strategies exist, there is no real standard of care because of poor predictability of response. I was fortunate to enjoy a reasonable quality of life on a treatment program that had been painstakingly pieced together by various medical experts over 18 years using over a dozen off label agents (approved agents used in unapproved applications).

My condition and treatment program were documented by the probation department and was prominently featured in its presentence report to the court. The report also included the opinion of a BOP medical director who said that my needs could not be accommodated in a regular prison setting, but they could make arrangements to transfer me to a higher-level care center to enable proper care. When the day for sentencing came, the expectation was that a date would be assigned for my "self-surrender," that is, I would be monitored under tight restrictions until a specific care place and plan could be arranged where I would serve out my sentence. That plan was unexpectedly abandoned at sentencing. I was taken directly into custody and placed immediately into the very same prison whose medical director said was not capable of providing me with adequate medical care.

My most immediate risk in custody came when it was time to eat. My condition was not caused by food allergies, but was widely aggravated by exposure to wheat, which happens to be the most common ingredient in the recipes served at the prison. My first encounter with Health Services in prison was a basic history taken by a nurse, primarily screening for TB. She was clearly put out but appeared to be dutifully recording much of my extensive treatment protocol. I explained my dietary needs to her and she quickly dodged saying, "I can't do anything about that. Talk to the doctor." I had not been allowed to bring any of my medications into the prison. I pressed her about when my treatment would resume. She withdrew for a minute to call her supervisor physician, and upon returning told me that Dr. wasn't prescribing anything. While disturbing, it was clear that the response given was not up for discussion.

My next medical encounter was four days later. A nurse practitioner performed a simple health screening and rated my health as "excellent." I had already lost a few pounds since avoiding my problem foods, left with only a very low-calorie diet. I was also starting to notice a number of symptoms usually prevented by missing medications. When these issues were raised, the prison doctor advised me to talk to food services about my diet and to report my increasing health problems as I experienced them. He said there was no way to continue my treatment because none of my treatments were on the prison's formulary.

I knew by then that the "food services" at this prison was just inmates supervised by a prison guard (CO) on a floor I could not visit. I also knew that neglecting my treatment amounted to unauthorized human experimentation. While I did not know when, I was sure that if their experiment was to continue, I knew the disaster it would end with would be me!

I did not know at that time that in one of these reams of BOP policies, it specified that every prison would make accommodations for special dietary needs—but only if ordered by the Health Services. Since Health Services wasn't going to order a special diet, all I was going to get was a dietary run-around.

It is nothing unusual for an inmate to have challenges adapting to a life in prison. I was sure I would need some food and medicine over the next 41 months, so I studied the inmate orientation handbook I had been given and discovered the Administrative Remedy Process. It is a four-tiered process that can be stretched out to almost 10 months. First, I would put my request for an appropriate diet and an effective treatment regimen in writing on a form BP-8. That form would be submitted to the staff who had already refused my requests. After an allowed delay of up to 20 days, I received a response telling me that "your records are being reviewed." Since these "medical records" didn't show my weight loss or advancing symptoms, I took the next step (the second tier), which was to put the same request on a new form called BP-9, a form that would go to the warden's office. The warden would have up to 40 days to respond. During these delays, the medical staff was discovering that it was bad for them to arbitrarily stop a patient's essential medications. After three weeks of complaining, they finally responded to blood work that showed that they had induced "an extreme hypothyroid state." Rather than restart the medication I had done well on for 18 years, they decided to experiment with another type, starting at too high of an initial dose and quickly induced a hyperthyroid state. They were also becoming aware of rashes, viral skin growths, and bacterial skin infections that was a product of their unauthorized human experiment. I was experiencing many additional problems but none that a casual observer could see.

In prison if a doctor wants to see you, you will be seen. However, if you want to see a doctor—good luck. You will be seen when they get around to it and those who do not fight for it hard enough will never be seen by the prison doctor. I wanted to see the doctor to get a reduced dose of thyroid medication, and for more blood work because they had previously ordered the wrong test to monitor my Job's disease. Neither of these things happened because I was ordered to "pack-out" which meant I was being transferred to another prison. BOP does its best to keep the inmate in the dark about why they are being transferred and where they are going. They call it a "safety issue." I knew I would leave in the morning and could only hope that my new prison recognized its affirmative duty to care for my unique medical needs. My transfer was standard fare, shackled hands and feet and packed into a bus for delivery. My transfer took four days including a weekend holdover at an intermediary located prison. Not surprisingly, my eating opportunities were very limited on the trip. On a typical day, I could salvage a couple of pieces of fruit, a bit of lunch meat and sometimes an ounce of potato chips. They did make sure to give me my daily overdose of thyroid medication, but I was able to make a rough adjustment by just biting off a part of the same tablet. I wound up in the federal prison camp in Lompoc, CA. In retrospective, I wonder if I were not a physician and did not understand the medication, I sure would not have made it thus far and already would be dead from heart problems caused by extreme hyperthyroidism due to extreme overdose. I wonder what happens to prisoners who don't know much about medications.

By first appearances, the camp would be a very tolerable setting to "do time." The camp was spacious, neatly landscaped with surrounding trees and views of local farm-lands as well as a distant view of the rocket launch site at nearby Vandenberg air force base. Upon arrival, I did go through a medical intake interview, which revealed that the Health Services at Lompoc hadn't been consulted at all regarding any special needs I might have. When I explained my medications and dietary needs, the nurse didn't seem to think that any accommodation was possible but said I would see the camp doctor in about two weeks and I should bring it up then. She was also unable to facilitate a simple adjust-ment of my thyroid medication—that would have to wait for the doctor as well. I had done well in my first six weeks of confinement to avoid any dietary mishaps. I was certainly hungry and losing around three pounds a week. My skin had gone from being clear to having an obvious red rash over about 40 percent of my body. The rash itself generally was just unsightly, while the deeper kind of itching and pain associated with the Job's disease was just starting to disrupt my sleep. I had been far more stable than I would have expected, and actually had more problems because of the mismanagement of my thyroid than anything else.

Things were about to change. The cafeteria at Lompoc Camp presented an unusual challenge. The meals were far less predictable than at my original prison. It was easy to avoid cereals, bread or pasta but there were more elaborate prepared dishes that were questionable wheat or gluten content. The food was made at a remote kitchen by one group of inmates. The servers had no insight on what ingredients went into the prepared dishes for the day. I spoke daily with the supervising officers and the best they could do was to say what was supposed to go into a recipe, with no guarantee of accuracy for a given day. This unfortunate uncertainty and excessive risk became manifest about a week after I arrived.

After my normal process of elimination, my first Sunday dinner at camp provided either another meal to skip entirely, or indulge in a serving of a black-eyed pea-soup that "never" had wheat in it. The soup was quite good, but it turned out that the kitchen had been a few pounds short of peas and had enough flour to provide adequate thickness to the dish. My immune reactions to wheat are delayed usually by 15 to 18 hours. So, I went about the rest of my day without suspecting any pending problems.

The next morning trouble woke me up. Like a pilot doing a pre-flight system check, my immediate sense was that all systems were broken. I had conflicting urges to lay quietly because many of my moving parts were complaining with pain, while I knew I had to get to the rest room before my abdomen would explode. I was experiencing a strong painful burning sensation on my scalp, neck and left ear that had permanently deformed that same ear a dozen years prior. Walking gingerly towards the toilets, I could see in the mirrors marked swelling and redness of those painful areas. That angioedema would persist for over a week migrating around until it had involved every inch of my face, nose and ears. The camp inmates had been dealing with the MRSA skin infections, so I was given a wide berth by other inmates because the problem was so obvious and nobody wanted what they thought I had. I knew the reactions were immunological, but not infectious. I did not know for another two days that the soup I had eaten was contaminated with wheat, so I wondered if my Job's disease had just returned suddenly with a vengeance. The reactions were similar to what I had experienced when I first contracted Job's disease, but in every sense the magnitude of my symptoms was far worse. For a couple of days, I simply rested, drank water and herbal tea, and ate sparingly, hoping that reactions would fade. Unfortunately, they continued to slowly build.

My face became so distorted from swelling that I looked like a different person each day—sometimes like a different species. Multiple joint pains and a penetrating feeling of illness were continuing. My abdominal pain was often intense. I experienced persistent diarrhea and developed rectal bleeding—a symptom I never had before.

I felt a small sense of relief when I received a Call-Out from the camp physician in the middle of that week. When I had initially been taken into custody, I was by all appearances in good health. My appearances made it easier to justify ignoring my maintenance therapy, though no less foolish to do so. This time there would be no question of what my immune system was capable of. I was a "full bloom." When I saw the camp doctor on Thursday morning, his interest seemed limited to the health screening questions he had to check off on his computer screen, possibly since he had a dozen other inmates scheduled to be seen at the same time. He was clearly not interested in discussing or solving any in-depth problem at that visit, but I was able to express to him my most immediate issue, which was the need for accommodation of my diet, the lack of which was the reason behind my continued weight loss from wheat avoidance and a causative factor in the exposure that led to my present set of distressing symptoms.

I was intent on him having my reactions accurately documented which elicited tension and hostility because the doctor just wanted to get through his morning schedule. At one point, he became obviously frustrated with the additional work I represented, suggested that my requests were unreasonable, and threatened to call the guards and have me thrown in the SHU (solitary confinement). That is certainly a "bedside manner" that can only be practiced by the FBOP. I was thankful he decided against that and quickly performed a cursory exam of my head and neck, stating "I see everything" when I told him to check out the swelling and the rashes.

After the exam, apparently to appease me, he promised to refer me to both a rheumatologist and an endocrinologist. I suggested that my thyroid dose could be easily adjusted. But he simply shouted, "I will refer you." After 18 years with this disease I was familiar with reasonable and effective treatments for the torment I was experiencing, but the camp doctor refused to provide any treatment saying it was "dangerous" and I would have to talk with the rheumatologist. He also said he had no authority to order a special diet and that I should contact the director of food services for help. "Next!"

I was already familiar with the dietary run-around, and now I was having my first referral gambit. I knew from talking with other inmates that visits with specialists rarely ever occurred and unless an emergency hospital visit was involved it would take multiple requests over months and sometimes years to see an "outside" physician. That left the net option of seeing the camp doctor as no treatment, no dietary accommodation for safety, and no follow up. What could possibly go wrong with that plan?

I was still very symptomatic and concerned about the ongoing progression of Job's disease. The Administrative Remedy program was very slow and unresponsive, but was necessary mainly to retain legal rights if my care continued to be neglected.

The next pathway to a solution was to have family and friends send a barrage of phone calls and letters to regional and national FBOP offices. "Going over their heads" led to a rapid breakdown of bureaucratic stagnation. Within a week, I was paged over the camp intercom to meet with an assistant to the prison warden. She said she needed to have eyes on the problem their office had been alerted to. She seemed attentive to my history but offered no solutions. I had already met with the food services director and it seemed that the camp just didn't have the resources to accurately know what was in the food served, or provide safe alternatives. The warden's office concurred.

In regard to my need for treatment and maintenance medicines, the assistant told me that the warden and the Health Services administrator were coming to camp soon and I should speak with them. It appeared that in recent months, there had been a flood of letters and phone calls from many Lompoc families, so the BOP had an administrative fire to put out. No one around the camp could remember when these administrators interacted with the inmates. I did get two separate occasions to sit down with the warden and Health Services administrator. The meetings were more cordial than my visit with the camp doctor. They reassured me that my requests were reasonable and that solutions could be found. I was to be one of the few who would be scheduled to meet with the regional medical director of the western region of the FBOP who would also be making a special appearance at camp. While nothing had been accomplished, the activity level seemed encouraging. The fact remained that a common dietary restriction and an easily accessible set of maintenance therapies seemed to be too much for BOP to handle.

Less than one month after my visit with the camp manager, I met with the regional medical director (RMD), Dr. Pelton in the same camp medical office. The RMD, Dr. Pelton, had all the authority needed to solve my medical access problems on the spot. He seemed well acquainted with my medical needs. He wanted to avoid the expense of transporting me to a higher-level care facility. We agreed that a simple dietary accommodation was clearly needed, but shouldn't be that hard to accomplish. He promised to work with a dietician to outline a plan to get that done at the camp. He decided that it shouldn't take an endocrinologist to put me on the same thyroid medication I had used safely and effectively for 18 years, so he promised to obtain and provide that. We had some mild conflict discussing my maintenance program. He noted that my treatments (including my thyroid) were non-formulary and wouldn't be approved under BOP policy. He offered two medications from the formulary that might help control some of my symptoms. Unfortunately, I had previously taken both, one causing ill effects and one simply proven ineffective.

I mentioned that my reactions were immunologic but not just allergic, and that the danger from non-treatment was greatest from long-term rheumatological complications. He agreed to approve a rheumatological consultation and to at least reconsider my maintenance program if recommended by the specialist. My meeting with the regional medical director was encouraging, but there was still far more promising going on than performance. My skepticism increased just days after the RMD meeting when I received my complete BOP medical records that my lawyer had requested though the court system.

This was the first time when I reviewed my medical records that I really understood and believed what some other long-term ill prisoners meant what they had been telling me all along, that promises of appointments with specialists and promises of medications and treatments was a scam and that the medical records were always forged, fabricated, and often sanitized to avoid all liabilities. I had only been in custody for three months so there were relatively few pages of medical records. I noted an odd pattern. It turns out that the word "wheat" or gluten or gliadin or health history was completely missing from the chart. By that time, my reactions to wheat were recorded in the Probation Report, in an outside physicians' consultation report, in all the Administrative Remedy forms submitted, and had been one of the main topics of conversation with at least six different BOP healthcare providers—each with one duty to discover and record my allergies and adverse reactions. The omission simply could not have been an accident, which meant that it had to be coordinated between both prisons. There were plenty of additional surprises. The notes provided by the camp doctor at the peak of my acute symptoms recorded a completely normal exam with no observed redness, swelling or tenderness. While comparing notes from prior notes showed a 19 pounds' weight loss, his notes reported, "No weight gain." His diagnosis was interesting— "dermatitis due to unspecified substance taken internally—Resolved." And, "allergy status to unspecified substance—Current."

The notes from the RMD were also skewed. He noted his recommendation for a BOP dietician, but gave no reason why. He did not accurately report the change he promised in my thyroid medication when he came to check on my Job's disease, he misidentified the underlying immunological imbalance, and recorded only the most superficial type of symptoms that could be called allergic. He then said that we had agreed that I should see an allergist, and that he had offered me symptomatic treatment which I declined (declined!). The medical records managed to obscure the dietary trigger, the underlying disorder and the range and severity of the resulting symptoms.

Medical records are considered legal documents and falsification of a patient's records is a crime, but BOP records are kept under the wraps. I probably received my records by accident because of the active involvement of the court in my case (medical records are often not released to prisoners despite their written requests and pleas), but through them, I was able to get a rare glimpse of how the BOP systematically deconstructs a real medical problem until it simply vanishes on paper. This might explain why it is extremely difficult for prisoners to have BOP release their medical records because BOP is concerned about getting exposed to the legal system. While the camp doctor mainly oozed incompetence, the RMD demonstrated studied duplicity.

I, the author, would like to add a couple of cents of my own from having reviewed scores of medical records (medical notes) by the prison doctor with regard to the health history of so many prisoners. There was one commonality that I noted, almost without exception, in the physician's diagnoses of very ill patients. His diagnosis and treatment at the end of every medical note of every prisoner patient almost always stated: "Dx: unspecified; resolved. Plan: unspecified and current." I noted these words over and over everywhere. These words essentially mean that the physician thinks the inmate has no significant medical problem and it is all taken care of, that is, resolved, problem solved. Every medical note is a happy ending.

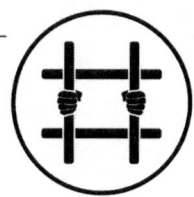

## CHAPTER 16

# TRUTH OUT FROM UNDER THE ROCK: IN REAL TIME

A S A SCIENTIST, I HAVE THE HABIT OF VERIFYING FACTS and duplicating results to make sure that the research data I have collected bears the truth with high probability with a smaller margin of error. I have measured p values in my own medical research on various research projects. The p value in medical research stands for probability and is associated with confidence levels as to the accuracy of the data obtained through experimental research. It occurred to me very early on in my prison investigation what a great scientific proof or disproof it would be if I could conduct a live experiment in prison. And what would be a better subject of this experiment than myself. After all, I was a prisoner as well as a patient in the same prison where I was conducting my investigation. If I could collect experimental data and directly corroborate or refute facts about the healthcare system in prison, it could only confirm or refute the veracity of what other prisoners were alleging. I had already obtained and reviewed the prison medical records of many inmates, that thus far supported the truthfulness of their claims, but I wanted to do more for confirmation. In science, we call it verification, duplication, and reproduction of the data so the theory will become actual science. Personally, it did not take me long to realize after arriving at the prison that the healthcare facade at the prison was tantamount to a scam; the prison was no more than an institution from where nearly dying patients were to be transported to the local hospitals only under extreme circumstances. Under normal circumstances, I would not have wasted my time in this environment to try to get any medical treatment from the prison clinic but I decided to do so for the sake of this controlled experiment, knowing ahead of time that my starting hypothesis was more than likely true.

I had some well-documented serious medical problems of my own, so I immediately went to work and made a plan to go through steps that other prisoners had gone through. I wanted to be able to go through as many remedy steps as possible within the limited time frame I had in prison to see if I noted similarities with what others had experienced.

I started off by keeping a paper trail and religiously followed up on each electronic BP-8 that I filed. My experiment corroborated everything precisely that I set out to find. My findings about the healthcare staff in the federal prison were consistent with my review of medical documentation of other prisoners and the written affidavits and testimonies they gave me.

Following is my story of seeking care, and the related documentation is published in *Prison Papers* under the fictitious name, Nigel. I used a fictitious name for myself as well just for consistency sake. My case with regard to healthcare in prison is a testament of what is going on in the federal prisons. I do not want this book to be about me but about tens of thousands of the very sick and elderly suffering in federal prisons—those without voice. My case only provides further confirmation of the healthcare scam in prison system because my own experience was so unbelievably consistent with the experience of other prisoners. I thought it would be irresponsible to leave my own story out of this book, because it strongly corroborates what I have discovered through my investigation of the healthcare available to prisoners in the custody of the Federal Bureau of Prisons. Following is my testimony and my story based on all internal documents obtained from the FBOP with regard to my "medical care" at the prison.

I am a 56-year-old physician who was sentenced to two-and-one-half-years, which would include six months to be served in a federal prison followed by one year of house arrest, followed by an additional year of supervisory release. I surrendered to the United States Penitentiary on June 20, 2016. (For those who want to know how I ended up in prison, I encourage you to read my personal story in *Guilty at Gunpoint: How the Government Framed Me*, which was launched along with the book in your hands on January 1, 2019.)

Prior to entering the prison system, I was on total disability. My physicians, my primary care doctor, the medical examiner, two neurosurgeons, and a neurologist provided my medical records to the Federal Bureau of Prisons two weeks in advance with prescriptions, a list of medications, treatment protocols, and recommended continuity of care during my incarceration. These records also became part and parcel of my presentence report prepared by and known to the Bureau of Prisons ahead of my self-surrender to the Bureau of Prisons.

221

One week prior to my surrender, my attorney called and confirmed that the federal prison at Lompoc, California, was in possession of all my medical records. The prison officials confirmed that they had received all my medical records. Now watch what happened to my medical records and my care after I arrived at the prison.

The prison doctor, Dr. Dhaliwal, saw me for an intake medical exam on June 22. Dr. Dhaliwal is a Punjabi, speaks the same language as I, and comes from the same part of the world. That I believe was a coincidence. This doctor spent about 28 minutes out of the total 30 minutes with me in this office visit filling in some data in the computer and spent only the remaining two minutes talking with me. During these two minutes, he took my blood pressure with the wrong cuff—a cuff that was meant to be used for prisoners twice my size. Apparently, the sphygmomanometer was recording abnormal blood pressure when he asked what was my usual blood pressure. I told him it was in the plus/minus range of 118/76 and I believe that he noted that number down in his computer instead of retaking my pressure with the right cuff. That is just a trivial detail however, compared to what I am about to tell you.

As he was working on the computer with some sort of data entry without any eye contact with me, I took the opportunity to give him a precise summary of my medical condition and then asked him to please read my medical records now in his possession. I also asked him to review my presentencing report in his possession, which confirmed my disability status due to the medical conditions listed therein as well. I informed him that I would like to continue my six medications and physical therapy care as instructed by my physicians. He told me that they don't have those medications that I was on and that he might give me a substitute. "How about physical therapy?" I asked.

"That will be too complicated," he replied. I did not know what he meant by that. He prescribed me a cane to walk and then called the next patient. He instructed me that I would fill my medication prescriptions through Trulincs, the prison's internal online electronic system created specifically for prisoners to communicate electronically with the prison staff.

A week later, Wednesday, June 29, Trulincs showed that two medications had been filled, Cymbalta (a substitute?) and metformin, one of my regular medications. The prison doctor substituted Cymbalta for all my other five medications. I was not sure what kind of substitute Cymbalta was because it was not a substitute for any of the other five medications I was on nor was this drug an indication for any of my medical problems. Cymbalta is an antidepressant, and depression or anything remotely related to it was not one of my medical problems. Later I learned in my investigation that this doctor substituted most prisoners' medications with Cymbalta, for any symptoms regardless of their medical conditions, ranging from cancer to broken spines to seizures, and for pain due to any illness, you name it. The physician was in his office, so I walked straight into his office without an appointment, taking the risk of getting into trouble, while he was seeing another patient and reminded him of the "substitutes" that he had promised. I also reminded him of the physical therapy that I needed in my right arm due to partial paralysis. I also showed him a paper he had given me on my prior visit with him, which said I had "myopathy." I reminded him of having informed him that I suffered from "myelopathy" and not "myopathy." Apparently, he did not know the difference. In the United States, most premedical students know the difference even before they enter medical school. He told me to come back on Friday to see him to discuss all my issues. I asked, "Do I need appointment?" "No," he replied. Just come in Friday morning. That he would see me while many prisoners had been waiting for months, even years, to get a Sick-Call appointment was a pleasant surprise. Perhaps he was trying to do me a favor, I thought; after all I was not only another physician but spoke his native language. Or so I thought. Was it some kind of favor?

As I was leaving his office, there were several inmates waiting at the door who told me that I took a huge risk, because walking into the doctor's office in the manner I did was a recipe for being locked up in the hole. This was the first time I heard of that word— "the hole"—and what it really meant. Later I learned that these prisoners were so right; many had been escorted to solitary confinement for violations of that nature, because these people who demanded medical care were considered a "security threat." Perhaps I got lucky that the physician did not send me to the hole. Frankly, I was still relatively new in prison at this time and did not know all the rules, which is why I barged into his office. The prisoners waiting at the clinic door advised me to fill in a form called the Sick-Call form and then wait to see my name on the Call-Out list. They also told me that once the Sick-Call request was made, it could take two months to a year to go on the Call-Out list, that is, if I kept coming back and resubmitting Sick Calls. They also explained that the clinic might respond to a Sick-Call request sooner if they knew you were seriously ill.

I ignored what the prisoners had told me to do, because the physician had already asked me to come back on Friday without an appointment; he was going to take care of me. Who was I to believe? Why bother submitting a Sick Call at that point, I thought to myself. I went back Friday morning as advised by Dr. Dhaliwal, and the nurse there told me that Dr. Dhaliwal comes to clinic only on Wednesdays for half a day once a week only. Later I learned that Dr. Dhaliwal often told prisoners, especially new ones, to come back Monday, Tuesday, Thursday or Fridays—days that he knew he was not going to be there. That upset me a bit. I went to the pill-line and when my turn came, I got a bit upset with the nurse (Ms. Pinnell, also the assistant health services administrator) for not receiving my medications or substitutes. The entire waiting room of prisoners simultaneously verbally jumped on me and instructed me to shut up and step away from the window immediately, which alarmed me. I knew I had done something wrong. I shut up of course, but did not understand why. Later, they told me that if I did not stop complaining, she would have called the guards who would have taken me to the hole; they were only trying to help. I was grateful that they helped me before it was too late. I had heard about the hole before, but didn't realize until this occurrence exactly how serious it was, a standard but devastating punishment for almost any violation, major or minor, in the Federal Bureau of Prisons.

Prisoners advised me again to submit a Sick Call, which I did right away. Then I went to the prison library and filed an online BP-8 to the medical staff the same day. The BP-8 form on the computer screen said, "Department of Justice, Federal Bureau of Prisons, Inmate Request to Staff," and on the bottom of the screen it stated that it might take three weeks to receive a response from the staff and that there would be no response if the inmate's question or complaint was not specific.

July 6, Wednesday, I went to the clinic to inquire about my Sick-Call form that I placed in the drop box on July 1. The nurse told me to submit another one because "no one looks into the drop box." I completed another Sick-Call request and handed it to her in person. She told me that I would get an appointment and I should look for my name on the Call Out schedule, which I did every day from that point on.

July 13, Wednesday, I went to the clinic and inquired about the Call-Out appointment for my two Sick-Call requests. The worker at the clinic told me that they do not have anything in their system that showed that I made a Sick-Call request and asked me to submit another one, which I did again on July 13 and personally handed it to the nurse.

On or about July 14, I saw an email from staff that seemed to be giving me an option of an automatic online medication refill request for the two meds that the physician had prescribed me. I requested refill for both the meds even though I still did not know what the Cymbalta was for.

I waited for two additional weeks and looked at the Call-Out schedules every single morning, but I did not see my name on the list. So, on July 29, I sent an electronic Inmate Request to Staff reminding them of my previous emails and Sick-Call requests.

Due to the nonresponse to the electronic Cop-Out (Inmate Request to Staff, BP-8), I filled in a handwritten Inmate Request to Staff (BP-8) on August 9 to initiate the Administrative Remedy Process. When the correctional counselor gave me the form to complete, to my surprise it was the same BP-8 form that I had been filing electronically. This was the first time I learned that there were two ways of making an Inmate Request to Staff: filling in a physical form or by completing a form electronically. The prison policy actually encouraged prisoners to make electronic filings. This time the counselor typed my complaint in her own words based on what I told her. She told me that the prison officials could take a few weeks to respond.

By this time my undercover investigation into the prison's health-care system had been launched aggressively and I knew of inmates who had been waiting for months and years for their medications, doctor's appointments, or radiology tests, and I knew I did not stand a chance; I was not even sick enough for them. Those who were waiting to get care were ten times sicker, weaker, and more vulnerable than I was, but I would want to continue this process to corroborate what others had told me they had experienced in prison. I desperately wanted to spend my limited time on conducting my investigation rather than pursue Administrative Remedies for my own healthcare that would have been fruitless anyway, but I religiously filed paper-work despite not wanting to do it. As horrific as the experience of sick prisoners were, my own experience was just as bad.

Following is a summary of my countless legal requests made to the Federal Bureau of Prisons in compliance with all the provisions of the prison policy for inmates' healthcare rights as well as a complete lack of response from the prison. The originals of the administrative records and my medical records (which I had to legally pull hair to obtain from the FBOP) are published in *Prison Papers.*

I made an electronic email Inmate Request to the prison's health-care services on July 1 through Trulincs, an internal email system set up for prisoners. In my first BP-8, I politely pointed out to the prison's Health Services that they were risking a public health disaster by not reading the PPD (purified protein derivative test for tuberculosis) test results within 72 hours of administering it to new incoming inmates; they had not read mine either and it had been 13 days since the administration of that test. Apparently, the clinic staff had been falsifying the medical charts by stating that PPD results were read as normal. That is what I suspected but I could not prove it to myself until I started reviewing some medical records. Prison is a high-risk place for the spread of tuberculosis just as it is for contagious infections such as scabies. In my BP-8, I also requested that the prison doctor review my medical records provided to him by my outside physicians and start providing me with a continuity of care with my regular medications. I pleaded with them that discontinuation of all medical care could risk worsening of the paralysis of my right arm and my left leg, myelopathy, and thoracic outlet syndrome. I also explained to the prison doctor the difference between *myelopathy* and *myopathy*. He had documented it as "myopathy" even though I explained to him that I had myelopathy and explained to him what it was. I also pointed out that the prison doctor, Dr. Dhaliwal, had prescribed me the wrong medications for wrong diagnoses—that is, for medical conditions I did not have. For instance, he gave me Cymbalta, a medication indicated for depression or diabetic peripheral neuropathy, an inappropriate medication for any of my medical conditions. I did not have any conditions for which Cymbalta was a prescribing indication. The prison doctor had discontinued all my medications that I was on prior to incarceration by saying, "We don't have them here." I reiterated the need for my medications, diabetic shoes, and an EKG for chest pain. I explained that my Sick-Call requests did not seem to get through to whoever scheduled for Call-Outs. I ended the BP-8 by urging a response from the prison officials whether or not I was going to get any care. I waited for three weeks for response as per the electronic appeal system's advice noted on the prison's computer screen but received no response from prison officials in the three weeks that followed.

Considering that "attend Sick Call" was the standard response from prison officials—if I ever received a response from prison officials—I continued to submit more Sick Calls for a month. I stood for hours at the clinic door along with scores of other prisoners. It was very rare for the nurse to even open the door to say hi to prisoners let alone address the Sick-Call requests they wanted to put in or had already put in weeks prior. I received no attention from the clinic staff in response to filing Sick-Call requests and waiting outside the clinic door for hours. I looked for my name on the Call-Out list in response to my written Sick-Call requests every morning but my name never appeared.

A month later, on July 29, I submitted another electronic Inmate Request to the Staff in which I complained about not receiving any response from the prison officials regarding my electronic BP-8s filed a month prior. I wrote:

> Your computer says that response may take up to three weeks. I have not heard a response to an electronic BP-8 that I filed on July 1. Please have the physician read my medical records in his possession and provide me with the appropriate available substitutes for my medications. I cannot sleep without them due to myelopathic pain. Also, please have the physician follow my medical examiners' instructions and provide me some continuity of care to prevent relapse into more severe symptoms, which is already taking place, primarily due to lack of sleep, lack of medications, and lack of physical and occupational therapy. I am here for a relatively short time, so please expedite. Also, please provide me an appropriate substitute for Cymbalta. Cymbalta is an inappropriate medication for any of my medical conditions. Thank you for your consideration.

Again, I received no response from Health Services. On August 8, I wrote a third BP-8 in which I explained that I had tried Sick Calls and electronic Inmate Requests to Staff but received no help. I again requested that the physician read my medical records to identify my medical issues and treat me accordingly. I pressed for my medications for continuity of care. I gave the physicians a list of all my diagnoses and regular medications since he was not willing to read my records. Once again Health Services ignored my Request to Staff, which was written to the attention of the Health Services.

I physically went to the office of the counselor, Ms. Hawkins to give her a handwritten BP-8 form. She decided to type my handwritten complaint in her own words. Ms. Hawkins rewrote everything in her own words after conducting an interview with me. She typed the following:

> **Inmate's Complaint:** The above inmate is filing a BP-8 stating that he has been attempting to receive care for his myelopathy and thoracic outlet syndrome with partial paralysis and pain in his right arm. The paralysis and pain have gotten worse since his arrival. He states that he was on 5 medications prior to his arrival here but now has been limited to two, one for pain and one for diabetes. He states that he has not been allowed medications for nerve pain, muscle relaxer and sleep medication.

> **Relief Requested:** Inmate is requesting that he be scheduled to see a physician with his medical records reviewed, so that he may start receiving proper medications, physical therapy, and all proper care for his conditions.

The counselor contacted the nurse, Ms. Pinnell, at the clinic, also known as the assistant healthcare administrator, who responded in writing: "If he is having issues he needs to sign up for Sick Call. He has not done so since he has been here. He was also seen by MD on 6/22/16. If he is not satisfied with this response, he is advised to proceed with the Administrative Remedy Process." The correctional counselor and the unit manager co-signed the nurse's decision on August 9 and handed it back to me with their signatures on it.

I wrote an electronic BP-8 on September 3 in which I reiterated that I met with Dr. Dhaliwal and he promised me that he had renewed my medications in his computer right in front of me. But when I looked in the system later I saw no renewals. I begged that my two substitutes (one of them an inappropriate medication in my opinion) be renewed immediately. There I was, now begging for the "substitutes," even for an inappropriate substitute.

There was no response from the prison health staff. On September 5, I wrote a direct letter to Dr. Dhaliwal in which I stated, "It has been a week since you re-filled my prescriptions 'in front of me.' I still have not gotten them. There is no online refill that you told me to look for."

There was no response either from Dr. Dhaliwal or from any of the prison's health staff. Finally, on September 14, I noted that the electronic system for refills showed a refill for medications, but these medications were a new list of medications, ones I had never taken in my life. I immediately wrote a BP-8 to the Health Services stating, "I am at a loss to know why I am being given Lisinopril refill? I do not have blood pressure problem, nor I ever was on Lisinopril, so why the refill. Meanwhile the medications I am on are not being refilled! Please explain this confusion, so I know what to do."

I submitted another electronic BP-8 to Health Services on September 18 in which I stated:

> I have not heard a response to the electronic request (BP-8) I sent on September 5 and all other prior email requests sent in the month of July, August, and September requesting the renewal of my medications. I do not understand why I am being renewed for Lisinopril (blood pressure medication), aspirin (blood thinner), and atorvastatin (anti-cholesterol medication)!!! These are not my medications; those are apparently someone else's medications. I have been waiting for the renewal of my medications for over two months now. I have sent several email Cop-Outs (Inmate Requests) in the last two months but of no avail.

There was no response to this BP-8 either. A pattern was starting to emerge that looked like what the other prisoners had been complaining about; they filed and submitted appeal after appeal for getting help with refilling their medications with no help coming forth. I was convinced that there would be no help no matter how many letters I wrote, but I wanted to continue to test my hypothesis to convince myself that the prison was in the business of mental torture and cruel medical punishment of inmates. I filed another BP-8 on September 30 in which I stated:

> Please renew my medications. I have been waiting for months for renewal after choosing the option of renewal online as I was instructed. Unfortunately, my release to the halfway house is somewhat delayed, as a result of my initial refusal of not wanting to go to the halfway house and then

changing my mind to go - [To my readers: I had deliberately delayed my release from the prison to finish some unfinished work.] - Meanwhile I have been without medications which has led to the worsening of my condition. I am in more pain now and there is greater numbness in my left arm and left leg which was not too bad before, not to mention that my right hand and right arm have become more impaired with greater pain and weakness. Please give me a 30 day of renewal till I see my own doctor soon after my release to the halfway house.

As expected, again I received no response. I wrote another Inmate Request to Staff on October 5. This time, I did not go into any details of all the complaints I had already filed umpteen times. This was just another test. This time around, I addressed my complaint to both Health Services and the prison pharmacy. My complaint said, "I have just requested on-line refill for Cymbalta. Please make it available as soon as possible so I have medication till I see my own doctor at the halfway house in the near future. I hope I can get 30 tablets to last till then."

No response, of course. I wrote another Request to Staff on October 11:

Once again, I see the wrong medication list in my online account. These are not my medications; these are apparently someone else's medications. Please replace this list with the list of my medications, which are gabapentin, Carbamaze-pine, Clonazepam, Norco and Metformin. I neither have blood pressure nor do I have full blown diabetes or diabetic neuropathy. My blood pressure is always in the range of

233

120/76 and my Hgb A1c is always below 6.00. A month ago, it was 5. 9 as per Dr. 's review of blood work.

After correcting the list of my medications, please disburse those meds to me at least for 30-day supply because I will be leaving the prison camp soon. I have not had my medications refilled ever since I came here, let alone get any physical therapy for my arm and leg paralysis. Hence, my disability has much worsened.

At this point, I was getting sick of submitting appeals for renewal of my medications. I submitted another appeal to Dr. Dhaliwal and copied it to Health Services on October 13, which read:

My "medication list errors" have not been fixed. The medications listed are someone else's medications which supposedly got refilled on 9/14/16 and are valid for refills till 10/31/16. I came to the camp a few months ago, with my list of medications that have never been given to me. I have been going to the clinic window (pill-line) asking for refills as well as requesting refills online as I am required to do. Nothing has come to fruition after months of requests for informal resolutions. Now I am on the brink of leaving the prison camp to go the halfway house.

Please give me 30-day supply of my medications before I leave here. I have listed those medications in my email Cop-Outs several times and I have given the list of meds to the pill-line window as well. Due to the lack of treatment and my prescribed medications, my extremities are going completely cold in the middle of the night so much so that I am unable to walk to the bathroom to urinate which I need often due to prostate enlargement. My symptoms of myelopathy, thoracic outlet syndrome and right-sided radiculopathy have gotten much worse. If there is any clarification needed about my presentence diagnosis prior to custody, please review my medical records submitted to you by my doctors through the Department of Probation. A back-up copy was submitted by myself and then by my lawyer and confirmed receipt by the Federal Bureau of Prisons, specifically by your prison. You are in possession of those records. It should be a simple thing to do; I wonder why it is so hard. Starting to take my medications as soon as possible will prevent further worsening of my symptoms which could become irreversible if no attention is given in a timely manner. I will be grateful if I can get at least 15-day supply of my regular medications if not 30 days. It will get me through till I see my primary care doctor for renewals. Please advise.

Please note that there was not a single response from the Bureau of Prisons to any of my Inmate Requests to Staff over several months. I filed them electronically all in proper formats and using the appropriate forms as per prison policy, and the prison staff ignored every single one of them in violation of its own written policy. I was also very specific in my complaints as the prison policy required. I wonder to this day, what is the incident of medication error in prison? Apparently, many prisoners are taking medications of other prisoners because of the prison staff mixing up information in medical charts. What happens to prisoners who do not realize that they are taking other prisoner's medications? They are not necessarily expected to know or understand what medications the prison doctor is giving them and why. What is

235

most frightening is that once wrong medications get listed under your name, no amount of appeals will change that list. That list is written in stone. Not even God could fix that error.

In anticipation of being released from the prison, I had already filed a written request for the release of my medical records on September 13, meeting the 30-day written notice requirement, but the prison officials never gave me a copy of my medical records till the day I left the prison. They had 42 days to release my records. I was dying to find out what was written in my prison medical charts. I was released to a halfway house in Salinas, Northern California, on October 25. I sent the prison a certified letter from the halfway house with a signed return receipt requested on November 8. My letter stated the following:

> This is a second request from Bureau of Prisons for release of my medical records (first COP-OUT request was made on September 13, 2016, while I was at the prison). Please release all my medical records to my address within 30 days (as per BOP policy). My address is: Attention: Nigel at [Address]. If you choose not to release all records, please identify what parts of the records are "not releasable" (as per your policy) and explain why those portions of the medical records are "not releasable."

I sent another certified letter with return receipt requested on November 20 addressed to the United States Penitentiary, Bureau of Prisons Medical Clinic, directed to the attention of Dr. Dhaliwal.

> Please release all medical records, and medical notes generated by Jaspal Dhaliwal MD related to my healthcare

during his medical treatment of me at the Lompoc South Camp prison. Please include all disability related records in custody of BOP (submitted to BOP by my private physicians for review prior to my incarceration on 6/20/16). Please also include RDAP [Residential Drug Abuse Program] related medical records/recommendations as noted by Doctor Dhaliwal and the prison psychologist.

If there are any portions of my medical records that are "not releasable per BOP policy," please list those and refer to relevant part/clause/section of BOP policy that deems or qualifies those portions of the medical records "not releasable" and explain why they are not releasable.

This is a third written request for my medical records. The first request was made through a written Cop-Out at the Lompoc prison on September 13, 2016. I anticipate receiving my records within 30 days of this letter as per BOP policy. If there is any fee for photocopying, please send me an invoice and I will be happy to pay for the cost, if any. If the fee is required in advance, please notify me and I will be happy to mail an advance check for fee prior to you releasing my medical records.

I had put the prison officials in a fix with two Green Card Acknowledgements of my Request for medical records, signed by prison staff and returned to me with their signatures. They now had no choice but to release my records or release something, anything that the prison chooses to call medical records.

My own medical records released by the prison authorities confirm the stories of prison abuse and the manufacturing of medical records. When I reviewed the copy of my prison medical records that the prison released to me, I noted a statement written on the top of each page in the records: "SENSITIVE BUT UNCLASSI-FIED—This information is confidential and must be appropriately safeguarded."

My prison medical records had more surprises for me than I could have anticipated. The first thing I noted right off the bat as I started analyzing the records was my actual medical records (which I estimate to be several hundred pages) were missing; only one page was included, which was a prescription from my physiatrist that listed the medications that I was on.

There is a clue here: If a court ever requests a prison warden to release a prisoner's medical records in a lawsuit, the truth is already hidden from the get-go by not releasing the prisoner's actual medical records to blind the judge so he will never have a chance to find out anything about the true medical history of the inmate who is suing the FBOP. Is this what the FBOP calls "unreleasable portions" of prisoner's medical records?

Then I started flipping through the approximately 100 pages; that my prison medical records were about 100 pages long was a bigger surprise. How did two physical encounters with a prison physician each one about two minutes long of history and physical exam translate into 100 pages of medical records was a mystery. I started to unravel that mystery by reading the pages.

The first thing I noted was that my two-minute encounter with Dr. Dhaliwal on June 22, 2016, had somehow translated into 43 pages of medical records. (Recall my story of being seen by Dr. Dhaliwal in a two-minute encounter on June 22, 2016, described earlier when I was wondering what he was putting into the computer for 28 minutes out of the 30-minute appointment.) Now it made all sense. The only entries on these 43 pages that were true were my weight and blood pressure and a notation of medications that I was on, which I had honed into his head during my visit to his office. The other 42 pages were fabricated records of extensive history taking and physical exams. I have never been examined so much in my entire life and no doctor has ever taken such an extensive medical history from me in my entire existence from the day I was born. His physical exams and history taking would be the equivalent of five different specialists doing a thorough history taking and a thorough physical exam, all compressed into one history and physical exam performed by Dr. Dhaliwal on me in a two-minutes encounter. This must have been magic. Then I flipped the pages and noted something particularly disturbing to me.

The assistant healthcare administrator, Nurse Marsha Pinnell, who was in charge of making medical decisions for 3,000 inmates in Lompoc prison complex and who had administered a PPD skin test on my arrival on June 20, 2016, noted that she read it as negative on June 23, 2016, 72 hours later, and it showed zero (0) mm of induration. I have been PPD positive for 30 years (once positive, always positive). In fact, it would not surprise me if a relatively large population in prisons are PPD positive because the majority of the people locked up are minorities from third-world countries, thus statistically more likely to be PPD positive. This one falsification in medical records of a prisoner alone is dangerous enough if you were to leave out the rest of the fabrications in a prisoner's health records. This should explain how the prison keeps it a secret when outbreaks such as TB occur in prison and prisoners die. This one violation alone is serious enough that this healthcare administrator, in my opinion, should be in jail for a crime of falsifying records that could lead to dangerous TB outbreaks in prison system that are resistant to all antibiotics. What the public health officials worry about the most now-a-days is someone contracting tuberculosis that is resistant to all currently developed treatment regimens. We all know tuberculosis is coming back to America due to resistant strains.

As I turned pages, I noted more fascinating facts, such as patient encounters with different doctors, nurses, and paramedics who I never met but are prescribing me newer medications just on paper and then filling in paperwork to show that there is a continuity of care and everything is being done perfectly. Sometimes it is called "new encounters." It does not say encounter with who and what? Apparently, these records are manufactured with obfuscating language such as "new encounter" to fool the courts where judges are not going to ask the FBOP what these encounters are. And then someone called Dr. Girone in a "new encounter" put me on a blood pressure medication (on paper) and then the paperwork was continuously generated by different people behind the scenes to show that everything was being followed up religiously with precision and accuracy to provide the best continuity of care, better than any medical practitioner or patient in the outside world could hope for. In other words, patient was never seen by a practitioner but hundreds of pages of medical records were created.

In short, my prison medical records were a combination of forgeries and carelessly tick-marked blank boxes of electronic forms, recklessly filled in by the prison medical staff; it had phony diagnoses and a list of medications that I thought all along belonged to some other inmate while I was still incarcerated. But in any case, it did not matter, because medications are given only on paper, not in reality.

Dr. Girone put me on blood pressure medication (just on paper of course), but a medical student before even entering medical school would know not to give blood pressure medication to anyone with a consistent history of blood pressure of 116/70. A person's blood pressure does not get better than that. I am glad medical care is provided just on paper; imagine if the guards had forced me to take this blood pressure medication or the doctor wrote in the chart, "patient declined" if I refused to take a medication that I should not be on anyway. You will see when reviewing other inmates' medical records where staff writes, "Inmate declined medication" when in fact he declined because the medication was inappropriate or dangerous for him.

The fill-in-the-blank electronic medical records were filled in and recklessly tick-marked to create a medical chart on me. Now imagine when these beautifully created medical notes are given to a judge in a prisoner's lawsuit. Who do you think the judge is going to believe? The prisoner or the Federal Bureau of Prisons? The judge is going to think, all these hundreds of pages of medical records cannot be possibly all false. He would never believe a prisoner if he claimed that they were all phony histories and bogus physical exams.

My HgbA1c is filled with random number from 7.0 or 5.0, numbers that represent from brittle diabetes to no diabetes at all. A paramedic chose to fill in an interpretation of my EKG as bradycardia, while the actual abnormal results of my EKG, which would explain my chest pain, were never reported to me. For example, the EKG machine detected left axis deviation and other abnormal findings, which I was never informed about. A nurse and a doctor chose to fill in to show that I had a periapical abscess due to diabetes, whereas, in fact, I am not even a diabetic. I have been taking metformin

241

just as a prophylactic measure to reduce the future risk of diabetes. Effectively these medical records confirmed my suspicion that it was not just a few prisoners' records that they had falsified—the ones I had reviewed. It confirmed that it was a universal BOP official program and practice, which also explained why it was such a fight for inmates to get the FBOP to release their medical records—their legal right both by law as well as by prison policy.

My short encounter with a prison optometrist and a dentist were accurately noted, but these are outside contractors, not prison employees, and their notes of history and physical exams were only a page or two long. This was a confirmation to me that these medical records are solely created to fool a court or the legal system to give it a semblance of a healthcare, something that an untrained eye of a medically ignorant court could never even begin to decipher. It is also reasonable to conclude based on my own prison medical records and those of others that it is not just Dr. Dhaliwal at Lompoc Federal Prison who is engaged in this criminally illegal practice but also nearly all healthcare workers at all federal prisons whose medical notes I reviewed. This is certainly true of the western and northwestern region prisons whose records I specifically reviewed. I have no reason to believe that the other four regions of the FBOP are not doing the same.

In further reviewing my medical records I noted that I had had appointments in many chronic and specialty clinics such as neurology, orthopedics, rheumatology, and diabetes, with the in-charge expert of all these specialty clinics being the same physician, Dr Dhaliwal. This is the same prison physician who had claimed to Kingsley (see Kingsley's testimony and records) that he was not authorized to prescribe him thyroid medication. But on my prison medical records, legally prepared for the court system, Dr. Dhaliwal was a neurologist, an orthopedist, a rheumatologist, a diabetes specialist, and subspecialist in all areas of medicine. How is this man, who is not authorized to prescribe a simple medication, a neurologist, an orthopedic surgeon, a rheumatologist, and a diabetologist? [Read about Dhaliwal's true academic qualifications in chapter 23: Care providers from Hell Trained to Torture.]

This reminded me of letter that Warden Langford wrote to the public defender assuring him that his client, Mason, was being seen in six specialty clinics, when in fact, he was seen only once in his entire incarceration period by Dr. Dhaliwal. I am glad I requested my medical records because it cleared some of these mysteries for me. With confidence, I can extrapolate from my medical records and those of many others that I have had the opportunity to review that there is an entire program behind the scenes in the Federal Bureau of Prisons in which an entire team of doctors, nurses, and paramedics are hired only to manufacture medical records—records that are presented to the court system when a lawsuit occurs—without the knowledge of inmates or anyone else outside the prison system. And this is done at every single one of the 122 prison complexes around the nation.

My medical records also stated that I was noncompliant with a medication, which caused them to stop it, something I had noted in many other inmates' records as well. These were verifiably untrue statements because when I asked these prisoners if they ever declined a medication, they laughed at my question. The only exception I found was when prisoners declined prison formulary "substitutes" imposed on them that were admittedly causing serious side effects and complications. My experience also confirmed my suspicion that the creation of false records by the BOP was not just for litigious prisoners as a protective measure of sort but also a systemic practice of the BOP health service employees across the board for all inmates because you never know who would want to sue the government in the future. I will return to this vital topic of manufacturing medical records in Chapter 18.

I have published originals of my prison medical and administrative records and electronic BP-8s in *Prison Papers*. None of these electronic documents of administrative records were released by the prison Health Services upon my written requests because these records have damning evidence. These are the ones that are deleted from the system by prison officials and may also be part of what the BOP describes as "unreleasable portions" of medical records. In simple terms, anything that will expose the corruption and crime of the prisons' healthcare officials is a "non-releasable portion." This is not different from when CIA classifies documents to cover up criminal activity. But I have been able to reveal this by publishing photocopies that I kept for my own paper trail before the prison officials had a chance to delete it from their email system. I have no doubt that these documents are an example of what the prison tells the courts are nonreleasable medical records. These are the kind of records that will simply vanish in most lawsuits, tilting the odds in favor of defense of the Federal Bureau of Prisons.

What prison defines as non-releasable portions of a prison's medical records for "security and safety" actually are parts of the records that expose corruption, the medical cruelty, and the human rights abuses in prison. The prison will never let anyone, not courts or judges, see this part of the prisoner's story about seeking basic medical attention through electronic BP-8s. Any piece of paper in a prisoner's medical record that exposes the prison officials' abuse, mental torture, emotional violence, medical cruelty, or violation of the inmates' civil and constitutional rights is a nonreleasable medical record, which explains why it is so difficult for any prisoner to be successful in any lawsuit that he may try to bring against the Bureau of Prisons.

All cases in the courts are presented based on the prison's documentation of an inmate's medical records, and if the records are false, good luck. It is not surprising then that only one-tenth of one percent of those who will sue the BOP or wish to sue will succeed in exposing the BOP in terms of what really occurred during their incarceration. If it were not for a book like this, I do not believe that the plaintiff lawyers representing prisoners have any source(s) of inside information. Their hands are tied. You cannot accuse the government of any wrongdoing when there is no evidence. Only the BOP has the evidence, that is, the secrets that are withheld from the courts.

The prisoners mentioned in this book have great luck in the sense that their medical records, including many of their nonreleasable prison records, have been made public through this book—these records that the Bureau of Prisons will never allow to come to light. In this sense, I have fulfilled my promise to these prisoners that the nonreleasable information belonging to their cases would be given open access to any lawyer they choose to hire to sue the BOP during their incarceration or when they get out or for that matter any civil rights or public service attorney who wishes to bring a class action suit or to any social and economic justice group that is striving to bring about prison reform.

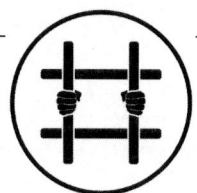

# MY DIESEL TOUR: THE TESTIMONY OF EASON

I WANT TO END TRAIL OF TEARS WITH A STORY BY AN inmate, Eason. The story is entertaining but sad in that it reminds you how low a species called homo sapiens can stoop to manifest the ugly side of its true nature. You can laugh at it because it is fun to read or you can feel disgusted and sick. I will leave that choice to the readers.

"Diesel tour" in prison language means that when BOP wishes to punish and make an example out of you, they can choose to transfer you with the intent of driving you around for weeks or months at a time without giving you adequate break to be able to eat, sleep, defecate, urinate, or rest. So solitary confinement is not the only form of cruel and unusual punishment; other kinds of punishments, which are blatant violations of human rights exist in the Federal Bureau of Prisons and Diesel tour is one of them. The prisoners transported in this fashion can include a mixture of prisoners: all ages, all sexes, and all kinds of offenses. It is like a school bus that picks up and drops off prisoners to different destinations, and very often without predetermined destinations. And that you are very sick or elderly or a non-violent criminal does not buy you any mercy on this school bus. Many prisoners around the country have experienced Diesel tour punishment.

The testimony in this chapter is written by Eason, a 67-year-old prisoner incarcerated for 15 years for a small drug-dealing crime. His own example shows that age does not matter, just as being sick does not matter. He informed me that in the diesel tour he experienced in which he was driven around in a van packed with people for four months also included a very sick, elderly individual. When it comes to punishment, the BOP of the Department of Justice shows no mercy on age or fragility, according to Eason:

> July 2009 was a nightmare. I was living in Gilroy, California, working on a horse ranch just seven miles outside of town. I was riding a bicycle to and from work at this time and one day when I was on my way to work, a Gilroy police car pulled me over to see whether I was carrying any drugs on me, which they do a lot around this area, being a small town of 80,000 people.
>
> So, the policeman patted me down, but found nothing. Then he ran a warrant check and what do you know, it came up that I had an outstanding warrant in Texas for marijuana usage of some kind. So the policeman took me into Santa

Clara County Jail, where I was held 45 days before my momentous journey was to begin.

A company from Nashville Tennessee entitled TPT, which stood for Tennessee Prisoner Transport, arrived and I was then put in this van that was made to carry a maximum of 6 passengers or so. The van had no air-conditioning, no windows and no vents. The drivers were from Tennessee. When I first was put in the van, there were 8 people inside, so we were super cramped. There were men and women of all ages. We were all shackled down and couldn't move much at all.

My first thoughts were that we were going to be taken to a larger bus transport nearby or something like that, maybe an airfield. But no, it turns out we were headed north to the state of Washington to pick up more people, and then to take them back to Texas, or Tennessee. The driver kept driving from Gilroy all the way to Los Angeles, California, then on to San Diego. Then we went to Reno, Nevada.

The drivers were not willing to stop and let anyone go to the bathroom. It was crazy and it was the middle of the summer. Temperatures were up to 95 degrees in the Central Valley, so you can just imagine how hot it was in that dark closed-up van, and without any water! Everybody sweating like pigs. It became like steaming sauna of sweat, piss and shit. Cause if you had to take a shit, you were out of luck, for the drivers were determined not to stop, no matter what.

We all tried to talk with the drivers, but they just got mad. Instead of letting us out of the van everywhere we went, the drivers kept adding a prisoner or two. We ended up with 12 prisoners in the van for two days driving north to Washington, then south again to California, then east to Nevada. We hadn't eaten or gone to the bathroom, or even been given any water to drink all that time.

So here we were, sweating like dogs in this van on the second day somewhere in Phoenix, Arizona. It was so hot, I finally passed out due to heat exhaustion, had heat stroke. Meanwhile TPT was trying to give us to this jail in Glade, Arizona, to see if the jail would accept us, but they (jail) wouldn't take us. The drivers tried to have the county jail there to take us, so when they opened the doors of the van I just fell out—totally being passed out. The jailers there refused to touch me because they didn't want any responsibility for my welfare, because I wasn't "wanted" in Arizona for anything. So TPT went looking for jails to house us. This went on for two weeks, while we kept picking up prisoners to go to jail in Texas or somewhere back east before finally they were able to get to a prison in El Paso, Texas. It took a total of 89 days of being held hostage in that van, with people pissing, passing out, getting terribly sick, vomiting, shitting all over and never being allowed even water to drink. It was an unbelievable experience that I thought could never happen in the United States. But it did. I know, cause I was there. Somehow, through God's grace I survived, although I was never given credit for the 89 days in that van, being held hostage by TPT [inmate is referring to getting 89-days credit toward his prison sentence]. There was one older man in that van who was very ill all this time, I will never forget him. It was heart breaking to see him suffering like this. I don't wish that for any human being.

Overall, we passed through 11 different states in the course of 89 days without TPT drivers giving us food, water, bathroom or telephone services. I will never forget that time of my life for as long I live. I do not wish that upon any human being to ever have to go through that. The only reason we didn't die was because every two or three days the TPT drivers would stop at a local jail where we would get out and allowed to enjoy a meal, a shower, and get a bag of lunch to go—and be off and on the road again in the hell.

I hope the above story gave you a break from the monotonous reading in this part of the book. Now let us move onto the most serious and important section of the book: "Reminiscent of War Crimes."

# SECTION III
# REMINISCENT
# OF WAR CRIMES

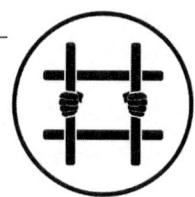

CHAPTER 18

# MANUFACTURING MEDICAL RECORDS

**O**UT IN THE CIVILIAN POPULATION, IT IS A WELL-KNOWN saying among physicians and medical malpractice plaintiff and defense attorneys that "if the doctor did not document, he/she did not do it," which emphasizes the legal significance of documenting patients' visits and encounters with physicians and surgeons. These clichés are traded like candy when a physician is being sued and he screams and hollers at the top of his lungs that he did do it but failed to document in his medical note. In the federal prison, however, the rule followed by healthcare workers is opposite. Every healthcare worker of the BOP must document in the chart that he or she did it and not worry about actually doing it.

The Federal Bureau of Prisons of the Department of Justice knows all too well what it means to our legal system that having documented something means that it was done—that is, the proof. So let the FBOP Health Services employees make sure that it is all documented, and it is documented flawlessly. The idea is why do something when documenting is all you need to prove your point. That is the proof to the judge, is it not? We will give the judge as much proof as he desires, and he dares not question it, because guess what? The proof being furnished is by the government that the judge works for. He dares not question his employer. So, why give medication to the prisoner when you can just document that it was given? This is an ingenious method; the Federal Bureau of Prisons of the Department of Justice has known this for one hundred years, since the inception of the Federal Bureau of Prisons. And it works for them. In other words, just falsify records to make life easy for everyone.

Let us talk about the specifics of the Federal Bureau of Prisons of the Department of Justice's routine practice of falsifying prisoners' medical records. They conceal prisoners' true medical records and manufacture documentation of medical histories taken and physical exams performed by the prison's "healthcare providers." The most powerful deceptive device prison doctors are trained to employ in forging medical notes on behalf of sick prisoners is a device I call "omission." It is a very powerful tool in all legal matters. The idea is to selectively omit from a medical history, physical exam, assessment, and plan anything and everything that puts the prison at liability for the treatment of a prisoner's medical condition. Omit the diagnosis that necessitates treatment, and substitute it with diagnoses that look like medical jargon but require minimal or no treatment. It is like pseudoscientists who use scientific terminology to fool those who are ignorant of science. Our courts and judges are certainly ignorant because not only are they not trained physicians, but even if they were, who is to argue with the government that the records being presented are false. This game starts on day one when a new prisoner walks into a federal penitentiary.

Those who are convicted while suffering from a current or preexisting illness and are sentenced to incarceration generally bring in medical records of their medical illness, diagnoses, current treatments, and medications—medical records that are often already embedded in the presentencing reports of the Department of Probation and court papers, where judges often have already ordered that such prisoners be placed in appropriate federal medical incarceration facilities. The moment such a convict is brought into the prison, often to a facility where there is no appropriate medical care available for the sick and often against court orders, the process of fabricating the prisoner's medical records begins in preparation for successfully defeating any potential future lawsuits. The prisoners' preexisting medical records are looked at by a nurse upon his arrival, his medication list is reconciled, and from then on God be your refuge and your fortress. ("Reconciliation" of a medication list in a medical chart refers to a process where the prison nurse is supposed to make sure that the patient will get the right medications, and in the correct doses and frequencies, that had been prescribed to him by his physicians in the outside world.)

Prisons preplan to deny most of the medications that the prisoner was on prior to incarceration because those medications are "not on the prison's formulary," the first and foremost reason for denial. If a drug that is not on the prison's formulary was the only issue, that would be a legitimate reason for denial and perhaps a reasonable excuse; after all the tax payer has only so much money to spend on prisoners to provide them medications of their choice.

But that is not the real issue: the real problem is that substitutes, often bogus substitutes, are given to prisoners regardless of the suitability of those substitutes for the medical conditions in question. The problem does not end there. The prisoners must constantly and endlessly battle to get a refill for those so-called substitutes. In most cases, these substitutes are not substitutes but just anything, most commonly a dirt-cheap, outdated, psychiatric medication that sometimes cannot be found in pharmacopeia. The previous diagnoses and treatments mentioned in prisoners' preexisting medical records are immediately concealed and blatantly disregarded as to their significance and always made to disappear from the prison's new medical chart (the prison's own medical records) now in the making. The vital medical history of the inmate prior to incarceration becomes nonexistent in a very short time. The prisoner's medical records from the outside world that obligate the BOP to provide medical care to the prisoner are systematically excluded from the new prisoner's patient chart, which is created in prison by the prison's healthcare workers.

For example, when physician inmate, Kingsley insisted that his diagnosis from his court papers and presentence report be accurately documented in his prison medical chart and he insisted that the prison physician examine him and accurately document his physical exam and diagnosis in the chart, he received a response from the prison doctor that his requests were unreasonable; the prison doctor threatened to call the guards on Kingsley and have him thrown in solitary confinement (SHU). This is interesting because a physician is threatening another patient physician to have him locked up in isolation because, in this case, the physician patient happens to be a federal inmate who understands his medical condition unlike many other prisoners. All he is requesting is that the prison doctor examine him and then document his physical exam accurately in prison's medical chart. Upon review of Kingsley's prison medical records, it became evident to me that the prison doctor reconstructed Kingsley's well-documented, rare genetic autoimmune medical disorder, called Job's disease, into a benign "unspecified dermatitis rash" or simple "allergic reaction" to some "unspecified substance" immediately followed by the words "Issue resolved." Kingsley's medical problem was systematically obfuscated and deconstructed by the prison doctor, for example, his 25-lb. weight loss in two weeks was omitted and documented as "no weight gain" and objective data of swelling and rash on physical exam was systematically obliterated from his medical records, while a nurse documented him in "excellent health." These prison medical records also stated that Kingsley declined the treatment—a lie. This lie was also found in the records of inmates Samuel, Kylo, and Walter, as well as my own medical records and many other prisoners who never refused any treatment because they were not offered any proper treatment in the first place.

One does not have to be a physician to see that these prisoners' medical records are crafted to deceive the legal system in the event of a lawsuit against the prison. The message is pretty clear. The BOP's intention is to not provide healthcare to anyone no matter how sick the prisoner is from day one of his incarceration other than symbolic gestures and occasional deceptive reassurances to those who are at the doorstep of death already. The BOP treats every prisoner's case as a potential lawsuit; they do not intend to provide medical care, which in turn also means that the BOP by necessity must start fabricating medical records from the day a prisoner walks into those hallways. This message became crystal clear to me as I properly analyzed hundreds of documents that became available to me, most of which I have published in *Prison Papers.*

For example, Pete's blood in the urine due to bladder cancer was systematically omitted or deleted from his medical records for five years. Diagnoses are almost always being put into some obscure "unspecified category," which in medicine means no diagnosis at all so that any physician can wash his hands of any responsibility. I was shocked to see how often diagnoses for serious illnesses were given an "unspecified" diagnostic designation, which requires little or no follow-up or medical treatment, allowing the healthcare practitioner to be free from any potential accusation of negligence or obligation to treat the sick. Such assessments and plans in the medical charts are followed by a bigger lie, which is "problem solved or resolved." Relatively nonspecific and benign diagnoses are often used to minimize patients' illnesses or conditions.

In the case of Elijah, his diagnosis of osteomyelitis is given to the admitting hospital by the prison doctor while concealing the truth about the serious criminal mismanagement that had taken place before making a referral for an MRI. The orthopedic surgeon had driven nails through the bones of Elijah's foot without first straightening his bones and then later told him not to worry because he would just amputate his foot. All these medical records that are clearly suggestive of intentional medical cruelty are obliterated from inmates' prison medical records. Only the trained eye of an experienced physician can understand the meaning of all these repetitive diagnoses that are given to prisoners, which essentially mean, 'nothing is wrong with you.' And therefore, no treatment necessary, or "take a deep breath, drink some water and go for a walk, and you will be fine." And prisoners must accept those diagnoses given to them. They can take it or leave it; they have no recourse for a second medical opinion or any other opinion from anyone else whatsoever.

Every act of malpractice and criminality perpetrated on Elijah was omitted from his medical chart. If it were not for the Saint Anthony Hospital, Oklahoma, radiology department report, the prison could have swept its wrongdoing under the carpet. If Dr. O'Brian's nurse did not whisper into Elijah's ear that the surgeon broke the middle screw while trying to take it out at an inappropriately delayed time frame after surgery or if someone had not whispered in his ear that the screws were driven into his foot without straightening his bones, omission of such facts from the medical records would not have become known to Elijah or anyone else. It was always an accidental release of some document or a whistle blown by some insider or outsider (an outside civilian hospital for example) that led to the discovery that the prison's medical records were forged, altered, sanitized, and omitted and the true records were substituted with fake records. In the case of Samuel, if it were not for exposure of truth by two major hospitalizations at Memorial Hospital and the long-term acute care hospital, the omitted details from Samuel's chart would never have become known to the prisoner and me, the physician reviewer of his medical records.

Elijah told me that by the time he gets out of prison after 25 years and seeks any justice for deprivation of medical care, it will be too late—not to mention that he could die in prison before his release as he is already 70 years old. Most prisoners, especially the sick, are so psychologically damaged by the time they leave the prison that they do not have the moral, physical, emotional, or mental strength to sue the prison for wrongdoing, nor do they have the financial means to pursue any grievances. What attorney is going to accept a contingency case for them anyway to fight a formidable enemy, the Federal Bureau of Prisons? These prisoners do not have any moral courage left in them. Their lives have been crushed and they just want to go on with the rest of their lives hoping to survive as they cling to their desire to continue to want to live and be accepted by some remote corner of society again. The prison system has a way of destroying that faculty in their brains, a faculty that they must keep alive to be able to exercise their right to want to seek justice or even understand what their human rights are.

In the case of Kylo, a note was forged by a mid-level practitioner, Mr. R. Camacho, dated March 7, 2016, stating that the patient had been seen and examined by Dr. Alfred who supposedly reduced his level of care from Clinical Care Level III to Level II. Based on my own review of Kylo's medical records, his allegations are true. Kylo claims that he was never seen by Dr. Alfred or any other doctor for downgrading his care level. There is no note by Dr. Alfred in his medical chart; this was fabrication of data. The prison officials lied to the Western Regional Office of the Bureau of Prisons that the prisoner was seen by Dr. Alfred who downgraded him to Care Level II thus disqualifying Kylo for a transfer to a medical facility. Mr. Camacho created a phony medical note to silence this prisoner's constant complaints that he be transferred to high level care due to his life-threatening medical conditions and because of the court's prior designation for him to be incarcerated at a Level III medical facility in Rochester, Minnesota. If anything, Kylo needed to be upgraded to Level IV Care due to his deteriorating condition in my own personal assessment of his physical condition as an experienced physician. The medical chart was forged apparently to prepare false documentation for the court system in the event of a lawsuit, especially because the prison had already violated court's order of not sending this prisoner to the correct level of care facility as ordered by the judge at sentencing. I verified this fact by reviewing the court papers that ordered Kylo to be sent to a Level III care facility in prison due to his myriad medical conditions.

Written reports of "Clinical encounters" or "New encounters" are generated in which prisoners supposedly undergo a physical exam and receive a treatment or have a physician devise a treatment plan for them. For example, in the case of Pete, prison doctor Nicholas Arafiles, upon order from the court, forged a medical note called "Chronic Care Pulmonary and Court Ordered." She neither examined nor interviewed Pete for this notation as the court had ordered. A false note is created for the court in response to Magistrate Kenton's order that the prison "examine this patient within 24 hours for his claimed medical conditions" and treat his condition and submit proof to the court of having done so. Even when a prisoner is at the brink of death and is expected to become a liability for the prison officials, prison physicians only conduct perfunctory medical exams that are intended not to help the patient but to tick mark some fill-in-the-blank or tick-mark-a-box paperwork to deceive a judge or fool the legal system. A medically illiterate judge who already has a blind eye and a bias in favor of the accuracy of the BOP's medical records, who is inclined to support the government case in the first place, cannot be relied on for any justice.

Pete's case is not an isolated one. Falsification of medical records is a reality and true across the board for all federal prisoners who are sick and in dire need of medical assistance, as you have noted over and over in the testimonies and true stories in this book. False diagnoses based on perfunctory make-believe exams are documented followed by treatment plans, which necessitate little or no action by the medical staff. Data on subjective complaints, objective histories, and physical exams of nearly all prisoners are falsified on check-in-the-box standard electronic forms where every box is marked as negative findings or "within normal limits." Prisoners' health histories contain only carefully selected benign health information and quite often have critical parts of health history, physical exam, assessment, and plan edited out and fine-tuned to purge and sanitize all statements of facts to reduce or eliminate liability for the Federal Bureau of Prisons.

The prison medical records are manufactured in such a way that it gives the appearance of good responsible care to any third-party outsider healthcare professional who is not in the loop. At its worst, the medical chart may appear to all strangers as no more than just a minor malpractice case in the event some information slips out into the hands of the plaintiff or the outside community physicians involved with the prisoner's care through emergency room ambulance visits or hospitalizations. The DOJ (BOP) wants to make sure that the medical records never show malpractice let alone criminal behavior on the part of the government. Even in the worst of the medical conditions, only the absolutely unavoidable medical information that cannot be blatantly overlooked is minimally referenced in prisoner's medical chart during custody. And BOP healthcare employees do not document it willingly; they document it because somehow it got imposed on the prison system without an escape route out of it.

Personally, I did not find a single case where the BOP appropriately noted in its chart the serious preexisting medical condition of anyone coming into the prison. The prison doctor and nurses seem to document everyone as in excellent health or good health on their first clinic visit in prison, which includes those who cannot walk, breathe, sit, or stand or those who the BOP knows will surely die an unnatural death in prison. The very extensive medical chart note of a prisoner's first Health Intake Exam in prison is sanitized and colored to create a foundation for all future falsification of facts, which is done from time to time on a needed basis throughout the prisoner's sentence. The outside reviewers will never find out about the inmate's true medical records or his medical condition from what is presented to the courts by the BOP staff when it is compelled to do so.

The BOP staff also amends medical records on a needed basis without specifying when an amendment was done and why it was necessary. The BOP presents records that were least relevant to the actual medical complaints of the prisoner that put him at risk of morbidity and potential mortality during his incarceration. Courts only accept the prison's version of the medical records, not the prisoner's version or his testimony. Prisoners' complaints are forbidden from becoming part of any documentation in the medical charts of the prisoners. Almost anything goes with regard to medical records of a prisoner if the prison officials know that they could get away with it. It is not surprising that the prison doctors and staff often tell the prisoners who ask for medical help for their medical condition that "there is no proof that you have a medical condition" or "your medical records do not support your medical complaints." Sure enough, there is no proof of anything, because the proof was destroyed or concealed by those who manufactured the prisoner's medical records in the first place.

Medical records that the prison officials consider undesirable or inconvenient are the ones that forcibly find their way into the prison's medical records because they are generated by outside doctors, hospitalizations, or emergency room visits. For example, when a prisoner collapses due to lack of care in prison and is transported to a local hospital emergency room or gets admitted due to a life-threatening medical condition, the outside doctors write extensive histories and physicals, thus unintendedly exposing the prior history of medical cruelty by the prison officials. You have read examples of emergency hospitalizations of inmates Mason, Samuel, Noah, Elijah, and many others in the Trail of Tears Section. Genuine medical notes generated by physicians outside the penitentiaries based on the medical evaluations of the prisoners returning to their detention facilities after catastrophic medical emergencies and hospitalization get rammed down the prison's throat, putting prison officials at risk and limiting their ability to continue to falsify information in prisoner's medical charts. Upon the prisoner's return to the penitentiary, the prison healthcare staff is forced to make at least a casual reference of the inmate's emergency hospital visit, but it is never more than a sentence, because the more they write, the more they expose their own malfeasance and criminality. And then they go on with their business as usual pretending the emergency situation that occurred was not significant until the next emergency hits again, when they have to once again figure out how to minimize and hide details of the new incident. They often fail to incorporate in prisoner's medical records any detailed description provided to the prison by private hospital emergency rooms or practitioners contracted with the prison system. In most lawsuits against the BOP, when a prisoner is successful, which is extremely rare, it is not because the prison medical records showed any liability through its own documentation, but because medical records of an outside source exposed the prison system by revealing the inmate's diagnosis for which that prisoner had no history of ever having received any treatment at the prison facility during his incarceration.

Many other situations can limit the ability of the FBOP to hide prisoner's health history. For example, in the case of Liam, his mother, who was made aware of her son's prostate cancer, put the Bureau's regional office on notice by making phone calls and writing letters to the regional office of the BOP. In the case of Elijah, two senators, Feinstein and Barbara Boxer, and Surgeon General Vivek Murthy were made aware and prison officials were notified that this matter was being pursued by the prisoner's family at various levels. There is no doubt that these outside politicians and government officials tossed Elijah's written pleas in the trash bin, but the word was getting out there, everywhere, that he was being subjected to inhuman treatment, thus increasing the level of exposure for the prison's deadly neglect of the prisoner. In his letter to Surgeon General Murthy, Elijah wrote, "I am very fearful of the retaliation for submitting this letter to your office, but am more fearful of going blind."

In the case of Noah, Congressman Campbell was made aware of the torture Noah was being subjected to daily. In the case of Wilder, Congressman Bercera from Los Angeles became actively involved, not because he cared but because there was tremendous pressure coming from Wilder's resourceful family. In the case of Mason, many outside doctors, specialists, and hospitals were already on the case prior to his imprisonment and then were regularly being updated as to the prisoner's maltreatment inside the penitentiary. In such situations, it is nearly impossible for the Bureau of Prisons to hide everything. It is very easy for the BOP to conceal medical information that is transmitted to it from its loyal sister government agencies such as the court system or the Department of Probation, but it becomes very hard to cover up the medical records generated by the outside public and private healthcare industry in which the doctors, simply doing their job as they are supposed to, unintendedly expose the government. The prison has to make at least a passing remark in the medical chart about on-site inmates' loss of consciousness and similar emergency events leading to hospitalization or ER visits that cannot go without any mention at all. But surprisingly, even those events often go totally undocumented in prison's medical records. They try to omit that information as well and pretend nothing happened if they know it is unlikely that deliberate omission will ever get discovered by anyone. The more emergency room visits, the more emergency hospitalizations, the harder it gets to custom-make and forge medical records.

In the case of Kingsley, he brought this falsification of records to the attention of the court as soon as he discovered it in the beginning of his incarceration. But such inmates with proper education, financial resources, and family support, often white-collar criminals who are on top of their game, are few and far between in the prison system. The rest of the prison population, 99 percent, is doomed as far as their health issues are concerned; they do not have much of a chance because they are minorities, Hispanics, blacks and poor whites.

The falsification of medical records explains, for the most part, why the BOP almost never gives a copy of medical records to prisoners upon first, second, or even third request made in writing as they are supposed to do per prison policy. The BOP officials are aware that written requests for the release of medical records by sick prisoners puts the prison officials at risk. For example, (a) any average prisoner will immediately find out that some parts of his medical records are omitted, specifically the ones that are most important to his medical history, health, and diagnosis; (b) some parts of medical records are either not released or possibly destroyed; (c) the prisoner is never given an official diagnosis with the pre-established diagnosis omitted; (d) all health-related administrative records are not released to him, which are at the heart of the denial of every health-related request ever made by the prisoner; and (e) there are frequent misrepresentations and lies in the medical records. Because of this awareness, the BOP continuously delays the release of medical records until it no longer can or it is forced to release them to reduce further liability. Records are finally released when the BOP sees that any further delay in the release of medical records can become a potential problem for the BOP because the prisoner or his family are persistent and won't give up. The records are then carefully examined and sanitized, and amendments made before the release. The FBOP does not resist the release of records when it perceives little or no risk for a relatively healthy prisoner who does not need much medical care anyway, in other words, one who could not possibly have grounds to sue the prison. But most healthy prisoners are not interested in their medical records in the first place, so it is a moot point. When records are requested by prisoners for review by outside physicians, or ordered by a magistrate or judge, there is often a great deal of resistance in releasing records because of the risk of immediate exposure. Frequently, there is contempt of court by simply ignoring the judge's order.

The BOP is known to sometimes simply defy court orders for providing care to the prisoner or release his medical records to the court. For example, both the warden and the prison physician ignored the orders of Magistrate Kenton in the case of Pete. The prison physician finally manufactured a phony medical note for submission upon pressure from the judge. The BOP manufactured a bogus medical record for Pete's medical chart after many written requests but never actually submitted it to the court, despite the judge personally calling the prison doctor. The prison doctor never examined Pete before forging a medical note despite the magistrate's order that he be examined within 24 hours for his medical condition. Judges often back off when the BOP resists, something for which it will hold any American citizen in contempt of court and place such a civilian in prison. Imagine you or I or any civilian showing a middle finger to the judge if he requests a document from you that he knows you are in possession of. We could land in jail for years for contempt of court. The reason for this double standard is the incestuous relationship between government agencies and the federal court system in which federal judges, appointees of the government, act as shields for the federal agencies and the executive branch of the government.

Noah was not given a copy of his medical records and copies of all his Sick-Call requests when he made this request in writing many times. Mason requested in writing many times over a period of one year that his records be released to his outside physicians for review but they were not released. Elijah authorized the prison in writing to release copies of his medical records to him to be shared with his entire family to be reviewed independently by outsiders, but he never received his records. Th BOP released records to Samuel upon request only when his two hospitalizations had documented his condition in ways that the prison could not have concealed his story any further. Walter requested his records of work injury in prison many times along with medical records of CT and MRI reports, ER doctor's report, Job Injury report, Safety Officer's report, OSHA report, Workman's Comp report, but received no response. A lower-level empathetic Health Services employee at the prison clinic slipped a copy of a forged note written by a mid-level practitioner, R. Camacho, to Kylo. If it were not for this kind-hearted employee, the prisoner would not have known about this forgery because they refused to give him his records when he requested them many times in writing.

The Federal Bureau of Prisons officially categorizes prisoners' medical records into two categories. This categorization is not made obvious to the American people or to the court system, but rather preached internally among the prison's healthcare staff. The first type of medical records is what they officially designate as "releasable portions" of medical records. This type, for purposes of FBOP internal communications, is also termed as "not classified but sensitive information to be guarded" by all FBOP facilities, contractors, and affiliates, and they internally have to share these medical records from time to time during a prisoner's transfer from one facility to another, for example. The second type is what they call "nonreleasable portions of the medical records"—nonreleasable for reasons that they will never tell anyone. The vague answer you will get as to why some portions are nonreleasable is "security matter" or a "safety matter"; they might say that this "release might be detrimental to the well-being of the prisoner." But they will never tell you what types of medical records are specifically hidden under the category of nonreleasable portions. They will say that the release of such information will endanger the security of the institution or be medically or psychologically detrimental to the prisoner. What they don't wish to tell you is that these nonreleasable portions will expose the barbarism, medical cruelty, emotional violence, and deadly neglect practiced by prisons' healthcare employees, not because these employees want to but because this is an institutional imperative that they must brutalize the sick. Some of these nonreleasable records have a history of prisoners' seeking administrative remedies for months and years with flat denials of their requests even in the direst of medically ill circumstances. Nonreleasable records certainly include all the actual medical records that the prisoner came into the prison with. It includes all electronic records because the prisoner was warned that they would be deleted from the system, and they were indeed deleted and made to vanish. Perhaps some of these nonreleasable records are shredded or destroyed or made classified in that they would not be revealed no matter who requests them including the courts. The courts will never know that such records exist. Only a prisoner could potentially reveal only some of those nonreleasable portions if he is legally savvy enough to keep a meticulous paper trail of all events, incidents, episodes, Administrative Remedy requests, Sick-Calls, and verbal communications, which is a herculean task when you are locked up 24/7 without money, resources, or a proper education and living under the threat of retaliation every moment of your life if you look the wrong way.

It is hard for any human being to comprehend how the release of medical records about someone's health can be a safety matter or a security threat to an institution called the Department of Justice or the Federal Bureau of Prisons. Yes, it is a security and safety matter for the prison industrial complex and those who profit from the prisons. This is a buzz word for prison staff, to call it a security matter, when they intend to hide something from the public. This security threat pretext works for the BOP when it intends to harbor criminal activity and engage in illegal, unethical, unconstitutional acts and cover up human rights abuse. All the BOP staff are instructed by the DOJ to "guard" even the releasable records from prisoners, as it is "sensitive information to be guarded." Why does it need to be guarded? Because they know it to be inaccurate, so the longer you can conceal it, the better the chance that it would not become part of any discussion and thus forever remain unquestioned and out of sight. Hiding public information in the name of security or safety is a brilliant method of telling the American people any lie at any time without the risk of ever getting caught red-handed.

From having read these stories, one can tell that the release of these medical records being detrimental to a prisoner's health is the least of the BOP's concerns. That the BOP could not care less about anything being detrimental to prisoners is so obvious to any insider who is a firsthand witness to the medical cruelty and neglect that prisoners are subject to every day. Everything detrimental to very sick prisoners is exactly what the prison officials persistently seek in prison's death culture that they so strongly espouse among themselves, as you have noted in every testimonial in the Trail of Tears. As afore-mentioned, many records of failed administrative remedies sought by the prisoners are one of the big parts of those nonreleasable records because releasing prison officials remedy resolutions or remedy responses would readily expose the FBOP's inhuman treatment of the prison population and human rights abuse even though the prison tries its best to give this administrative work as much legal cover as possible, pretending they are just following prison policy and FBOP regulations. Again, the only way at least some of these nonreleasable records can be brought to the attention of the court is if a prisoner has the ability to keep a meticulous paper trail of his own, which is not easy in prison environment. Imagine being a hen in a henhouse and trying to keep paperwork to indict the fox who is in charge of your henhouse.

The unwritten policy of the BOP has yet a third type of medical record that one would never know even existed simply because they are made not to exist as soon as they surface. The prison culture adopted by prison healthcare employees knows that there are some things with regard to denying health assistance to inmates that should never appear on any piece of paper, let alone a medical record. These medical records that are destroyed before they are born are worse than classified information. At least some parts of the classified information have a chance of becoming declassified sometime in the future, but the declassification of information that was obliterated out of existence, that is, destroyed or never jotted down anywhere, is impossible. It is like asking where Mr. Mike Jones is, who was actually aborted as soon as he got conceived in his mother's uterus before anyone knew a conception occurred. I am alluding to the genuine medical histories of the sick prisoners, including verbal complaints that contained the subjective complaints and objective signs and symptoms of sick prisoners and parts that every nurse and physician knows is supposed to be part of a SOAP Note (a medical progress note with four parts to it—Subjective, Objective, Assessment, and Plan), that were purposely left out of any discussion or actively omitted or obliterated because of their medical–legal nature.

In all the prisoners' medical records that I had a chance to review, I noted that the subjective part of the medical note is simply omitted for the most part, especially patient's complaints and history that would require any medical treatment. The prison healthcare staff deletes, omits, or modifies any serious subjective complaints that would put responsibility on the shoulders of the BOP. The objective part of the note is worse because it is almost always nearly 100 percent falsified with the only exception of blood pressure and weight. The records are sometimes a bit accurate only when someone is healthy and has no medical illness, a situation in which accuracy is not of much consequence to the BOP. For example, if you write a healthy inmate's blood pressure as 110/72 or 128/84, it would not matter because both readings are normal blood pressures that suggest low risk or no risk, because no treatment is required anyway—so pick your number. Such a patient will not sue you even if you falsified because such false documentation has no legal repercussions. There is also no need to falsify medical records of a healthy young prisoner because there is not much to falsify and no good reason to do so. The third part, the Assessment, where a physician is supposed to write a diagnosis, is the most sinister part. As per a prison's unwritten policy (as opposed to the written policy made available to the American people and to the courts), the prison doctor is never allowed to write the real diagnosis of a sick prisoner. I will be the first one to tell you that there is probably no official mandate that tells the prison doctor not to write the diagnosis, but it is apparent to him from the day he begins employment in prison what is expected of him. He is expected to write a directed diagnosis, the one that is so crafted that the prisoner might not require more than Tylenol or Motrin or a cream or a lotion in physician's final Plan for Treatment. He is also expected not to recommend any drug or treatment that the prison formulary does not have or anything prison officials simply do not want him to prescribe. He has no authority of giving anything to any prisoner without first asking the health services administrator who is usually a poorly qualified, criminal-minded nurse. A physician is not allowed to recommend any medication for a prisoner even if he knows that a certain medication or treatment will save the prisoner's life and an improper and ineffective formulary drug would prove fatal with worsening health condition. He is often some poorly qualified physician with past problems with his license or medical education, who cannot get a job elsewhere and is willing to work for the prison for cents on a dollar and to be used as a rubber stamp for the prison officials and generally treated like shit. Pardon my French.

The moment the prison officials become aware of a prisoner's intention to sue for deprivation of healthcare, they intensify their efforts to custom-make his/her medical records, like in the cases of the patients Kingsley and Kylo, which occurred in front of my eyes during my stay at the prison. I saw this process taking place in real time. My own direct interactions with the prison's health staff regarding my health issues further corroborated the fact that the prison actively engaged in fraudulent acts of falsifying most prisoners' medical records.

The BOP has a written policy and programs to show to the courts and to the American people, but its unwritten policies are only verbally shared among its employees. One of the most criminally insane practices of the BOP through its unwritten policy is to give a bogus doctored diagnosis instead of an actual medical diagnosis to sick prisoners who come through the system, no matter how ill the prisoner is. Surprisingly, this includes prisoners who are fatally ill and who came into the prison with clearly well-established, life-threatening diagnoses given by outside physicians prior to their incarceration. Prison officials often say, "These outside doctors do not tell us what to do," as they told Samuel and Mason—the two prisoners who almost died in the hospital due to the prison's barbaric treatment and gross negligence. Whenever a prison physician is compelled to give a diagnosis to a prisoner, for example, by circumstance or by the court order, the physician still likes to give only a directed diagnosis or a diagnosis that warrants little treatment such as take a walk and drink more water, don't worry about it, or you will get used to it. If someone in our government who has the power and integrity of sending a qualified overseer of healthcare professionals to audit medical charts of 1,000 prisoners at random in federal prisons, as was done under the auspices of Federal Judge Thelton Henderson for California prisons in 2009, I assure you that they will rarely find an ill prisoner with an accurate diagnosis—not because the physician made a human error but because of a systematic contrivance of medical charts by the BOP under a systematic protective shield of the Department of Justice. The only exception where you will ever find a diagnosis given that is technically considered accurate is where the physician already knows that the diagnosis requires no medical treatment, or if it does, the treatment is the same that your grandma would generally do a much better job at home; in other words, it requires no treatment because it is self-healing. Fortunately, the human body has tremendous capacity to heal itself especially if the condition is relatively non-serious. This practice of prisons' healthcare culture is tantamount to criminal activity, not a simple violation of human rights.

Some prison health officials openly tell sick prisoners that they would not be given a diagnosis, their rationale being, "If I give you a diagnosis, then I have to give one to everyone else." This is as though giving a diagnosis of MI (heart attack) to a heart attack patient is doing him a special favor. This is the answer Kylo received when he requested that he be given a diagnosis with an already well-documented history of diagnoses of heart attack, congestive heart failure, hepatitis C, asthma, COPD, chest pain, retrolisthesis, hypertension, glaucoma, cataracts, pancreatitis, and shortness of breath. It is the same answer Jacob, a brittle diabetic, received when he asked that he be given a diagnosis of uncontrollable type I diabetes and treated with an insulin pump that he desperately needed. Instead he was told, "there is no proof that you have diabetes." Prison doctors often say, "If I were to do this favor for you, then I have to do this for all others; sorry no favors folks." The BOP sees the act of giving someone a diagnosis as undertaking an unnecessary liability that would warrant a treatment for that diagnosis. So the BOP's solution to the problem of having to provide healthcare to prisoners is a simple solution to a huge problem: Don't give a diagnosis to anyone. This will relieve us of the chronic headache of having to provide medical care. If the prison physician's health assessment of the prisoner could say that the inmate has no medical problems or the prisoner is in excellent health, it solves all issues instantly without further ado.

This also explains why the BOP avoids exposing its prisoners to outside help at all costs until such point that they run out of all options to conceal liability in that the prisoner could die if he is not immediately transported to the nearest ER. After all, when someone collapses, the rest of the prisoners are watching and they are potential witnesses, so in such situations, the prisoner must be transported to the hospital because too much has been exposed. It frightens me to think how prison officials would handle such a situation if they knew that no one saw the prisoner collapse or lose consciousness. The BOP's healthcare workers are forced to write a notation in the chart in such circumstances noting what they knew the prisoner had all along but tried to omit or hide it for as long as they knew they could get away with. The BOP fights tooth and nail in its resistance to send any prisoner to an outside specialist or a consultant or a hospital because of the fear of being exposed about the prison abuse up until such point that they are pinned against the wall. The BOP only privately discusses the issues of its budgetary constraints to provide healthcare, which is only a small part of the problem, not the global problem of a prison's death culture, which views prisoners as less than human. Treating prisoners as less than human is a presupposition, not up for discussion—a much greater problem than the budgetary constraints.

When I reviewed the cookie-cutter, fill-in-the-blank, or tick-mark-in-a-box electronic records, it appeared to me that I was reviewing the same records of the same prisoner over and over because different prisoners' records were filled with the same or similar false data. Every sick prisoner whose medical records I reviewed seemed to be in great health with most or all of the physical exam noted as being within normal limits, (which was an exam that was never done but noted in the chart.) This included prisoners who were ill with devastating and terminal diseases. Every chart had screening tests, blood pressure, weight, blood work, EKG, chest X-ray, hemoccult test, a dental visit, an optometric visit, and a visit with the prison's psychologist, whether the prisoner needed it or not. If any abnormality was found on any of these screening tests or routine screening consultations, however, it was never followed up with any treatment until the inmate found out about abnormal results and then fought hard with the BOP to get at least some perfunctory care. Why bother doing the screening or consulting? It seemed that the underlying purpose of such screening by the prison officials is not to follow up on any abnormality detected on screening—they did not even bother to review the results in most cases. Rather the purpose of routine screening is to keep the prison machinery going by letting contractors continue to profit from taxpayer money by doing tests on everyone, including those who do not need it. The rule is do the tests on all inmates, tests they don't need, but never do the test that a prisoner actually needs to stay alive. The contractors have to make an X amount of profits or they will refuse to work for the prison; the contractors are already upset because they say they make a fraction of what they make in the private industry. They need business. At the end of the day, this entire showbiz ends up creating some seemingly credible "medical records" to an untrained eye such as those of judges, while at the same time unscrupulously, secretively, and intentionally ignoring the healthcare of all prisoners, not just the sickest and the most vulnerable. This is the BOP's way of giving an appearance to the courts that the FBOP is taking care of its prisoners by giving it the semblance of medical care. A judge is neither medically qualified nor necessarily trained enough to see that such medical records are meaningless and deceptive in a clear majority of the cases. They look like a bunch of decent medical interventions to a judge who can't tell the difference between his elbow and his ass; pardon my expression. A screening test intervention without a follow-up is no intervention at all; it is a bogus and ill-intended measure designed to fool a naïve person who is not trained in auditing a medical chart to look for deliberate negligence. Only a trained independent physician such as myself could tell that the real medical records in each inmate's case were omitted, deleted, edited, concealed or redacted from the prisoner's charts as manifest from healthcare workers' notes that sometimes contradict one another because of recklessness and bad communication among themselves before the fraud is consummated by them. As the saying goes, you have to be perfectly trained to commit a perfect crime.

Routine screening tests are also done because some blood lab or prison contractor, part of the vast network of the prison industrial complex, is making obscene profits off this enormous volume of testing without follow-up care for those who were found to be screen positive for a medical condition. It should be clear, therefore, why there is an entire industrial complex of profiteers that seek contracts with the prison system through their political links and lobbying, from commissary at exorbitant prices to food supplies of expired food products to healthcare contracts, none of which is intended to help the sick prisoners or any prisoners at all. Too many vultures are making money off the most miserable and the most vulnerable in our society.

The judge who is a shield for the government and is already biased in favor of the government will never try to understand whether these medical records presented by the BOP in its defense have any relevance to the actual medical ailments or conditions for which the prisoner is suing the BOP for not getting the care that he actually needed. Many of these records are created and custom made without the prisoner being examined or interviewed by the prison's many "care providers" who only saw the prisoner once for the initial screening intake when the manufacturing of medical records began, with endless lies to be added on later as needed to create a larger, bewildering set of unmanageable volumes of paperwork that no one could decipher without a deep professional analysis and expert audit.

The BOP claims that the Centers for Disease Control and Prevention (CDC) maintains a healthcare record containing medical and mental records on each prisoner. This healthcare file is separate from the prisoner's central file. The medical and mental health record should document all contact between a prisoner and CDC medical or mental health personnel, as well as records of any examination, surgery, doctors' orders, medical chrono, and so forth. Nobody has seen these CDC files. There is no doubt in my mind that the prisoners' charts with the CDC are copies of the prison's bogus charts. It will be interesting to open that Pandora's box to see what is in there, supposing that these CDC files do exist. And if they do exist, does the CDC, another government agency, care what is in those records? Has the CDC ever looked at them?

The FBOP further claims that a prisoner may review his or her medical and psychiatric records on request. The procedure, as per the BOP written policy, states that the prisoner should make a written request to the medical records department at the prison. The prison policy orientation manual says that the prisoner should be prepared to file an appeal if prison staff do not act on his request to let the inmate review his medical records. It is hard to understand why prisoners always have to file appeals instead of being able to review their so-called medical records upon their first written request as per prison policy. I believe the reason for not releasing any records upon first request in violation of prison's own policy is obvious enough that it requires no deep thought. The American people will never find out the truth as to why prisoners are not allowed to review their records or receive their records upon written requests unless someone of the caliber and integrity of Federal Judge Thelton Henderson orders a third-party independent investigation of the BOP prisoners' medical charts and interviews those prisoners at the same time. Government agencies, DOJ, FBOP, and halfway houses under the jurisdiction of the BOP all cover for each other, cut and paste reports from one another without questioning even though they are all aware of the cover-ups.

I reviewed a "Level of Care Memo" dated August 12, 2006, which was an exchange between the FBOP and federal judges in which a federal judge asks the BOP: "How can a judge help for proper level of medical care for sick prisoners?" The BOP replies, "Until an inmate comes into the prison and is evaluated by the BOP healthcare provider, the Presentence Report is the BOP's principal source of initially assessing medical conditions." I felt nauseated when I read this. I know that both the judges and the BOP are well aware that their statements are false. As you have seen clear evidence in this book thus far in umpteen case histories (read the original documents published in *Prison Papers*), the presentence reports, with or without court orders for a certain level of medical care to be given to a sick prisoner, are immediately discarded by the DOJ (FBOP) as soon as the prisoner leaves the courtroom with or without handcuffs. You can imagine the FBOP leaving the courtroom with the prisoner in hand-cuffs and then turning around and shooting the judge the middle finger and then saying to the prisoner, "Forget about what the judge said, you are mine now."

The DOJ or BOP absolutely have no respect for what the prisoner's medical designation is or what the judge ordered. They do with the prisoner anything they want once they have him in custody. Judges know this too, and they know it well that their orders will not be honored, but they are hypocrites. It is as though utter disregard for the medical conditions of a prisoner as documented in his presentence report is not enough for the FBOP's satiety; a prisoner gets only a make-believe intake evaluation by the prison physician once he enters into the prison. If I were to be appointed as an independent investigator by the government, I would challenge the FBOP to show me 1 out of the 1,000 randomly selected sick inmates' medical charts in the custody of the Federal Bureau of Prisons that truly reflects the medical conditions with which a genuinely sick prisoner was inducted into federal custody.

How the medical records are produced, created, manufactured, delivered, transferred, or released in the DOJ (FBOP) system is a subject matter of investigation for a PhD thesis because of falsified records, loopholes, and secretive information. It would shock the American people what this PhD dissertation would reveal. This area of discussion is the most mind-boggling of all. Under the BOP mission, it states that "prisoners have the right to obtain copies of 'certain releasable portions' of their medical records." It took me months of work, investigation, and diligent analysis to figure out what "releasable records" and "nonreleasable records" really meant in this story of the dark and dangerous world called the American prison.

Occasionally, there is an accidental leak of a medical wrongdoing without prison staff realizing that there is a serious discrepancy in medical records or when sometimes records make no sense at all and no one thoroughly scrutinized the records before releasing them. Very rarely an employee, often a lower-level employee or someone who does not intend to work long-term for the BOP, purposely sneaks out a piece of paper to a prisoner out of anger or resentment for either moral reasons or righteous indignation or personal resentment for getting paid very little for him to have to do the unconscionable burdensome task of lying all day. The medical records are kept secret just like classified information and the healthcare staff is instructed to treat it as such and "guard it" even while releasing information with a prisoner's written consent.

The area of the clinic where medical records are kept has an impenetrable iron fence, more secure than the highest underground security prison in the United States. This shows that the BOP is clearly aware of the affect that these prisoner medical and administrative records would have if they were to ever be stolen or exposed to the public. These records would reveal a story of torture of Americans at home, not just what we hear about our government doing at

Guantanamo, Abu Ghraib, Bagram, and other black site US prisons in foreign lands. If these records of mental torture were to ever be released (leaked), they would be of the same remarkable significance as the National Security Agency top secret reports that were leaked by Julian Assange and Edward Snowden. Such revelation will also be consistent with the stories described in this book; however, there would be tens of thousands of such stories revealed, not just the few leaked out through this book.

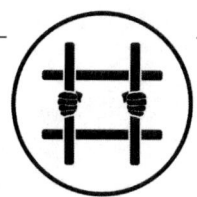

## CHAPTER 19

# SISYPHEAN REMEDIES

I N THE GREEK MYTH OF SISYPHUS, GODS HAD CONDEMNED Sisyphus to ceaselessly roll a rock to the top of a mountain, whence the stone would fall back of its own weight. The gods had thought with some reason that there could be no more dreadful punishment than futile and hopeless labor. Sisyphus kept on rolling the stone in the hope that he would eventually succeed in bringing the stone to the top. Little did he know that gods had done their calculations in that he would never be allowed to reach the top. Imagine a human falling into a deep well and trying to get out with no pegs or holes to grab onto. You already know the fate of such a person. I would like to show in this chapter how every prisoner in the Federal Bureau of Prisons is a Sisyphus who falsely believes that something is about to happen in the course of seeking Administrative Remedies that will get him to overcome this unsurmountable mountain.

Sick prisoners who are relatively new to the prison system live under the impression that the BOP's policy of Administrative Remedies will eventually get them the medical care they desperately need. Those who have been in prison for too long, however, already know that the Administrative Remedy process exists only in the minds of those who are new to the prison and still hopeful. There is no actual Administrative Remedy process in place for anyone. The process exists only on paper and in the prison policy manual under the title Administrative Remedies. This policy is calculated to be implemented by the prison staff in ways that any prisoner who tries to climb the four-tier system of the remedy ladder will never be allowed to reach the top. The system of Administrative Remedies in prison is a four-tier device. It starts with what is called a BP-8, which is a complaint to the prison staff for an informal resolution of the prisoner's complaint. If not resolved, the prisoner can file a BP-9, which is a formal complaint to the warden of the prison complex. If that fails as well, he could file a Regional Level Appeal to the Regional Office of the Bureau of Prisons, called a BP-10. The final level of appeal is to the Washington, DC, Central Office of the Bureau of Prisons. This highest level of complaint is called a BP-11. A prisoner must have tried all four levels of Administrative Remedies before courts would allow the prisoner to sue the Bureau of Prisons for barbarism and medical cruelty. So, the methodology is simple: Don't let the prisoner exhaust the four levels of remedies, which would disqualify him forever from suing the BOP. The prison officials are trained to sabotage prisoners' efforts from climbing above Level III of the tier before pulling them right back down to where they started. This cycle of rising and falling continues cyclically until the prisoner is so exhausted of trying that he simply gives up. This process goes on till the federal inmate finally falls to the ground and has no vital energy left to start climbing one last time because he is all bloodied from too many unhealable wounds.

The courts insist that a prisoner must exhaust all remedies before he can sue the FBOP. Never being able to reach Level IV (BP-11) to establish proof of denial of care disqualifies well over 99 percent of all sick prisoners from suing. What an ingenious way of keeping the prisoners from suing. Let us see how it works, first with some background information.

I have appropriately called it the Department of Justice's Sisyphean curse on the prisoners. The gods of the BOP administer their remedies to sick prisoners in precalculated ways, so the prisoner would never be allowed to climb the proverbial mountain to level BP-11, which is the peak of the mountain before he can even begin to imagine what may lay on the other side. The prison officials are trained and equipped with flawless techniques and "devices", as one court called it, to make the prisoner come tumbling back down to BP-8 from the height of BP-9 or BP-10. There are numerous tricks that the BOP uses to make it impossible for a prisoner to reach the top of the ladder where he can say that he exhausted all the remedies and now has a recourse to the legal system. Based on my research, I estimate that only 1 out of every 1,000 very sick but also very resourceful prisoners who try to seek remedies will reach the tier level of BP-11. The remaining tens of thousands of prisoners suffering from medical conditions in our federal prisons—those without families, friends, and physical, emotional, or financial resources—will be barred from suing because they cannot prove to the court that they exhausted all administrative remedies. Most of them will not even try hard enough because they know that it would not get them anywhere. They wait to die. Based on prison policy's designated deadlines, calculations show that it should not take more than a total of six months to exhaust all remedies before one can qualify to file a formal complaint with the courts. But the prison culture and well-trained prison officials can make a prisoner spin around for 5, 10, 20, or 30 years trying to exhaust remedies and still being unsuccessful. An average prisoner will never figure out what is preventing him from exhausting remedies, and if he does, he has no option but to keep trying or to simply give up with no light seen at the end of the tunnel. And it is not even a matter of how smart or legal minded you are; they know how to hold you down, so you are unable to get up. Most give up after a few years and leave it to their fate in the end. To understand how the DOJ (FBOP) accomplishes the task of keeping sick prisoners in a never-ending spiral, a bureaucratic circular loop in which prisoners keep spinning forever, let us review some of the techniques or devices used by the BOP to accomplish this masterful villainy. As you read the following, just imagine a lab rat spinning in circles; you have all seen that circular gadget used in laboratories that conduct experiments using rats.

The prison staff is supposed to answer a prisoner's tier level I (BP-8) complaint within 30 days as per prison policy. Prison officials can seek a 30-day extension to respond. The warden is required to answer the tier Level II complaint (BP-9) within 20 days, with an extra 20 days of written extension by the BOP if necessary. The Level III remedy that goes to the regional office of the Bureau of Prisons has 40 days to respond with the possibility of an extension of an additional 40 days. Finally, the BP-11 complaint filed with the Washington, DC, Central Office of the Bureau of Prisons has a 30-day requirement to respond. One can easily calculate that this process should not take more than a few months to exhaust all remedies even with the added extensions sought by the prison officials. How does this six months' time limit magically turn into years and decades? The idea is to somehow make prisoners reach the level of BP-10 over a period of one or two years and then knock them down from what they have already accomplished back to square one where they have to start at the BP-8 level over and over till they are so exhausted that they collapse in body, mind, and spirit and stop insisting on seeking medical care.

Meanwhile, a prisoner is not allowed contact with outside lawyers even if he has the means to hire one; every phone call by prisoners is monitored, recorded, and translated for interpretation when necessary. The prisoner must correspond with a lawyer, and the correspondence reply from the attorney will be opened and reviewed by the prison officials, and a prisoner is not allowed to communicate with his attorney through email. Prison officials say that they open the letters from lawyers in front of the prisoner and don't read them, but the fact of the matter is that these letters are already open before the prisoner receives them from the prison counselor, which means that prison officials have already opened and read them. So, the prison officials already have a heads-up regarding what the prisoner is thinking in terms of any allegations of wrongdoing against the prison, so that the prison doctors can get busy in sanitizing and custom writing medical records to prepare for a defense. Listening to phone conversations also gives the prison officials a heads-up about any legal threat that they are likely to face with all the confidential details of conversations between the plaintiff and his attorney, which puts them ahead of the game. This is not the worst part, however; this is only one of the problems faced by prisoners. Those who somehow manage to get to that level of communicating with their attorneys, which is very rare, now face routine retaliation from the prison guards.

There are innumerable tricks, techniques, deceitful methods, devices, and contrivances used by the prison staff to spin the bureaucratic paperwork around the Administrative Remedy process forever. While some of these methods are at risk for revealing themselves by their very nature, others are more secretive and subtler, not easily decipherable. The first technique employed by the prison staff is simply not to respond to the Inmate's Request to Staff or to an Administrative Remedy Request. The second and most common technique employed across the board is to respond to prisoners' remedy requests by saying to them that they are required to sign up for a Sick Call to have their issues resolved, to attend Sick Call to refill their medications, and so on. What they don't tell the prisoners in this type of Administrative Remedy response is that the so-called Sick-Call system in prison is so bureaucratically crafted that it may take weeks, months, and in some cases years for a very sick prisoner to see a healthcare practitioner in response to his written Sick-Call request, only to receive some verbal reassurance or 200 mg of Motrin or some equivalent in the end, and this is regardless of the seriousness of an inmate's illness, condition, or diagnosis. It does not matter if you are dying from cancer, you will be lucky if you get some Motrin for pain after waiting six months for this Sick-Call appointment. If an inmate is lucky to finally see his name on the Call-Out list in response to his endless Sick-Call requests, the prison doctor simply won't recognize the inmate's well-documented diagnosis or medical condition that he suffered with when he first entered the prison. The nurse or the doctor will say that there is no evidence of a medical problem in prisoner's medical records. They will not tell the prisoner what medical records or whose medical records they are alluding to. And it is the responsibility of the prisoner to prove that he is sick; it is not up to the prison physician to establish that the prisoner is sick, it is up to the prisoner. It does not matter that the prison authorities have all the information on the health condition of the prisoner in their possession, which they received from the Department of Probation's Sentencing Report or court orders that they are willing to pretend does not exist. Imagine a prison Sick Call is like going to an imaginary hospital ER room where a nurse comes out to the waiting room to greet you and then tell you, while you are bleeding or in the middle of a heart attack or stroke, that the ER waiting time is six months before you can be seen by the ER doctor. This kind of offer of "anytime free access to the Sick-Call remedy" renders the inmate helpless because he is not allowed to go to the next level of a BP-9 remedy until he can show that he did everything to seek a resolution for his medical care with the lower-level prison staff at the BP-8 level (Inmate Request to Staff). The prisoner must do everything he can to resolve this issue at this informal level. He must prove this or prove that.

Most BP-9 forms (Appeal to the Warden Remedy) designed by the federal prison have a question for the inmate: What have you done to resolve your issues at the BP-8 level? And if the prisoner cannot prove that he has been through the odyssey of this Sick-Call scam for months and months, his BP-9 will be outright rejected. Similarly, an inmate is also not allowed to go to the BP-10 level remedy with the regional BOP office until he can show that he complied with the prison policy to get help for his medical condition from the warden of the prison first. And good luck with that. And a prisoner is not allowed to file a BP-9 unless he can prove that he sought an informal resolution through BP-8 and provide proof of that paperwork. And he is required to submit copies of the BP-9 paperwork from the warden to file a BP-10 to show that his request was denied by the warden. But the problem is that the warden and the prison officials will never say in their written responses that they are denying care, but they have a way to deny everything. The warden's phony BP-9 responses are then used by regional BOP offices to throw inmates back into the hands of the local prison warden where they are suffering unbelievable medical tyranny. The prison warden's responses to prisoners' remedy requests always note his responses as "for informational purpose only." They use this cautionary legal jargon because they know that they have lied about everything by referring to these prison's medical records that they have falsely generated.

This sounds strange. How can you deny everything and yet never say that you are denying anything? The prison officials use this ingenious technique of denying but not denying, allowing themselves to engage in behaviors that can only be considered nothing short of criminal at best. The prisoner will be automatically rejected at a higher level (tier) of appeal because he can never prove that he was denied care at the lower level because the paperwork he submitted with a BP-10 appeal is generated by the prison officials in ways that it looks like they are doing a great job and doing it by the book, according to prison policy and programs. So the prisoner is kicked back to the lower level to start the process over and over till he is exhausted and gives up or starts with a BP-8 again, if he still has any emotional strength left.

The matter is already made much worse by the prison staff simply not responding to prisoners' requests no matter how many times they make that request. This should be familiar to you, my readers, as you have seen it in almost every well-documented story you read in the Trail of Tears. Now, how will a prisoner show that the prison official rejected his complaint if the prison staff chose not to respond to his request in the first place? The prisoner is not allowed to file next level of appeal until prison officials respond. The next level in the Administrative Remedy or appeal will automatically reject the prisoner's case if he is not able to submit multiple copies of the paperwork from his lower-level appeal—the paperwork that he never received. This one trick alone is the great evil that works at all levels of remedy request denials in that the BOP may choose to give a delayed response or no response at all to send the prisoner spinning around in a never-ending cycle, like a lab rat spinning in his wheel.

The BOP written policy made available to prisoners deliberately conceals from the prisoners the fact that they are entitled pursuant to CFR title 28 subsection 542.18 to file the next step when no response is forthcoming within the designated deadline as per BOP policy. This information about their legal right is diligently prevented from becoming known to the inmates. Nowhere does the prison written policy say that if the prison officials default in meeting the required deadline in responding, the prisoner is allowed to move on to the next level of Administrative Remedy in filing his paperwork. I believe that this part is deliberately removed or deleted (or not incorporated) in prison's orientation handout that prisoners are able to read for reference. This is the prison's unwritten policy, a powerful weapon used by its healthcare workers who are essentially ordained exterminators. If a prisoner tries to file a BP-10 because the prison warden has defaulted in responding within the allowed deadline, the prison warden will refuse to forward the prisoner's BP-10 Regional

Appeal to the regional office of the Bureau of Prisoners. The warden is in full control over the inmate's ability to get his appeal in the hands of the regional office. If the warden chooses to block the inmate's Regional Appeal from going forward, he can block it forever. If the prison chooses to block the prisoner's outgoing mail, it can do so when necessary. Prison officials frequently open outgoing mail even though they are allowed to open only incoming mail by prison policy as discussed earlier. There are six regional offices overseeing 122 federal penitentiaries in the United States. A prisoner must appeal to the regional office that oversees his penitentiary complex through and with the permission of his institution's warden. The regional offices of the Bureau of Prisons fully participate in this fraudulent practice by rejecting prisoner's appeals to regional by responding, "You must wait for your institutional response before you can file a regional appeal." Prisoners have tried to file Regional Appeals directly through the mail by bypassing the institution or filing BP-11 appeals directly to the General Counsel in Washington, DC, but it does not work because they are not given the paperwork of denial that they need to show that they have tried lower-level remedies. This paperwork will never show that the prisoner was denied care; it always shows that the prisoner received fabulous healthcare at the institution on the paperwork that needs to be submitted for appeal at the higher level. The regional offices and Washington, DC, also know this game and they participate in it. It is apparent from the examples that I published in *Prison Papers*.

Both Mason and Kylo tried to exercise this right under title 28 but the BOP at the higher regional levels of the North Central Regional and Northwestern Regional blocked their efforts, knowing fully well that it was within prisoners' legal right to appeal at a higher level if the institution defaulted in failing to respond. This shows that the corruption in the Bureau of Prisons is not just at the institutional level of penitentiary complexes but at higher levels as well. When I reviewed a document given to me by Kylo, which the regional office accidentally released to him, it confirmed that the regional offices in the Federal Bureau of Prisons engage in the use of the same illegal devices that local prisons do in falsifying dates to prolong the Administrative Remedy process for the prisoners, thus incapacitating them to move forward in the process.

There are other ways to reject these appeals with responses such as "Your appeal was untimely," that is, "received late," and then the inmate is asked to prove with staff verification that it was not his fault that it was late. What they don't tell prisoners is that it was prison staff's plan to forward it late or stamp it with a receipt date of their choice on purpose to sabotage the prisoner's effort to meet the deadline. What are the odds that the same staff will provide the inmate with verification that it was not the prisoner's fault, the same staff that denied his request in the first place? This game of using arbitrary dates is played at all levels. For example, I reviewed the regional director's response to Kylo's BP-10, which had two red stamps on it. One of them said, "Received May 21, 2015," and another stamp right underneath said "Received on July 27, 2015." How can one receive the same document at two different dates two months apart? Apparently, the clerk at the regional office did not pay attention to his/her own forgery before sending the response to Kylo.

When you engage in illegal acts on a regular basis, you are more likely to expose yourself accidentally. Commission of crime becomes a second nature for a criminal after a while. So, it is only a matter of time when an accidental release of some inculpatory evidence will occur. These illegal behaviors by the BOP cannot become public knowledge until these issues are brought out for public scrutiny and laws are passed that require release of all evidence hidden by the government officials, including the evidence that contradicts the government's own false claims against prisoners.

There are several examples of prisoners in this book where the BP-8, BP-9, and BP-10 responses from the prison officials have phony dates of receipt stamps on their paperwork proving to the prisoner that his appeal paperwork was not received before the deadline and thus rejected. The BOP can literally put any date of receipt stamp on the prisoner's complaint. It can hold onto it for several days before putting a stamp on it, or the BOP might deny that it ever received a request or request a resubmission from the inmate, and they do so all the time. No inmate can dare question prison officials or guards as to why they received the inmate's complaint one month after its actual submission date. When push comes to shove, the government officials can simply choose to ignore all requests from the prisoner even if they are filed meticulously and accurately meeting all the specific paperwork requirements of the BOP policy.

Prisoners are stuck in dead-end situations and reach an impasse with no choice left but to wait for an answer before they can move on, if they can move on at all to the next level. As the reader, you have noted in almost every prisoner's documentation described in this book (with originals published in *Prison Papers*) that sometimes they are submitting BP-8s and BP-9s over and over for a period of months with not a single response from the prison staff or warden forthcoming. For example, the prison officials did not respond to scores of BP-8s and BP-9s filed by Pete over five years. Instead, in response, they transferred him to different BOP facilities and sometimes locked him in solitary confinement in retaliation for being too demanding. He was able to file his suit pro se after 15 years of filing requests and appeals before he was able to reach a level of BP-11 to qualify to sue the BOP. He was still looking for a lawyer who would be willing to represent him when I left the prison. The question is, who is going to represent you when you are locked up in prison and have no money? And mind you, Pete was no ordinary inmate; he was resourceful and proactive and fully supported by the Jewish community outside the prison. Likewise, Noah filed many BP-8s and BP-9s without response from the BOP for months. He eventually wrote to Congressman Campbell: "They have an Administrative Remedy Process here that I have been trying to comply with for two years with obfuscation and more delays." Inmates Elijah, Samuel, Liam, and Arthur, and many other prisoners quoted in this book filed several level BP-8s and BP-9s, one after another, without any responses from the prison officials.

Once the prison officials take note that the prisoner has put them on the spot in an informal resolution BP-8 or Administrative Remedy BP-9, a kind of complaint they simply cannot ignore due to the high degree of liability, they can give themselves an extension by doubling the time limit that allows them opportunity to discuss among themselves as to how to respond in ways that appear to be legitimate and give them extra time to alter records if necessary. It is not unusual for the prison staff to almost always timely respond to the very first BP-8 filed by a prisoner after coming into the prison because the prisoner seems to pose very little or no legal liability to the prison at this initial stage. It also works out for the prison to give the new prisoner an impression that the prison plays by the rules before things start to change slowly and magically. The initial remedy request and response also gives the prison staff opportunity to assess the level of liability that a prisoner poses to them so that they can start planning how they will deal with inmate's unique medical complaints and the extent of his aggressiveness with which he might pursue demanding medical attention from them. It takes a while for the prisoner to begin to comprehend that the prison staff intends to do nothing to help resolve his health issues. In this way, the prison loves to give the remedy process the semblance of a legitimate remedy process to all the new arrivals. This is the prison's way of creating an illusion of confidence for the prisoner regarding the legitimacy of the Administrative Remedy process as soon as he walks into the prison. This buys them adequate time to assess the overall risk of liability that the prisoner's medical condition poses the government.

In situations where prison officials choose to respond to the prisoners' requests for Administrative Remedies, they frequently give delayed responses to prolong the process. On the other side of this coin, they strictly impose with an iron fist the time limit deadlines for prisoners' responses without fail. The prison policy rules are applied only to prisoners but not to the prison officials. This is called exercising rights without meeting legal obligations of an affirmative duty. I did not find any approved Remedy Requests by the prison officials among hundreds of Administrative Remedy responses that I reviewed personally. It was a denial 99.9 percent of the time. Frankly, I do not recall seeing one example of clear acknowledgment of any inmate's medical complaint, no matter how serious or emergent, of the thousand that I reviewed. I should say 100 percent denial, not 99.9 percent, but I am using the number 99.9 just in case I missed something in my reviews. The prison officials always have a reason why the request had to be denied, or they framed it in a way that it did not look like a denial but you could see it was a denial if you had an IQ over 70. For example, the prison staff denies or rejects the prisoner's appeal remedy because the prisoner did not file the paperwork correctly, being that it wasn't legible or was on more than one page, and the list goes on. And then they give the prisoner five days to resubmit the corrected paperwork or the prisoner risks having to start the remedy process all over again. This always leads to the inmate having to start the remedy process again at the BP-8 level because it is impossible for him to refile within five days. By giving a five-day deadline, the BOP already knows that they have succeeded in shutting down the prisoner for some time because it would be impossible for him to prepare complicated paperwork in five days, even with help. It will be hard even for a law firm in the outside world to respond in five days with all the specific requirements for the paperwork, let alone a prisoner who works in the American Gulag for six (6) cents an hour, who has no money, has very little education, and almost always depends on some jailhouse lawyer to do the drafting and typing for him. The jailhouse lawyer may or may not wish to help the prisoner so expeditiously within five days or may not want to help at all. And if he does, he may be at risk for retaliation or punishment by the prison officials for practicing law. If the prisoner handwrites it, the prison officials can always say it is not legible. Many of these reasons for rejection are not to be found anywhere in the BOP's Administrative Remedy Policy. Not to mention that the prison guard may choose to put a note on the library typewriter that states that prisoners are not allowed to use the typewriter for more than 15 minutes at a time in addition to lining up in a long queue to access the only working typewriter in the library. What are the odds of preparing your case and responding to the warden within a five-day deadline under such prohibitive circumstances?

Let us suppose an aggressive, resourceful, intelligent, and educated prisoner manages to meet the insurmountable paperwork requirements for seeking remedies in prison in a timely fashion, prison officials can always move on to their next trick in their unlimited arsenal. The response from the prison officials to the prisoner will be that he has not described his complaint specifically enough, therefore it is rejected. Let us say the prisoner, like the powerful Sisyphus, manages to write a specific complaint and still meet the five-day timeline as per the prison officials' demand. The response from the prison might well be that there is more than one complaint in the inmate's description and that he needs to file separate BP-9s for each specific medical complaint. This is a very powerful and an intractably fraudulent method that the BOP uses against helpless sick prisoners. There is no physician expert in the universe who can tease out what is specific, unspecific, or nonspecific about a complaint from a patient who is terribly sick with a life-threatening condition(s). When was the last time you had full-blown cancer and had only one specific symptom, for example, a headache? And if a prisoner with a terminal illness has 20 symptoms, how is he supposed to write 20 separate appeals for 20 different signs and symptoms (20 different legal documents for 20 specific complaints) within the five-day deadline afforded to him? And it better be done professionally typed, legible, and meeting all the many written, unwritten, and unknown requirements of the prison policy filing guidelines for Administrative Remedy paperwork. Only God could meet that demand. But wait a minute, God cannot meet that demand either, because the BOP can always say that the complaint does not meet the various requirements and that now God needs to go back and read the BOP policy one more time, a policy from which many clauses that describe prisoners' legal rights were left out.

For example, Pete's complaint of blood in the urine was as specific as it can get, but many federal prisons where he was locked up from time to time chose to ignore this specific complaint for five years, ignored at least 30 remedy applications, and put him in the solitary confinement more than once for insisting on getting medical care for his bladder cancer. When a prisoner is not specific in his complaint, his appeal will be rejected, but if he is specific, it will be ignored anyway. So, what is the point of trying, prisoners wonder. There are umpteen other creative ways of not addressing the Administrative Remedy appeals such as, "Your request has been forwarded to the appropriate department," "Your matter is being looked into," and so on. Then the remedy resolution reports always end with: "This is for informational purposes only", washing BOP hands of any responsibility.

In the best scenario, let us say a prisoner managed to write several BP-9s with several specific complaints as requested in the FBOP's denial. The warden can always give a fill-in-the-blank response, which the prison healthcare staff is trained to complete. Such responses from prison officials have the same pattern. I reviewed hundreds of those. This cookie-cutter response has three parts: (1) repeat the prisoner's complaints verbatim, literally copy and pasted; (2) find clues from already falsified and fabricated medical records and respond to the prisoner by using a template of a language, "A review of your medical records reveals that your medical problems had already been addressed in the past and medications have been given to you on such and such dates"; (3) state, "This response is for informational purposes only." Well you would think that "remedy" means help to resolve a prisoner's health issue, not "for informational purposes only." Nowhere in prison policy adopted by the Department of Justice does it say that the remedy responses from the DOJ to address prisoners' healthcare problems would be just a letter issued "For informational purposes only" and not for actually remedying their medical grievances. If it is just for information, then is it really a remedy? The BOP learned a long time ago that this language is suitable for any stupendously stupid legal-minded federal judge, who understands law but lacks common sense or simply does not care in the event a prisoner ever poses the government a legal threat. Finally, this fill-in-the-blank method of response always ends with the statement: "If you disagree with our 'information purpose only' then you may file for BP-10." This reminds me of a diploma mill college that was caught in a legal battle with its pants down when it gave its students the false impression that they were earning accredited academic credentials, but after the diploma mill lost its case in the court, it modified its language for future legal defense cases against plaintiffs by changing the wording in small print to "endowed diploma/ degree is for information purposes only." Now any student who tries to sue the diploma mill for giving him/her a false diploma will be shown the small print, which said, "information purpose only." The college devised this small print after writing in bold letters that its school was accredited by x, y and z agencies to wash its hands of being accountable for giving false impressions to new students that their diplomas were regionally accredited.

Out of the hundreds of cases of prison responses that I reviewed, I found only two cases where the FBOP response told the prisoner to file a BP-11 if he disagreed with their decision. The reason such a response is so seldom is because the BOP does not want the prisoner to go there. Going to BP-11 is going too close to the live wire; if the prisoner gets over that hump, he would then have exhausted his remedies, which would qualify him to sue the Bureau of Prisons.

If the prisoner does get over the final impediment, the BOP is not particularly worried, because it will make it so hard for the inmate to sue the BOP that he would rather commit suicide than have to deal with the retaliations and solitary confinements for posing a legal threat to the prison officials while still in custody. That is why you will rarely see a case in a federal court where a prisoner is suing the BOP while he is still incarcerated. And if the prisoner is incarcerated for life, good luck; the BOP is in charge and he is in bad luck. If he tries to sue the BOP while still in custody, the BOP also has ways to take him back to court and increase his jail time for this or that serious violation. They can set him up to show that he committed serious crime while incarcerated. If he is incarcerated for 10 to 15 years, prison officials will do enough damage to the prisoner's mind and spirit over that long-time span that when the prisoner gets out, if he gets out alive, the last thing he would want to do is sue the prison. The prisoner will struggle every day to find a way to survive and be accepted by society, especially if he already has many medical problems. No one will even bother to look carefully into his background to see that he was incarcerated for 20 years for just smoking some weed and not hurting anyone.

So it should be crystal clear to you, my readers, by now as to how local federal correctional institutions and the regional offices do everything in their power to make the prisoner go around in a circle between BP-8 and BP-9 (within prison complex) and occasionally BP-10 to the regional office only to be thrown right back into the hands of the local institution where the risk potential for prisoners' abuse is most serious, sometimes fatal, because the prison officials and guards are in complete control and they do whatever they want with the prisoner whose body, mind, and spirit they own.

If the prisoner gets to the level of the BP-10, the regional office makes sure that it will be automatically denied based on the false BP-9 documentation submitted by the warden, actually a standard bogus fill-in-the-blanks form generated by the warden's clerk. In other words, the prison officials have already done the dirty work for the regional office to make its job easy. This is because the prison officials force the prisoner to submit with the BP-10 all the BP-9 resolution documentation from the warden, which was doctored in the first place to tie the regional office's hands back to the original denial. The regional office must go by the BP-9 version of the warden and must reject the prisoner's written version of his medical history and related complaints. The orchestrated response from the regional office then becomes part of the BP-11 appeal if the prisoner ever gets lucky to get to appeal to the Washington, DC, level. The general counsel at Washington, DC, will use the same false paperwork generated at the level of the inmate's penitentiary as the basis for final denial. What goes around comes around. The local prison officials will always win in the end. As I stated before, one of every thousand prisoners working hard at it will manage to get to a very high level with the help of their loved ones, families, friends, outside lawyers, and sometimes families pressuring congressmen, senators, and local politicians. All other sick inmates in 122 US federal penitentiaries will eventually languish or die rolling that Sisyphean stone up the hill.

When the prison officials note that something is too close to call to become a liability in that the prisoner or his lawyer is insisting on obtaining the prisoner's medical records, they avoid giving him the medical records by giving him a false promise or hope of an imminent appointment with a specialist or an imaging test already "approved to be scheduled.". You have seen many examples in this book: "We already placed you on a Call Out" to see a physician, "Your request for medication has been approved," and "We are actively working to expedite your case." Appointments with specialists are scheduled to be scheduled to be scheduled or approved to be approved to be approved, only to be cancelled later to start the process of approving to be scheduled and rescheduled, which in most cases are only for medical chart documentation. A real approval or actual appointment rarely ensues after such promises.

These bogus deceptive promises in patients' medical charts give the prison officials extra time, the prisoner backs off from demanding copies of medical records in the false hope that finally the prison is paying attention, and then unbeknown to him the prison officials go right back to their old behavior. This also gives the FBOP new opportunity to throw the prisoner back in time, making all his efforts thus far fruitless because these false promises make him miss his current deadlines for written response per prison policy. The prisoner had hope that the prison officials were finally ready to help, not knowing that such false promises were meant to dodge the prisoner's attempt at exhausting his remedy options, which was his only ticket to his freedom from suppression and way out of the never-ending spiral. Even if an inmate knew this game (and many prisoners do), he would not be allowed to go to the next level of remedy seeking because the prison is now giving the appearance that they are finally ready to help treat the prisoner's condition by offering an informal resolution. If a lawsuit is initiated after exhausting all remedies up till the BP-11 level, then the BOP is ever ready to present sanitized, falsified, and often colorably forged medical records to the court system.

A case in point is the story of Pete and that of Toliver, a Mexican immigrant who sued the BOP, and the BOP presented manufactured medical records in its defense. Another example of the BOP's preparedness for such eventuality is in the case of Benicio in which the prison warden provided false information to the public defender and totally convinced him (the public defender) that his client was well taken care of in the "six chronic care clinics"—clinics that don't exist but are somehow made part of Mason's medical records as though he is routinely being seen in these six specialty clinics. It was not till the public defender corresponded with his client that he found out that it was a false narrative provided to him by the prison warden. If a lawsuit ever were to be filed by Mason after he gets out of the prison in December 2017, it is the same forged medical records that the FBOP is going to present to the court with perhaps more forgeries added to it as and when it became necessary before his release. At least three other inmate health-related medical records published in *Prison Papers* show that the prisoners were being seen in these imaginary "six chronic care clinics." This includes Kingsley, Benicio, and Kylo. No one has ever seen these clinics on the prison complex in the form of a building or a physician specialist present or a time schedule posted on the clinic door for such clinics, nor is there a prisoner to be found in the entire prison complex who ever saw such a "chronic care clinic specialist" at any time during his incarceration, including those who have been there for almost ten years. Only a doctor from the regional office shows up occasionally to help intervene with the cases of those prisoners who are actively threatening to sue the prison officials for cruel and unusual punishment to put out some blazing fire. He visits the prison to give these "trouble makers" (complaining prisoners) false promises to buy more time hoping that the provision of medical services somehow could be postponed until the inmate's release from the prison.

As I have stated before, if a prisoner does not keep a paper trail of his own medical records in the most meticulous manner possible, he has a zero chance of winning the case in the court of law. And a prisoner must keep perfect records of his Administrative Remedies without which he would not have a case. The fact that the medical records were doctored could not be easily proven even if an inmate managed to obtain copies of his medical records from the prison. The court system that is a shield for the government has no interest in questioning the veracity of the prison's medical records written by the prison doctors and nurses. The burden of proof is on the prisoner to prove that these records are false. The prisoner is really like a little fish in a pond where he files a case with the crocodile against the crocodile in a court where the judge, the jury, the executioner, and the one he is accusing of a crime, are all the same person: the crocodile.

I like to reiterate another important point which I have already stated in this book earlier. This point is so important that it cannot be emphasized enough. A prisoner who makes $10 a month by working 40 hours a week is allowed a maximum of a 15-minute phone call that costs $3 in a federal prison. [In some prisons the cost for a 15-minute call is as much as $20 levied by predatory phone companies that Department of Justice does business with], and the conversation is recorded and monitored, not to mention that he (the prisoner) does not have the money to make that phone call in the first place. Imagine a $20 phone that allows only 15 minutes conversation which is a prisoner's two months' salary after hard labor working 40 hours a week for two months. What attorney wants to represent a prisoner who cannot afford a 15-minute phone call and is rotting in prison while providing free slave labor without earning any money to pay the lawyer? Only those are able to make a phone call whose families have enough money to support them, but they are not allowed to receive more than $300 a month.

More than 90 percent of the prisoners make anywhere between 6 and 7 cents an hour. A clear majority of prisoners who work in many areas of the prison make only 50 cents a day for eight hours of labor; this is enough money just to make two photocopies of a document from the prison law library (20 cents a copy). You must also know how to read and write, which many prisoners are not good at. You must know how to type, and the prison guard may not allow more than 15 minutes on the typewriter per prisoner. And then you may have to wait in line for your turn to type and there may be two hours of wait in the queue. By the time you can get to the typewriter, it is time to go back to your cell for the CO's prison count. You must buy your own wheel and ribbon for the typewriter, which could cost $50, which is the equivalent of five months of salary for most prisoners. For example, I made $10.25 per month for 40 hours per week of hard physical labor. Many other prisoners in many other departments made between $10 and $18 a month for full-time work. Some prisoners who oversee certain departments such as the kitchen, the construction projects, and dairy that has 3,000 cows, old-timer prisoners who are like the CEOs of these departments, may make as much as $3 to $4 a day, but such prisoners have been working for years, have the highest level (level IV) prison jobs, and work long hours including the weekends with no extra pay.

Prisoners are a not allowed to send an email to the Office of the Inspector General (OIG), DOJ, Special Investigative Service (SIS), the attorney general's (AG) office, or the Washington, DC, Office of the Bureau of Prisons. Any such emails are not forwarded, and they are completely deleted from the electronic system 60 days later.

This is to wipe out any evidence of prisoners' attempts to directly complain to any higher up authority in the system of justice outside the prison. The FBOP also has a special representative for prisoners' complaints in Washington, DC. Surprisingly, the BOP does not allow any inmate to send an email to that office either. So why have a special BOP representative? When prisoners write these emails, and they often do, emails are deleted by the BOP staff. If any warden of any federal penitentiary in the United States is asked why they delete prisoner's emails to the Department of Justice, every warden will explain that somehow it is an institutional security matter. One has to be naïve to believe that this has anything to do with prison security; it is to prevent the stories of prison abuse from getting out. Every email from a prisoner is screened and analyzed before forwarding it to his family members. Sometimes emails to family members are held back for scrutiny for days before they are electronically released to the family. Inmates have to be very careful what they write in their emails or what they say on the phone because they know the consequences. Permission is not granted to send or receive an email from any attorney representing an inmate.

Whenever I accessed the prison email system, I noted a message on the bottom of the screen: "Messages sent to SIS or DOJ will not be saved in your sent box and staff will not be able to reply. DOJ and OIG messages are reviewed during normal weekday business hours." It also stated: "Response may take up to 3 weeks. Messages older than 60 days will be purged." These self-given rights provide the BOP a free-for-all to destroy all evidence before it gets out.

As stated earlier, the government attorneys are given instant access to a prisoner who is threatening to sue the FBOP for cruel and harsh punishment, which puts the government attorney miles ahead in a lawsuit. And it gives the government attorney a chance to directly threaten the prisoner with consequences and further deprivation of healthcare if the prisoner insists on suing the government for lack of medical attention or refuses to settle the case amicably. Inmate Pete told me that the US assistant attorney, Ms. Cameron-Banks, allegedly blackmailed and threatened him on the phone to settle his lawsuit against the government if he wanted to see a neurologist for his Parkinson's disease, or else he must suffer like he had suffered with his bleeding cancer without being seen by a doctor for five years. He was told that if he dropped or settled the lawsuit, the government would let him see a doctor. This was right after Pete filed a pro se lawsuit against the BOP in late 2016 for $300 million of damages for ignoring his bleeding cancer for five years. I reviewed the letters that he wrote to Ms. Cameron-Banks in this regard which are self-explanatory and I have published them in *Prison Papers* under his fictitious name.

Retaliation is much too common for posing legal threats to the prison staff. For example, According to Kylo, they took away his betablocker (the only medication he had to lower the risk of recurrent congestive heart failure) as a consequence for having reported the prison officials for not treating suffering prisoners from scabies for one year. He was also downgraded to level II care for threatening the prison staff with legal language in his BP-8 and BP-9 appeals. Prisoners threatening to sue the prison often face retaliation of the most egregious kind from the prison guards and the prison healthcare staff, the standard punishment being sending them to the SHU for longer and longer periods if the inmate continues to challenge the prison officials.

Any threat of a lawsuit to the BOP by anyone can meet with severe punishment or retaliation with solitary confinement. A prisoner has to be extremely polite throughout the process of Administrative Remedy Appeals and show extreme caution or else he will find himself in the SHU for "threatening the medical staff" for putting "prison's institutional security" at risk. Any excessive demand for healthcare or medications is considered a "security and safety" issue by the prison's healthcare staff, which justifies putting the prisoner in the SHU. Even an 80-year-old prisoner with cancer, on the verge of death, can be put in solitary confinement if he shows any frustration for lack of care, because "he is a threat to prison security." It is hard to understand how an 80-year-old fatally ill prisoner with a nonviolent past, who can barely breathe or walk, can be a security risk of any kind to the prison staff and/or to other inmates.

Some naïve and new prison staff, who are not yet groomed into the prison culture of "civic death for prisoners," or those who are renegades and do not intend to work for the prison system for any length of time, or are simply kind-hearted, have naively (and sometimes plain honestly) told some prisoners that they do not stand a chance to see a medical specialist, no matter how serious their condition is, if their total sentence is less than five years. Examples in this book are Arthur, Liam, and Mason. The nurse at the clinic told Mason that he will not be seen by the neurologist because of his short sentence of two and half years (although such promises to him would be routinely made, she told him). Imagine if you cannot see a medical specialist in prison for five years if you have had a stroke, a heart attack, weekly seizures, and/or blindness. Who else is sick enough in prison to qualify to deserve an appointment with a medical specialist in less than five years? And if you are there for more than five years, consultation with a specialist, blood work, or a radiology test does not become an automatic right within the five years period;

you have to constantly battle and put pressure on the prison through outside family members to get it done. Some people die waiting for a test because it is too little, too late for them. Generally, family, financial resources, or sometimes political connections are necessary to get a test or surgery done or even obtain a life-saving medication. There are many prisoners described in this book who were able to get some treatment only after the involvement of influential people from outside the prison, for example, in the case of Wilder, Congressman Bercera from Los Angeles was involved in getting him the surgery and chemoradiation for his invasive prostate cancer that he desperately needed. But I met with four other people with active prostate cancers who had simply given up battling with the prison, hoping that they won't die before they finish serving their sentence. Others told me they simply won't bother seeking any help.

Often, the involvement of politicians does not help either. It is useless unless the politicians continue to be harassed by the prisoner's family. Occasionally, an inmate may be a lucky winner of falling in the lap of some kind-hearted healthcare professional temporarily working for the prison who has become too aware of the prison's death culture and his conscience can no longer handle it. I met with one such employee in prison who quietly helped me with good inside information at a huge risk to his own well-being. I wish there were more people like him in this harsh world to help those who are helpless.

If a prisoner gets too close to receiving a consultation with a specialist or a CT scan or an MRI that has been promised for five years, then another device, an ultimate weapon, frequently applied is to transfer the prisoner to another FBOP facility before the test is done, where he must restart the process of Administrative Remedy to get that MRI test, prolonging the process possibly by additional five years. This explains how a six-month remedy process can magically change into 10, 20, or 30 years for those who try hard. Those who are not able to try simply don't count; they are invisible and they must die. For example, Arthur was transferred after waiting for an MRI for two years following the recommendation for an MRI and hip surgery by two different orthopedic surgeons at two different times while in the same prison. Pete was transferred from one facility to another multiple times to avoid dealing with his constant demand that the doctors address his need for treatment of his bladder cancer. He had to start all over again with his Administrative Remedy Requests to whatever penitentiary he was transferred to. The prison staff often tells the prisoners, "We don't care what was done for you at the other facility. You are new here. Here you have to line up for your turn and start over like everybody else." The BOP holds back prisoner's medical records for apparent reasons when they transfer a prisoner to another facility. Because if they sent his important medical records with him, it would defeat the purpose of transfer, which was to deny him healthcare. This is not to say that all transfers are done for the purpose of denying healthcare to inmates. I am sure there are many other legitimate reasons that warrant transfers from penitentiary to penitentiary but transfer is one of the tools used for denying medical attention.

It is important to remember that the main problem in the Bureau of Prisons is not that there are some bad actor employees (this is probably how DOJ would defend its position in lawsuits). The truth of the matter is that the problem is across the board, and mistreatment of prisoners is not a consequence of a few bad and unethical employees; it is due to a deliberate systematic medical cruelty practiced in prison culture. So it is not just one bad apple but the entire barrel that is contaminated with corruption. It is not a coincidence that Pete, who was bleeding with cancer for five years, begged at least ten different prison doctors and innumerable nurses at many different federal prisons around the country and always received the same answer: denied.

As I have indicated earlier in the discussion, it is tragic that the courts have held (42 USC § 1997e (a). that prisoners need to raise issues in the grievance system of his/her institution and pursue them to the fullest extent there. It prohibits the prisoners from litigating until the remedies are exhausted. But the DOJ (FBOP) makes sure that it is extremely hard for the prisoner to exhaust those remedies, which disqualifies them from suing, not to mention that 99 percent of them don't even have the wherewithal to even begin to seek any justice at all.

Rarely a prisoner always prints a copy of electronic BP-8 requests that they make to prison officials before the prison warden gets a chance to delete the electronic written evidence. Keeping records by making a copy every single time is a hard challenge as is, not to mention that you must come from a family who can afford to regularly send you money every month. Know that with the exception of some white-collar criminals, the families of 99 percent of the prisoners who are minorities, blacks, Hispanics, native Americans and some poor whites are unable to afford to send any money to their loved ones who are incarcerated. Most of the prisoners don't even have any families; they lost their families a long time ago. Elijah, who lost his infected foot due to lack of treatment, told me that he had been trying to find a lawyer to help him file a case for 20 years but had not been successful; now he is five years away from his release. This shows how difficult it is even for an educated and resourceful white-collar prisoner to sue the Bureau of Prisoners while he is locked up and not allowed access to the outside world and has limited access to money.

The take-home message from this message is that these remedies exist only in the FBOP policy, programs, and manuals; there is no remedy available. Thus, the epithet Sisyphean remedies is the appropriate expression. Sisyphus was a cruel king of Corinth condemned forever to roll a large stone up a hill in Hades only to have it roll down again on nearly the top. All prisoners are Sisyphus in that when they get to the level of BP-9 or BP-10 at the most, very rarely would one reach the level of BP-11; they are made to roll back to BP-8 so that they will never have a chance to exhaust their remedies, which means they would never be able to sue the Bureau of Prisons. Nearly 100 percent of the applications at the levels of BP-8 and BP-9 are denied. The rest are killed at the level of BP-10. The prisoner's health information that local prison officials provide to the regional office is designed to kill the prisoner's appeal at the level of BP-10. This supports my evidence-based hypothesis that if 1,000 sick prisoners who were denied medical care were to try to actively sue the BOP, perhaps one among them would be successful, the one who is the smartest, the fittest, the most motivated, and with the most resources. As prisoners file for higher and higher level appeals they are given the confidence of illusion that there is hope but they do not discover till much later, sometimes years or decades later, that it is all a coordinated effort by the FBOP at different levels to make sure that their remedy appeals always fail for one reason or another, mostly by using carrot-and-stick techniques.

As explained earlier and noted in the Trail of Tears Section that many prisoners request transfer of care to the prison's Level III medical facilities due to lack of care; the prisoners' original records published in *Prison Papers* have hundreds of written pleas to the prison warden requesting for a transfer to a higher care level medical prison facility where their medical condition might be treated more appropriately. I interviewed many prisoners who had been transferred from Level III to Level II (in the reverse direction) only to discover to my surprise (and to the surprise of these inmates) that the care at these so-called higher-level III medical facilities were not a great deal better than what it was at the level II medical facility. The FBOP has just about enough room for about a few hundred prisoners who are terminally ill out of a population of tens of thousands of prisoners who are critically ill and continue to terribly suffer in silence in the federal prison system. They are in desperate need of medical help but they will never get it.

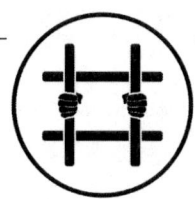

CHAPTER 20

# THE SICK-CALL SCAM

JUST ABOUT ANY EXAMPLE FROM THE TRAIL OF TEARS should be sufficient to convince you that the Sick-Call system in the Federal Bureau of Prisons is tantamount to a scam. For example, prison officials' remedy responses to Mason, a terribly sick prisoner with stroke, heart attack, epileptic seizures, and blindness and a history of regular emergency room visits and hospitalizations, are all about asking him to attend Sick Calls. And when the prisoner makes requests for a Sick Call, it takes him six months of weekly written Sick-Call requests to be seen in the Sick Call only to get some token reassurance in the end. This shows that the BOP's definition of "emergency sick call" could mean six months to a year of waiting, and mind you that is only for the extremely sick.

A nurse, Ms. Blitch, threatened to throw Samuel in the hole when he begged for a Sick-Call appointment before he was about to collapse and be transported to the local hospital that took two months of hospitalization to save his life. If a prisoner is not about to die, his Sick Call may have to wait for five years or perhaps never come around on the BOP's Call-Out waiting list. And then you would think when a prisoner is finally seen in Sick Call, his medical needs are addressed in some reasonable way. Far from the truth. Prisoners are often denied care after such long waits. This is the BOP's definition of "emergency help" for the sickest of them all. When Mason tried to file for more Administrative Remedies, he received the same responses all over again: "You are required to report to Sick Call in order to be medically assessed by a doctor concerning your medical issues." He received a response to another Administrative Remedy request: "In order to get your medications refilled, you must report to Sick Call." Then the cycle of filing for Sick Calls started all over again for him, just like the cyclical repetitive process of filing Sisyphean remedies over years of begging and pleading by him and many other prisoners. Despite these recommendations to attend Sick Calls through the Administrative Remedy responses to Mason, according to him, he was seen only once by the prison physician during his entire incarceration, which was really for the Initial Intake Screening upon entry into the prison, which every prisoner goes through like a meaningless ritual. This shows that the prison healthcare workers lie to the sick prisoners till they either finish their sentence and get out alive or die waiting for medical treatment in prison. I ask the American public that if such false medical documentation by the prison staff ever gets out and becomes public information in a court case, who do you think the court judge will believe: the government's defense lawyer representing the DOJ and FBOP or the prisoner?

One of the very reasons that triggered me to conduct an investigation from inside the prison was my direct observation of these Sick-Call visits by Benicio, my neighbor in prison camp dormitory. He was very sick and kept on going to the so-called Sick-Call Clinic every day and got turned down for one reason or another. (You may want to go back to recall that story in Chapter 1.) Benicio's denials at the Sick-Call Clinic made me suspicious about this Sick-Call Clinic business that could not address the basic emergency needs of a prisoner who was critically ill. When I inquired as to why Benicio was not being seen by the doctor in the clinic, a prisoner who had been incarcerated for seven years told me that there was no such thing as Sick-Call Clinic in prison. "The only clinic that they have is a line at the pill-call- window," he said, "that opens an hour in the morning and an hour in the evening for those who were on certain regular medications such as insulin." Later, I discovered during seeking care for myself that the actual doctor's clinic at the camp opens for only half a day a week where a physician comes to screen the new weekly batch of prisoners who are brought into the prison. Many prisoners, old timers, confirmed my suspicion that the initial intake visit is the only one time a prisoner is seen by the prison doctor during his incarceration not to be seen again, does not matter how ill you were. While the healthy prisoners will never be seen again no matter how many years they are at the prison, the very sick prisoners are seen once in a blue moon only to put out fires and deal with dire emergencies, not with the intention of providing any medical assistance. I was told that the Sick Call existed only for those who could potentially die within the next 24 hours. And what was called a Sick Call really meant a transfer to a hospital via ambulance for life-threatening emergencies only. Then I heard a prisoner joke around with a new comer who was on his way to the Sick Call, stating, "Do you mean you are going to the Death Call?" I asked this comedian what he meant by that. He was serious. He told me some prisoners called Sick Call a Death Call because prison healthcare workers do not consider prisoners sick unless they are convinced that the prisoner is going to die if they did not take him seriously enough. And it is the job of the dying prisoner to convince them that he will die; it is not based on any evaluation by the prison doctor. "Death Call" sounded a bit strange to me but as I started conducting my own investigation, I found much truth to this expression. The logistics of it were not exactly the way it was described to me, but my research showed striking similarities that convinced me that Sick Call being described as Death Call was not an exaggeration.

For example, when I followed around the progression of the illnesses of Benicio and reviewed copies of his prison documents, I found out that he had been requesting a Sick Call from the prison officials in the form of Administrative Remedies on a weekly basis for six months and then finally when he was seen, care was denied to him. Apparently, someone who is legally blind, walks with a cane, has neurological deficit due to a history of strokes, has had a heart attack, and has weekly epileptic seizures and several hospitalizations is not sick enough for the prison officials to deserve emergency Sick-Call medical attention even with a vastly unqualified and undesignated healthcare worker in prison clinic. With such healthcare, yes, I have no hesitation in calling prison's Sick Call a Death call, especially if a prisoner with the illnesses of this magnitude must wait for six months to be granted a Sick Call, a clinic visit where nothing is going to be done for him anyway. If this does not qualify a prisoner to be defined as sick in the eyes of the prison's healthcare workers, then I wonder what does.

The staff tells prisoners when they go to clinic for a Sick-Call request that they must complete the paperwork for Sick Call and they would be put on the Call-Out list after submitting the paperwork. Then magically this paperwork disappears and they are never called out. They look at the Call-Out list posted every morning with anxiety but they never see their name. The only names that are posted are either those of new weekly arrivals or those who have to go through the prison's ritualistic appointments so that prison officials can generate some medical records on them. The fact of the matter is there is no real Sick-Call Clinic or a genuine Call-Out list. Only those who are at the brink of death get attention for a day or so and then are immediately forgotten the moment it appears that they are out of the woods for now. If you have read the prisoners testimonies, affidavits, and documentation in *Prison Papers* carefully, you have already noted that these prisoners have requested a Sick-Call appointment from months to years without having been able see a nurse or a physician or even a medical assistant. When prisoners line up at the clinic for hours to submit their Sick-Call request paperwork, they have to be very lucky if the nurse or the paramedic working inside unlocks the door to them to say hi. After hours of waiting, they start knocking at the door. If the nurse chooses to open the door, he/she will question the first one in the line as to why he needs a Sick Call, and if the inmate manages to convince him/her about his emergency needs, she may take the paperwork from him or may tell him to come back with his paperwork the following day (which is the most common response). If she does take his paperwork, she will tell him, "We will put your name on the Call-Out list, "Come back next week (or tomorrow)," "Sick Call is full today," and so on. Then she shuts the door on the other inmates who had been waiting to submit their written sick call for hours. Those who know it, know very well that there is no Sick Call going on inside that mysterious door. Perhaps some fires are being put out on some cases that have gone terribly wrong because the prison officials have put some prisoner at death's door, which they are now trying to salvage or cover up. After waiting half a day, the prisoners are forced to leave the clinic door because now it is mandatory count time back at the prison, or it is lunch time for which they must report to the chow hall within the designated hour or else go hungry until dinner time. The one lucky inmate who was able to submit his paperwork now waits for weeks at a time to look for his name on the Call-Out list every morning and then has to go back to the clinic to find out what happened to his Sick-Call request that he submitted, only to find out that his paperwork somehow got lost or misplaced. The paperwork gets lost not just occasionally here and there but almost always. You wonder. The clinic has "no evidence" that the inmate ever came to the clinic to submit his Sick-Call request paperwork. The prisoner is the one who has the burden of proof to establish that he submitted his Sick-Call request paperwork. If he has a photocopy of his Sick-Call slip he filled in, there is "no proof" that he submitted the original of that photocopy. Now he is asked to resubmit his paperwork again. Those who leave their paperwork in the labeled drop box inside the clinic waiting room will never see their name on the Call-Out list because those Sick-Call requests are removed and tossed into the garbage pail from time to time.

Some of the common responses from the healthcare workers that inmates get when they knock at the clinic door for a Sick Call are to come back with the paperwork tomorrow, the nurse (or doctor) is not here, and Sick Call is full today. The staff is trained to give ambiguous, false, and vague answers to the prisoners' questions, answers that are meant to deceive and deny medical attention. For example, Noah states in his letter to the warden that he has made countless Sick-Call requests and he submitted photocopies of all those requests to the warden as evidence, and he never saw his name on the Call-Out list, not once in response to all those written requests. The prisoners are always told in responses to their Administrative Remedy Requests that they "must report to Sick Call" if they want medical care or to get their medications refilled. You will see documentation published in prison *Papers* that inmates submit Sick Call after Sick-Call request without ever seeing their name on the Call-Out. Their Sick-Call request paperwork seems to always slip through the cracks. This Sick-Call request paperwork submitted to prison officials is also one of those "nonreleasable portions" of the prisoner's medical records but the BOP will never tell the court in the event of a lawsuit what "nonreleasable" means.

Samuel submitted innumerable Sick Calls; Jacob submitted weekly and daily Sick-Call requests with no help forthcoming throughout his incarceration; Elijah submitted umpteen Sick Calls. Pete submitted Sick-Call requests for five years. Every time Pete did succeed in seeing a prison doctor as a result of filing scores of requests for Sick Calls, the Sick-Call appointment turned out to be another ploy, a scam, a cruel joke, in that he received no care. Some prisoners who express too much frustration at the clinic door are on the blacklist to be either transferred elsewhere or thrown into solitary confinement under the label of "security threat" to the institution. The best a prisoner can hope in prison when he is the lucky winner of getting a Sick-Call appointment with a prison health professional is to get a promise, which almost always turn out to be a lie: "I will schedule you an appointment with a specialist," "I will have the doctor or the PA call you or come and see you at the camp," and so on. The prison physician or nurse sees a prisoner for a Sick Call only when the prison is up to its ears with pleadings, complaints, letters, emergency episodes, and Administrative Remedy Requests, but the intent behind such doctor's visit is often not to provide any medical help but rather to fill in some new paperwork to show that something was done to provide medical assistance based on the nurse, PA, or doctor's diagnosis of choice—a diagnosis that requires no treatment or requires minimal intervention for the prisoner's medical condition. An example would be to avoid the medical attention that the prisoner really needs by giving two tablets of Motrin for pain to a prisoner who has active malignant cancer while concealing the prisoner's actual complaints about how cancer is eating his organ systems. I ask my readers, if you have anyone in your family who is suffering from active malignant cancer, ask him/her if Motrin would alleviate his/her pain. It will be like making fun of a very ill person who is dying. You dare not tell your loved one a joke like that.

When an inmate is told to come back tomorrow and then he does, the response he always gets from a different employee at the window or the door is, "I know nothing about it," "Nobody told me about you coming back," "Why don't you come back tomorrow; the nurse from yesterday that you spoke with will be back tomorrow to address your issues" These devious behaviors of healthcare employees are documented ad nauseum in this book. Prisoners are told by the staff to come back on certain days knowing fully well the clinic would be closed on those days. The prison healthcare staff and guards are trained to make false promises to sick prisoners, which is one of the techniques prisons use to deny medical care. As Walter, who was constantly lied to with false promises of being scheduled to be seen by a physician for his Sick Calls, states in his testimony, "It appears that BOP does not keep its stated promises or goals and is placating inmates with intentional untruths." This is also exactly what I found to be the case with my own healthcare pleas and those of many others that I encountered.

The prison doctor comes to prison camp only half a day a week. He is also the one and only (and much underqualified) physician at the entire correctional complex of 3,000 inmates. He rotates at different prison clinics on the prison complex: the medium-, low-, and minimal-security complexes half a day each, taking care of a population of 3,000 prisoners. The prison manual of course advertises to the public and to the court system, as well as in their policy manuals, that the prison complex has a physician on call for 24 hours a day for all emergencies. During my entire incarceration, I noted only one episode when the physician was called later in the evening by a naïve new healthcare employee because he suspected a prisoner had a heart attack. The physician answered the phone but said it wasn't his problem and to take the prisoner to the ER. This physician, Dr. Dhaliwal, is rarely called by the prison staff for any emergency because they know what to expect. They are lucky if he answers his phone. The physician already has a grievance that he works for pennies on a dollar salary. Dr. Dhaliwal is a foreign graduate who barely speaks any English and has no credentials of any formal medical training of practicing medicine in the United States. The prison manual's advertisement that there is a "physician on call 24/7" is a deliberate and shameless lie told in many federal prisons around the country. This underqualified physician who is not employable at any other job outside the prison, who is paid half to sometimes one-third the salary of his counterparts in the civilian population refused to come to see a prisoner who likely had a heart attack or stroke on prison grounds. And even if this physician were to show up to see this prisoner, he would not have a clue what to do with the prisoner or what was wrong with the prisoner, so why bother.

Prison officials know of course that there is no such thing as a physician on 24-hour-call or duty in prison, but that is not the impression the prison officials give to the courts. The courts are made to believe that everything is in place for prisoners' healthcare. The only option for emergencies during the day or at night is a call for an ambulance for the local community hospital. This is true across the board for all federal prisons. Mortal emergencies where a prisoner must be taken to a local hospital immediately are the only Sick Calls that exist in prison, if you choose to call them Sick Calls.

Those who are moderately sick in prison quickly learn not to bother to seek help because it would be a waste of their time, so they hope for the best to recover on their own if they fall ill or their preexisting condition worsens. They would rather go to the chapel every day to pray for their health than to the clinic where they know they would be turned down. They pray for their spontaneous recovery but the messiah almost never comes around to do any healing. Inmate supervisors (senior prisoners) are often kind to sick prisoners working under their supervision and let them recover before they go back to work as long as the prison guards don't notice that the ill prisoners are not working or absent. If a prison guard does not like a prisoner, he could make him go to work with a broken leg or spine and no one can challenge his decision. Any objection from the prisoner would mean more punishment for him. For example, McClinton, a prison guard, sent Arthur weed-whacking eight hours a day on Labor Day weekend in 2016 despite the fact that he was so severely disabled that he could not walk due to a broken hip for which the prison clinic had refused to give him any medical attention for two years. After that episode, Arthur was unable to walk on his own more than a few steps at a time. Would you like to know how I know about this story? Because I was sent with this inmate to face the same punishment on that Labor Day weekend. So this is eyewitness news.

I hope that you, the reader, are convinced by now based on the evidence already provided, backed up with originals published in *Prison Papers*, that the Sick-Call system in the Federal Bureau of Prisons is neither genuine nor deserving of such an epithet. The term is used only to provide a confidence of illusion to the American tax payers who are supposedly watching, which they are actually not watching at all, to the benefit of the institution called the Bureau of Prisons. The Sick-Call situation described in this chapter is analogous to a war scene where many people are dying or seriously injured, a scene where very few paramedics, who are poorly qualified or unqualified, are at the scene and have no idea how to triage the scene, all looking at one another for guidance as to what to do. Also, imagine a scenario where these nurses and paramedics are also deployed at the war scene by the winning army responsible for maiming the injured in the first place, so none of the deployed health professionals truly believe that the seriously wounded enemies deserve any medical help. The injured are our enemies after all.

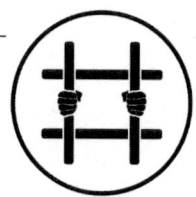

CHAPTER 21

# WITHHOLDING
# LIFE-SAVING MEDICATIONS

YOU HAVE NOTED IN PRISONERS' DOCUMENTS AND THEIR testimonies that they repeatedly ask for their medications, and the medications are being denied even to those who are at risk of losing their lives. The BOP's biggest defense with regard to the disbursement of medications and healthcare in prison is that they "are providing appropriate care and medications in accordance with program statute 6031004 (Patient Care and National Drug Formulary)." This program allows the federal prison to provide prisoners with cheaper drug substitutes that are on the program's national drug formulary. That would be in fact a reasonable argument for the BOP to make if the problem was limited just to the substitution of drugs. There are many health maintenance organizations (HMOs) and private and government healthcare organizations in the civilian population that also provide more cost-effective drug substitutes, which is regarded as an acceptable and reasonable practice. This is also done because of budget constraints. Why give someone a $10 pill or a $20 brand when a substitute that costs a penny will do the same thing or have similar drug benefits. This makes sense and I am sure this is a legitimate and reasonable BOP program that rations a reasonable quota of taxpayers' money from its limited resources to the prison population. Let it be known, however, that this program statute is not the real issue, just as the substitution of drugs is not the real issue with medical barbarism in the federal prisons. The real issue is not giving prisoners any drugs at all in most instances or giving drugs in the beginning for the first two weeks of incarceration and then withholding them as a form of punishment, not to mention that the prison staff will push for a substitute drug even if the prisoner has a severe allergic reaction to the drug, putting him at serious risk of potential death. No one will ever know the names of those who have died as a result of such behaviors, and it will forever remain a prison secret for us and future generations.

You have noted in the Trail of Tears Section of the book that even the prisoners whose outside doctors prior to their incarceration warned that the prisoner would be hospitalized or die if he did not receive his medication(s), the prisoner is told repeatedly to go to Sick Call to request a refill or attend the next Sick Call to request a refill for his medications, or he is told that he must request a refill electronically online. In the majority of these cases, prisoners fail to receive their medications. Twice-a-day insulin injections are about the only drug that is routinely given to prisoners suffering from diabetes, and it is given in the most unsupervised fashion humanly possible, making it one of the most dangerous practices in the federal prison system. These doses are given without any sense of safety and with utter disregard to the dangerousness of mega-dosing or under-dosing. As you recall when Jacob, a brittle diabetic, told the nurse that the high insulin dose she was about to give him would kill him, her reply was, "Don't blame me if you die. You are the one who wanted more insulin. This is what the physician prescribed and this is what you are going to get." This reply came from a nurse who is the assistant healthcare administrator of the prison complex, the one who is essentially in charge of running the show and making all medical decisions and who frequently falsifies prisoners' records, even the prison physician is not allowed to make any medical decisions like she is authorized to. In fact, the physician would be fired if he is noted to be aggressively treating or empathizing with sick prisoners by showing a soft spot.

As discussed in the previous chapter, the Sick-Call Clinic, where the prisoners are supposed to attend to request refills for their medications, does not exist for the most part or exists only in the mind of the prison officials and new prisoner arrivals. The electronic online medication refill requests are rarely answered. And yet the prison officials insist that prisoners refill their prescriptions only electronically through a system set up for them to be able to obtain their refills. There is a rare exception when electronic email or an online request for refill is responded to. For example, when Benicio complained in an Administrative Remedy for refilling his medications, he was told "that I must refill online, but it is never refilled when I request online." I, the author personally requested an online refill for my own medications at least six times over a four-month period and it was never filled, as my BP-8 records published under *Prison Papers* will show. Sometimes the physicians only write scripts in charts to give it the appearance that a medication was given to the prisoner, but it is not actually filled or disbursed by the pharmacist. If it is disbursed, it is disbursed only in the form of a paper trail that is now called a medical record. Often the pharmacist does not even know that such a request was made in the medical chart by the physician because the note in the medical chart was not intended to become known to the pharmacist, the actual disburser of the meds. The note in the medical chart is not written with the intention to refill a prescription but rather to create records that look like medications are being prescribed and disbursed in a timely manner and on a regular basis. Like Kylo states in his Administrative Remedy Request, "A script was allegedly written but it was never filled." When prisoners complain that they never received their medications, the response from the warden is a prewritten standard letter that almost always has the same wording: "Current medication summary report in your chart reveals that you were given medications," or "A review of your records reveals that your medications were reconciled and disbursed to you." Once you see the same notation written for the twentieth time in the administrative record of a prisoner who is complaining about not being able to refill his medications, it does not take a genius to figure out that the prison doctors are falsifying the prisoners' medical charts by stating that medications are being disbursed when they actually are not. It would be insane for every single sick prisoner to be complaining of the same thing a hundred times over if each prisoner was receiving his medications. You can have one insane person in prison complaining of the same thing over and over but not hundreds complaining of the same thing.

Experimenting on prisoners with substituted drugs to which they have a severe life-threatening allergic reaction, a serious side effect, or death causing contraindication according to pharmacopeia is another issue that warrants brief discussion. It is hard to tell if this is the government's experimental program on which they are collecting data to test the limits of the human body or whether it is just the result of prison culture in which prison health employees are formally trained to torture inmates. I noted many examples of such experimentation based on talking with inmates and reviewing their records on their medical history in prison. It may sound bizarre in the twenty-first century to believe that our government would do such a thing to humans, but if history is any guide (and it always is and should be), remember that our government, the CIA, has experimented on prison populations on many occasions up until a few decades ago discovered through declassified and sometimes leaked documents. This may sound like a conspiracy theory to some, but if the government did this in the past, there is no good reason to believe that they have stopped this practice altogether. Government has a policy not to declassify information of this nature till the next generation, almost 40 to 50 years later. The idea is that the next generation wouldn't be too interested in finding out what occurred in the past or would be more forgiving or more accepting of the past because it would appear to the future generation that this is something that occurred way back and does not pertain to them or is no longer relevant. And remember today's present will be the past of the future. This reminds me of Noam Chomsky who says that we should always correlate today's claims with the lies of the past.

I personally cannot vouch for such experimentation taking place in prison one way or another because I do not have enough evidence. All I can tell you is that I noted so many cases where the prison health service employees continued to tell inmates that the drug or its substitute being taken by the inmate was not harmful to them despite the fact that it had become well established through the inmates' outside emergency visits that the drug was wreaking havoc on their health and the side effect, contraindication or the allergic reaction could potentially lead to death. Perhaps this experimentation is not official but rather is the result of the personal enthusiasm of some health service employees or wardens who are curious to know how far they could stretch it to see what could happen as a result of such experimentation.

For instance, Noah was made to take meloxicam with aspirin even though he protested against taking it because he was aware that it was contraindicated. His doctor at the hospital had warned him not to take meloxicam if he was already taking aspirin. Not only was it double dosing with the same kind of medication (NSAID, a category of medications) but also it was a contraindication to his already seriously compromised kidney function that was about to bring him to the brink of dialysis. A much bigger and a clear-cut case of this is Samuel on whom the prison health officials tested the limits as to how much the human body could withstand the most serious chemical allergic reaction from a drug before it gives in. The Health Services experimented on him for more than one and a half years. If it were not for costing the BOP a fortune in hospitalizations, I do not have the slightest doubt that the prison staff would have continued to persuade Samuel to take this medication for his own good and that this medication, which was "so important for his breathing," was "not the cause of the allergic reaction." In the case of Kylo, the medical staff insisted that he take Neurontin despite the warnings from outside physicians that his diabetic nephropathy and failing kidneys were due to the side effect of this medication.

They made Grey take Motrin on a regular basis even though they knew that it was Motrin that was causing his rectal bleeding, which caused his hospitalization and need for blood transfusions due to Crohn's disease. It is hard to fathom why the prison staff would give Mason one-third of the dose of Keppra when the ER doctors and neurologist from his weekly hospital ER admissions, as well as his primary care doctors and specialists outside, were repeatedly sending warnings to the prison staff to give him the right dose of the correct medications to prevent his recurrent epileptic seizures. Was that just another experiment to find out how far an inmate can go with increasingly longer episodes of seizures before he dies? I met many prisoners with epileptic disorders who were put on miniscule and inappropriate doses of seizure medications to punish them with more seizures, Mr. C. being one among them. I saw Mr. C. seizing every other day in the dormitory and taken to the hospital almost every other day in the month of October 2016 when I was getting ready to leave the prison. All the prison had to do was to give him the medication that the hospital emergency room stated he needed to prevent further epileptic seizures. Obviously, there was a method to the madness of prison officials in denying him the correct dose of the right seizure medications. This kind of experimental program in prison becomes more credible, and less of a conspiracy theory, when you start seeing cases where the prison staff insists on continuing the secret experiment despite warnings from the outside physicians who detected the problem upon an inmate's ER visit or hospitalization and properly and timely warned the prison about it.

What is considered an inmate being a security threat by prison officials is another issue that deserves some additional comments. When prisoners persist in demanding their medications, they are considered to be a security threat and sometimes land in solitary confinement as a result. And it does not matter if you are 84 years old and six months away from dying, you are a security threat if you challenge a clinic nurse or the doctor. Sometimes you are put into isolation for "safety reasons." How would you like to be locked up in a small dark room 24 hours a day, 7 days a week without seeing any sunlight for your own safety or anyone else's safety? How is the demand for medications by a blind man, like Mason who has had a stroke, seizures, hospitalization and emergency ER visits, a heart attack, and advanced CPR resuscitation in prison pose a security or safety threat to the prison by asking for his medications is beyond anyone's comprehension. He faced the threat of being thrown into a hole if he did not stop complaining.

How can one justify threats of throwing Samuel in the hole for begging for a life-saving medication at a time when he was already in acute respiratory failure, only moments away from collapsing and getting hospitalized for being on the brink of death? Hospital records show that he did actually almost die at the hospital. He was hospitalized twice for two months due to the denial of medication by prison officials despite the hospital doctors on his first hospitalization warning the prison not to force Asmanex on him due to its fatal side effects. The prison doctor continued to encourage him to take Asmanex because he "would die of suffocation if you do not take it," despite stern warnings against giving him that medication to which he was having increasingly bigger episodes of allergic reactions with the passage of time. Any physician knows that continual intake of a medication that one is allergic to can end up in the most severe catastrophic, irreversible, and sometimes fatal allergic episode. Deceptively forcing Asmanex on Samuel in this criminal manner can only be regarded as the most barbaric of all punishments by the prison doctor, with full foreknowledge that the patient was severely allergic to that medication. Samuel alleges that it was malicious of the prison physician to misinform him that Asmanex was good for him and that the allergic reaction was not due to the Asmanex. And I totally agree with him having analyzed his medical records from the hospital. After returning from a long hospitalization and demanding his medication that was mandated by the hospital physicians as the only safe treatment, Samuel, who was diagnosed with hypoxemia and respiratory failure, toxic epidermal necrolysis, and asthma by the hospital emergency room with his heart already not working well due to a congenital heart abnormality, was told by the prison nurse, Ms. Blitch, "If you don't leave right now, I will have guards put you in the hole." She also said to him, "These hospitals doctors cannot tell us what to do." These comments from her mouth came hours before he was again hospitalized. He would have sure died if they further delayed his second hospital admission. How Samuel was a security threat to the Federal Bureau of Prisons again, is beyond comprehension.

These are just examples of what kind of emotional violence sick prisoners in our federal prisons face. These prisoners referred to previously are all nonviolent offenders and elderly, incapable of hurting anyone, and they are not a security threat to anyone. Only one of the 20 plus prisoners identified in this book has a violent past, but he too is very old now and can barely walk or breathe, how is he going to be a threat to anyone when you can gently push him and he will fall on the floor. Every prisoner noted in this book except one is a nonviolent criminal with no prior history of physical threats to anyone inside or outside of the prison. I will not single out even his fictional name to avoid distraction from the main gist of this book and because this can lead to his identification, which could subject him to further retaliation.

Samuel is denied medication for over a year until the regional medical director of the BOP decides to write in the chart that it is time to give him the right medication because these "hospitalizations have been too costly to the BOP." He recommends giving the prisoner the medication, not because it would save his life, but because if the BOP did not give this medication, it would continue to cost the prison too much money in additional hospitalizations. This can be interpreted only one way: It is ok if the prisoner dies if BOP could save money. The priority is the cost to the prison, not a person's life—an American citizen who is entitled to equal healthcare under the Eighth Amendment of the Constitution while he is incarcerated. Prisoners' demand for medical attention is their constitutional right. This BOP's regional medical director could not have cared less if Samuel died, as long as it was cost-effective for the institution. And, thus, the reason for this long-awaited ultimate decision to give him medicine was an economic one, not necessarily to save the life of a nonviolent criminal who committed a minor offense, or perhaps no offense at all as Samuel claims.

This is not to suggest in any way that the prison should be allowed to torture criminals with a violent past and spare the nonviolent ones; it just denotes the extent of barbarism one can experience in prison, no matter what your offense. You could be one of our American heroes who is locked up in prison because you blew the whistle on the government's corruption and you would be treated no differently. You could be just a dissident or a political prisoner and you will get no special medical attention. It was hard for me to fathom when I saw an extremely ill 77-year-old inmate, Walter, being escorted to the low-security prison to be put in a SHU because he would not stop demanding medical attention. How did he become a security threat? How did Jacob become enough of a security threat that he needed to be sent to the hole for demanding more than two sugar testing strips for his brittle diabetes? This nonviolent criminal is so frail and 50 pounds underweight due to failing kidneys that he could hardly be a security threat to anyone let alone deserve to be locked up in solitary confinement for demanding a medication, which is his constitutional right.

Inmates are constantly lied to and misinformed about their medications in prison. For example, Mason was constantly lied to by the prison officials that they would give him a diabetic card for the chow hall, knowing full well that no such diabetic diet or diabetic card even existed. If it does exist, no one knows where it is and which prison official is in charge of it, no one has seen this diabetic card. Finally, when the day of promise to give him a diabetic card came, he was told that they don't believe that he is a diabetic: "There is no proof you are a diabetic," "We don't believe inmates. They are liars." This was the final answer given to Mason, who was living with half of his body organs terminally damaged due to unmanaged diabetes.

Even during war times, the prisoners of war have some healthcare rights as it is laid out in the Geneva Convention. I do not understand how any healthcare professional gives occasional Motrin for pain to someone like Pete, who is suffering from cancer-related pain for five years, let alone offering surgery and/or chemoradiation for it. Those who are familiar with cancer know that the pain can be excruciating, something you can understand only if you have experienced it; there is nothing like it. How do we explain giving very low doses of Motrin as pain medication to prisoners who have broken spines, crushed vertebrae, and fractured hips due to work injuries such as in the cases of Grey, Arthur, and Walter? Let's not forget the denial of treatments and medications for many of their other clearly defined medical diagnoses. We deny medications to prisoners at Guantanamo Bay because we decided to change the expressions in the English dictionary from 'prisoner of war' to 'enemy combatant' just so we could deprive them of POW's rights under the Geneva Convention. But what about prisoners at home, American citizens on our own soil, are they 'enemy combatants' too? Perhaps those who specialize in prison torture techniques, such as Dick Cheney and Rumsfeld can answer that question, the ones who invented new terminology, 'enemy combatant' to violate Geneva conventions, which supersedes all our domestic laws.

When the prison nurses or doctors are willing to give some medications, they don't seem to care whose medications are being disbursed to whom. Once prisoner X starts getting prisoner Y's medications, that is the way it is going to be for the next 20 years or for the entire sentence period of his incarceration. Such an error is written in stone and there is nothing a prisoner can do to change it even if the prisoner is aware of the error and alerts the prison officials of the mistake. One hundred thousand patients die in American hospitals every year due to medication errors, how many die in American prisons for the same reason? No one will ever make medication correction in the prisoner's chart. An inmate, if he is aware, can only protest and complain but it won't work. This only means that many inmates in prison are taking someone else's medications or wrong medications for diseases they do not have, and then they suffer from unnecessary side effects from these meds. An average inmate cannot be expected to understand what he is being given and why, especially when they don't tell the inmate what he is receiving. Prisoners are not supposed to ask, at least not ask more than once. Most prisoners are not very educated, so imagine such a prisoner taking someone else's medications for 20 years. What long-term consequences will he have to his body as a result of such poisoning for decades? For example, they could be giving blood pressure medication to a cancer patient and vice versa, and in most cases the prisoner would never know because he does not read, understand, or know the difference. He takes these medications in good faith thinking that the doctor must have given him the right medication, because he is a "doctor" after all.

No one in prison clinics, including their physicians, seems to know the difference between 10 milligrams and 10 micrograms, which means they could give the patient fatal doses, 1,000 times the prescribed dose. When patients die, the cause of death is kept secret; the courts or the family will never find out because a newly devised medical chart can be produced at any time on demand and presented to the court. All they have to do is to "amend" the chart notes and change 10 milligrams to 10 micrograms in a new print-out and stamp it with "Amendment." Yes, the prison (the government) is allowed to do that. In a civilian population, a physician could lose his license and go to jail for altering medical records, but our government is exempt from such crimes. The real chart notes will become the "nonreleasable portion" of the medical records for mysterious reasons. The judge will not ask the prison officials for the actual medical records because those nonreleasable portions disappear and the judge will never know that they even existed. If the nonreleasable portions do exist somewhere, the prison will deny their existence. It is no different from what the Department of Justice does in concealing exculpatory evidence that contradicts the government's cases against US citizens who are accused of crimes. There are no judges out there who have the guts to force the BOP to reveal all records or dare ask what BOP really means by "nonreleasable" and what are the contents of these "nonreleasable" documents, and how these nonreleasable parts of the records are a safety or security matter for the inmate or for others. What does releasability have to do with a person's health? And how is a judge to order the release of a medical record that the prison officials claim does not exist? If the judge asks again, he will be lied to again, and he is expected to accept the government's narrative as the truth. Such a judge may be charged with contempt of government, just as he charges citizens with contempt of court, if he remotely suggests that he does not believe the government's version about the facts of the case. Such a judge will become the DOJ's target. These human rights violations inside the prison are tantamount to the recent story of government prosecutors sending thousands of innocent Americans to federal jails by concealing exculpatory and inculpatory evidences in the last three decades. The rule that the courts follow is that the government never lies, and if a plaintiff or a defendant against the government says anything that contradicts the government's statement, he is a liar, even if he puts forward evidence that contradicts the government's claims against the innocent.

The American people as electors of our government should be outraged to know that a nurse, working for the Department of Justice who wants to give Jacob a fatal insulin dose is the assistant health services administrator and authorized to be solely responsible for making healthcare decisions for 3,000 inmates at one of our federal prison complexes with prisoners with the most complex of ailments. There is a clinical director and healthcare administrator and a prison physician above her, but they do not make health decisions; they are too busy enforcing discipline on prisoners on behalf of the BOP. Some of these clinical directors and prison physicians are potentially without a medical license. (This possibility is fully supported by the intergovernmental literature put out by the BOP.) All of the decision-making authority is delegated to this assistant health services administrator.

I was told that the clinical director of the prison where I spent time did not have a medical license. I had no way of verifying that fact. It is not uncommon for the FBOP to hire physicians who have no medical license. This is mentioned in the FBOP policy in the prisoner's Handbook and the FBOP and DOJ documents. Our federal government has entitled the BOP to engage in the kind of practice of medicine for which it will send a civilian physician to prison for—practicing without a license, forging medical records, and prescribing dangerous medications, not to mention that many of these so-called health providers in the federal prisons have questionable pasts. (This is again supported by the facts related in the hiring policies of the BOP.) The BOP reports submitted to the OIG office in 2015 and 2016 strongly suggest that BOP often hires doctors without licenses or suspended licenses to take positions that are very difficult for them to fill because no qualified physician wishes to work for the prison at half the average salary of a physician out in the open.

DOJ's Training manual for prison officials (parts published in *Prison Papers*) strongly suggest that the Department of Justice promulgates a death culture that says prisoners have no human rights and that they have met their civic death by having committed crimes against society, and therefore, it is ok to punish them by denying life-saving drugs or medical care. I also noted during my prison stay that psychiatric drugs are pushed on prisoners who have no psychiatric diseases. For example, I discovered that the prison doctor, Dhaliwal, gives everyone his favorite psych medication, duloxetine (Cymbalta), for countless unrelated physical medical conditions for which there is no indication for a psych drug; he prescribes it for pain as well, regardless of the cause of the pain or no pain, including serious bodily injuries. I was given Cymbalta, an antidepressant, as a substitute for many physical conditions such as thoracic outlet syndrome, myelopathy, paralysis for my right arm, and so on, conditions for which Cymbalta would be considered blatantly inappropriate treatment by any trained medical professional. The fact that the prison does not want to refill prisoners' medications is a blessing in disguise in such situations where the psyche drugs are inappropriately prescribed or even have serious contraindications as listed in the pharmacopeia. No drug is better than a dangerous or wrong drug. The prisoners' actual medications that they really need refilled in a timely fashion are rarely renewed, and if ever refilled, are never filled on time and with regularity and often given in the wrong doses. Such high fluctuations of high and low concentration of the drug in a person's blood stream can cause strokes, heart attacks, fatal seizures and so on depending on the drug administered. If the prisoner complains that he is not receiving his meds, it is somehow his fault because the "patient chart says that it was refilled," so it must somehow be the prisoner's fault that he did not get it. The reasons often given in Administrative Remedy Responses include "Prisoner declined it," "He did not refill it," or "He did not show up." One of the prison doctor's most favorite lies documented in many charts is that the prisoner "declined it." How can a prisoner decline something that was not offered to him in the first place? Or, how is it a decline when the prisoner actually refused a dangerous drug or drug dose that the prison nurse was imposing on the prisoner who was too aware and he declined it to save his life? Once it is documented in the chart that the prisoner "refused it," it gets easier to ignore all his further requests for refills for which he had been kicking and screaming all along to try to get refilled. Now the mantra of declined in the medical records would prevail defeating all other reasonable arguments to the contrary. Bottom line: It is always the prisoner's fault, no matter what really happened or who wrote what in the inmate's chart.

The pain medication on a 77-year-old elderly inmate, Walter, was discontinued within a week of his serious work injury and he was asked to go back to work with potential broken microfractures after taking a 5-foot fall into a hole in the ground at the Lompoc Horticulture Farm during his afternoon shift at work. How sensible is it for the BOP to make this prisoner work on the farm full-time for slave labor at six cents an hour in this American gulag when he could barely walk after a major injury? This is the prison's way of punishing a 77-year-old terribly sick inmate with debilitating pulmonary sarcoidosis and multiple other medical conditions including five vessel heart stents surgeries, hypertension, diabetes, and low renal (kidney) function, not to mention the fresh work-related injury. When Walter asked for a stool softener caused by the pain medication given to him right after the incident, they told him to "use the spoon," which I have yet to figure out what it means in prison talk. Narcotics are known to cause severe constipation in the elderly.

Joseph lost his leg due to a preventable MRSA-related small blister on the sole of his foot because the staff at the pill-call window told him that the "pharmacist was too busy" to fill an oral antibiotic prescription for him. This was after the laboratory had confirmed in a written report that he had a severe infection with MRSA, which is an indication for immediate intervention with hospitalization even with the most marginal standard of care anywhere. I saw many prisoners' feet infected with either fungus or suspected MRSA due to the work-boots. Some of these prison work shoes are very old, sometimes with nails sticking out inside, which could be very painful to walk on. This might explain many recent MRSA epidemics in US prisons. Exposure to rusted iron can also cause tetanus. The prison never provides any vaccinations although they religiously document in everyone's medical chart that they are reviewing their vaccination history and risk factors. The prison doctor or nurse has never once talked with a prisoner about vaccinations let alone offer them vaccinations. The American people are not allowed to know about these outbreaks of MRSA, fungus, scabies, and other eruptions that occur in prison from time to time. Our mainstream media does a great job in serving our corporate government by hiding any such news that only an investigative journalist such as myself might reveal.

Out of all the things I witnessed at the prison that saddened me the most was that the healthcare staff at the prison wish to give medication with a known serious side effect to a prisoner as a device for punishment. They convince him that the medication he is taking is something he must take or else he would die and that the medication he is taking is not the cause of the symptoms (side effects) he is experiencing. One cannot imagine a more sinister way of punishing anyone than giving a dangerous drug with the foreknowledge that it would further deteriorate the prisoner's health or may even kill him. The only other explanation one can have is that the prison's healthcare doctors, nurses, and pharmacists simply have no knowledge that medications can have adverse side effects. One does not have to be a nurse or a doctor to know that drugs can have adverse reactions and that when someone is experiencing sudden unexpected horrific symptoms, one has to consider the possibility that it is not a worsening of the disease but a potential side effect of the drug itself.

The malicious intent of prison healthcare staff became apparent when the local hospital ER staff continued to warn the prison officials that Samuel was having a life-threatening allergic reaction to the Asmanex, yet the prison nurses and doctors continued to tell the prisoner that it was not the Asmanex that was the cause of the problem and that the inmate must take Asmanex or else he could die. Healthcare workers were telling this to the prisoner with a note in front of them from the hospital doctor that clearly showed them in bold letters: "Please do not substitute with Asmanex, patient is severely allergic." The prison doctor continued to tell Noah to take an NSAID, meloxicam, for pain knowing fully well that it was contraindicated in someone with limited renal (kidney) function and could damage the kidneys further. They continued to tell Kylo to take Neurontin despite his low renal function that was making his kidneys worse and then forced him to take an NSAID on top of that, another contraindication—that is, two medications that were contraindicated for his failing kidneys. They made Grey take Motrin when he was bleeding from his rectum due to ulcerative colitis and Crohn's disease, bleeding induced by Motrin in the first place, knowing fully well that Motrin will make the bleeding worse or could even punch a hole in his gut, not to mention that prison did not once even entertain the idea of helping him with his severe form of ulcerative colitis that had made his life miserable.

It is hard to believe that healthcare workers at the prison are completely ignorant of how medications work and their usage, indications, and contraindications. It is hard to believe, but it is possible.

I will let my readers judge this on their own based on the following chapter that talks about the qualifications of prison healthcare staff who are hired by the Department of Justice and given the responsibility for the health of a very sick prison population.

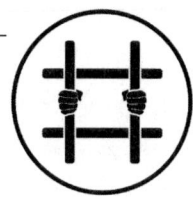

CHAPTER 22

# MEDICAL CRUELTY, EMOTIONAL VIOLENCE, AND DEADLY NEGLECT

I N MY LAST MONTH IN PRISON, OCTOBER 2016, I STARTED re-interviewing prisoners whose prison records and medical histories were to be published in this book to get last-minute updates from them. I knew I was at the end of my journey in prison and would not be able to follow up on obtaining additional inside scoops with regard to the health issues of these folks. First, I spoke with Liam and he informed me that he had no luck with scheduling an appointment with a urologist for his active prostate cancer diagnosed by prostate biopsy, despite aggressive intervention by his mother through the regional office of the Bureau of Prisons and the general counsel in Washington, DC. Liam was still waiting for a response from the regional office for his BP-10 appeal on the day we parted our ways.

I spoke with Mason and he told me that his federal public defender, Ms. Park had been making written requests to the prison warden to try to set up a atty-client phone meeting with Mason for a year. His family would like to sue the BOP but his health came first; however, the warden would not allow his public defender to set up a phone meeting with Mason. He reiterated that in his letter to the public defender, the warden had perjured himself by writing that Mason was receiving excellent care in "neurology, endocrinology, general, lipid, mental health, hypertension and diabetes clinics, —the "specialty clinics" that everyone knew did not exist—and that his "medical treatments by these clinics were on target goals." Now that Mason told the public defender that the warden had lied to him, the defender wanted to set up a confidential conference with Mason as soon as possible to pursue the matter legally, but an attorney–client privilege was not allowed. Later in the afternoon, after I re-interviewed Mason, I saw him collapse in the dorm. He had started to have more frequent epileptic seizures in October, on an average of twice a week, and was hospitalized each time. He returned with medication instructions from the hospital emergency room but the prison refused to give him the correct medication in the correct dose. As a result, the frequency and the duration of his epileptic episodes continued to increase.

Mason also informed me that when he went to the clinic and told the nurse that he needed to be given the right seizure medications in the right doses as prescribed by the hospital, the nurse replied, "These outsiders don't tell us what to do." He emphasized that he had been seen only once by the prison physician during his entire incarceration period. He showed me his paperwork to prove that the prison was aware that he was prescribed 750 mg of Keppra by his private neurologist before he came to the prison, but the prison had refused to give him more than 250 mg, which was triggering seizures every other day. Local ER physicians had further increased his doses to re-stabilize him, but he was not receiving the ER-recommended dose at the prison camp.

I observed another prisoner, Mr. C., two bunks away from Mason, have three generalized epileptic seizures in three weeks and was hospitalized each time. Other prisoners told me that Mr. C. was not getting his usual epilepsy medication, which was causing his seizures. I asked Mr. C. directly if he would share with me what medication he was on prior to coming to prison and what was he receiving, if anything, from the prison doctor. He refused to talk with me about it. Mason informed me that Mr. C. was afraid of retaliation by the prison guards if he discussed his case with anyone. "They did not punish Mr. C. but punished the guy who was trying to help Mr. C. by locking him up in the SHU." Every time Mr. C. had a seizure, I saw prison guards and health personnel let Mr. C. seize and then lay unconscious on the floor for as long as an hour before taking him to the hospital, all along hoping that he would recover on his own and avoid the need to be transported to the hospital. They called the ambulance only if he continued to be nonresponsive for more than an hour, and they brought him right back to the dorm without any medical evaluation if he became responsive on his way to the prison clinic while waiting for the ambulance to arrive. Prison guards regarded his medical condition a nuisance that they had to deal with every other day. I asked the prisoners, "Was he not just taken to the hospital an hour ago? How did he get back so soon?" They explained that they brought him back because he started responding as he laid in the wheelchair waiting for the hospital paramedics to arrive. I said,

"He should still be taken to the hospital to be checked even if he started responding." They started laughing when I said that.

I did not know much about Mr. C. because I was not in the loop, but I continued to observe Mason whose case I knew very well. I saw him collapse again due to epileptic seizures in the dorm on September 26 and then again on September 29. A paramedic, nurses, counselors, unit manager, lieutenants, clinical director, case workers, warden, and about 15 employees came running to the scene; it seemed like most employees of the prison complex. None of the healthcare workers knew what to do. They stood there for 45 minutes calling one another on the radio. Not a single person checked his pulse or blood pressure. He laid on the floor till paramedics from the hospital arrived. Once again, it turned out to be another seizure and it was due to a suboptimal dose of Keppra medication. He had been asking for the correct medications and the correct doses prescribed to him on his hospitalization, but the prison refused to give it to him. On October 2, he had yet another seizure in the dorm followed by another hospitalization. I noted altogether four people with different medical conditions in dormitory A collapse multiple times in the months of September and October 2016. I tried very hard to see if I could lay my hands on the medical records of some of these people but I could not due to scarcity of time and lack of cooperation from these people, for lack of trust. Some of them were starting to think I was some sort of investigator implanted in prison by the government. They did not trust me enough.

I re-reviewed Mason's outside medical records that he brought with him to the prison in January 2016 to check his seizure medications and doses; these were medical records that the prison doctor had pretended all along did not exist. These medical records from Mason's own physicians clearly showed that he was on 750 mg of Keppra XL (extended release) for partial seizures. The prison put him on 250 mg of regular Keppra (nonextended release). Regular Keppra for partial seizures is the wrong medication. The treatment medication for partial seizures is the extended release form of Keppra; regular Keppra is a treatment for generalized tonic clonic seizures. Purposefully giving the patient only one-third of the required epileptic medication dose is not just inappropriate but a criminal act. Every physician in the outside world should and would know that considering the instability of Mason's partial seizures, he should have been up to 3,000 mg of Keppra XL per day with 1,000 mg serial increases at two-week intervals till his seizures had been brought under control. Giving 250 mg of medication to someone who might need up to 3,000 mg daily is not simply malpractice but a criminally insane experiment, especially if the patient could die from lack of treatment that is readily available. But this is normal behavior in prison because it is done for punishment, not necessarily because the prison doctor is ignorant of the treatment protocols. Mason did not even receive his suboptimal dose of the wrong kind of Keppra in a timely manner; he got it after putting up a big fight through remedy requests and appeals, despite outside doctors' clear directions to the prison clinic regarding his dependence on these medications. Mason had several seizures in his bunk in September and October that I directly observed. His hospitalization records will bear that out, the medical history that I am willing to bet has also been carefully sanitized from his prison medical chart and that I don't have access to.

This under-dosing with a wrong medication made it clear as to what was going on with him. I observed Mason experiencing yet another major epileptic seizure on October 14 from which he took a very long time to recover. I did not think he was going to make it this time, but he did. He was taken to the hospital because he simply would not respond, and it took the hospital four days to stabilize him. Every time he returned from the hospital the doctors at the hospital sent him back to prison emphasizing that the prison had to initiate a proper dose of seizure medication with an initial loading dose of 1,000 mg of Keppra, which the prison staff refused to give him. He had another seizure on October 17 in my presence and was taken back to the hospital; he returned with a new prescription of Tegretol along with a much higher dose of his previous medication, Keppra, but they again refused to give him the prescribed medication in the doses that hospital doctors requested. He informed me that when he told the clinic that he needed the correct doses of the correct medications that the doctor at the hospital prescribed him, the nurse told him the same thing that she had told him before: "The outside doctors do not tell us what to do." Mason also informed me that he needed ten other medications, NPH insulin, blood pressure medication, cholesterol medication, atorvastatin, hydrochlorothiazide, B12, sitagliptin, and gabapentin, and he had not received any refills for any of those either. Whenever he requested medications through a formal Administrative Remedy Process, he was told, "You are required to attend Sick Call to get your medications", a standard response.

Because of the limitations of time at my disposal, I moved on to get as many updates and new stories that I could before they booted me out of the prison. So I obtained a last-minute update from Pete to see if there was anything new with his case. He informed me that he had sued the government for $300 million for medical cruelty and torture. He gave me a verbal testimony of which I took notes, which

I would like to paraphrase as follows as accurately as possible to the best of my ability and recollection.

On August 26 (2016), Assistant US attorney Ms. Indira Cameron-Banks called me and said that I needed to settle my case with the government. The attorney told me "I guarantee you will lose. If you settle, I will help you get an appointment with a neurologist." I stated to her that "my Rabbi called here and was helpful in motivating the warden to promise me an appointment with a neurologist for my Parkinson's." She (the US federal attorney) replied, "Forget the Rabbi; if I come there and tell the warden you need an appointment with the neurologist next week, I guarantee you it will be done before the end of this week. But you have to settle the case first if you want to see a neurologist. I guarantee you will never win." I told her, "Show me first that you can help me get an appointment with the neurologist and then we will talk about the settlement."

Pete showed me his notes of this phone call from the Ms. Indira Cameron-Banks who represented defense for the government in Pete's pro se lawsuit against the BOP, which he had just initiated with help from a jailhouse lawyer, Chris, who had kindly and quietly prepared legal paperwork for him just before his own release from the prison. Pete told me that that Ms. Cameron-Banks was given on-demand instant phone access to Pete at the oddest hours of the day. Contrast this with Pete having been trying to access a lawyer from the outside world for over a decade which was his legal right. Also compare this with the senior federal public defender and senior litigator, Ms. Park from Hawaii who sought permission from the warden to have an attorney–client phone conversation with her client, Mason for a year, having no hope that it would ever occur despite letters, emails, and phone calls for months. This is the equality before the law we have in the United States, this land of "liberty, equality and justice." How is this different from the former Soviet Union?

I read Pete's notes and the related court documents subsequently generated by the Assistant US Attorney, Ms. Cameron-Banks and it was clear to me that she was trying to incentivize this prisoner with settling his case with the government as a trade-off by offering him some medical attention for his Parkinson's disease. I found the underhandedness and behind-the-scene government blackmailing of this prisoner very disturbing. Ms. Cameron-Banks was asking him to drop the case or settle it in exchange for medical attention that he was entitled to by sheer human decency as well as his Eighth Amendment fundamental constitutional right to medical care. And she did not want the court to learn about this secret negotiation with the inmate. It made me nauseated when I learned this. The prison torture of Pete for five years by letting him live with malignant bladder cancer was apparently not good enough punishment for what is ironically called our Department of Justice. Now Pete was starting the process all over again trying to seek care for his Parkinson's. This will be the same story of torment repeated all over again, but I would not be able to follow up on that because I was about to be released from the prison and would never see Pete again. It would not surprise me if it took another five years for Pete to be able to see a neurologist for apparently an advanced Parkinson type of neurological disease that he is currently suffering, but I will not know because I am no longer there.

Pete sneaked some more paperwork in my hands a few days later, at the last minute, to update me as events occurred with his case. The paperwork clearly shows Pete's allegations that the government lawyer falsified to the judge that Pete had agreed to make a joint request to the court for an extension for the deadline for government reply to the judge's stipulated response deadline. Pete immediately notified the judge that the government attorney, Cameron-Banks had falsified what occurred in her phone conversation with him. [These letters are published with Pete's real name, case number and identity redacted in *Prison Papers*.] Pete alleges that he never agreed to give the government any extension to reply in that phone call from Cameron-Banks; in fact, Pete protested against any extension at all. He vowed that he would not agree to talk with the government attorney ever again. None of this came as a surprise to me personally because I have seen the government commit perjury way too many times in my own case, the kind of perjuries for which any American citizen would be charged with felony and face a very long jail sentence, while prosecutors enjoy absolute immunity for committing any crime against American citizens, no wonder they are not afraid of any wrongdoing.

Pete's lawsuit against the federal government for $300 million has already become public information now and my readers are welcome to publicly verify the veracity of Pete's allegations published in this book. But I am afraid that because Pete is already in his 70s and very ill and has several more years to go before he is released from the prison; the chances are that he might die in prison before he has a chance to see justice. That makes him a very vulnerable plaintiff in this lawsuit. Once again, the corrupt prosecutors who had unlimited access to him in prison will continue to intimidate him and bargain with him in offering him 'medical care or justice, pick one or the other', till they get what they want. The rule of thumb is that the government must win at all costs against this sick elderly man whose hands shake like Jell-O from Parkinson's. He is on the verge of death with his various medical issues and he is not being given access to any private attorney outside the prison, while the prosecutors enjoy instant access to him 24 hours of the day to negotiate with him at their own terms. There goes equality before the law in this great country of ours that claims to stand for liberty and justice for all. As I am now editing the draft of this manuscript that I completed in prison, I wonder what is going on with this poor fellow behind bars; he still has five more years to serve to complete his 25-year-long sentence. He was incarcerated for some drug smuggling charges at Israel's airport 20 years ago.

I moved on to Kylo and asked him if he had any last-minute updates for me. I wanted to understand why he was constantly complaining of chest pain despite the use of a beta-blocker that I knew he had managed to intermittently get from the prison, so I asked him to show me his medication bottles if he had any. It bothered me that Kylo could barely walk twenty steps before being out of breath, having to stop or sit down five times on his way to the chow hall only 100 yards away from the dormitory. I noted on his medicine bottle that the prison doctor was giving him 50 mg of regular metoprolol (the immediate release type) once a day, which is supposed to be a treatment for myocardial infarction (heart attack). Kylo's well-documented diagnosis was congestive heart failure (CHF) for which the treatment is supposed to be 200 mg of metoprolol of XL or ER type (the extended release) to keep his heart pumping and decongested from CHF. Due to long-term negligence at this point, Kylo also needed at least a dose of 200 mg due to a long-standing history of chest pain and his poorly controlled advanced congestive heart failure. A newly recognized CHF is supposed to be treated with metoprolol ER 25 mg then doubled every two days to reach 200 mg/day. This explained why he continued to have chest pain. He was being treated for a heart attack while his medical condition was congestive heart failure, which is why he was dying a slow death exacerbated by a whole host of other serious medical conditions, including hepatitis C, COPD, pancreatitis, and retrolisthesis—medical conditions for which he was not receiving any treatment at all as well as being denied his regular medications.

Was this being done to him on purpose? Kylo alleges that at one time, they stopped giving him the beta-blocker altogether as a punishment for trying to report prison officials in Florence Prison in Colorado for neglecting 100 prisoners with scabies who continued to suffer without treatment for one year. The prison doctor took away his pain medications and beta-blocker for his congestive heart failure as well as his HTN (blood pressure) medication, barred him from being seen by healthcare workers, and threatened to put him in SHU if he continued to demand his beta-blocker. Kylo said he would rather be in solitary confinement than not have his beta-blocker, which he believed made his heart keep going, because not taking it, he said, would kill him. It was not unusual for very sick prisoners to tell me that they would rather live in the hole and get some medical help than receive no medications at all and possibly die in freedom they enjoyed under minimal security. Prisoners such as Kylo are a special category of prisoners who no longer fear retaliation from the prison officials, because they have nothing more to lose. They will die for lack of medical treatment, so they might as well fight for their rights even if it meant pissing off the prison officials, as Kylo asserted.

Kylo informed me that the prison officials told the inmates who were infected with scabies at the Florence Prison complex, Colorado that their "rash is due to barometric pressure, don't worry about it," while according to Kylo at least 100 prisoners were itching their skins for one year, to the point of becoming suicidal. Kylo updated me with a "Clinical Encounter" medical note that he obtained from a clinic employee, which said, the "prisoner is using gym regularly" and therefore healthy enough to be downgraded to Level II care. I asked Kylo if it was true that he was using the gym. I wondered, how could he use the gym with constant chest pain, heart failure, and obesity? In response, Kylo took me to the gym and showed me the machine that he was using for five minutes a day. The machine seemed like it was designed for disabled prisoners to help them stretch and mobilize their muscles in a stress-free, protected, sitting posture with back support for safety. According to Kylo, this forgery of documentation appeared in Kylo's medical chart note after he had become a nuisance to the medical staff by persistently demanding transfer to a Care Level III facility as the court had ordered for him. Kylo said that the prison officials wanted to make an example out of him for blowing the whistle on prison doctors in a town hall meeting about treating prisoners' scabies with athlete's foot fungal cream. The photocopy of this bogus clinic note from his medical file was slipped into his hand by a lower-level employee at the clinic who did not like the treatment of the prisoners by prison authorities and was planning to quit his job, so he did not care if prison officials found out that he released medical chart information to the patient— "sensitive information" that healthcare staff is instructed by the FBOP to guard and prevent from being leaked. This employee was just going to say, "Oops," if he was ever discovered. He couldn't care less; he was prepared to be fired or quit his job. Kylo's medical condition had gotten so much worse since he came to the prison that he was now a walking "atomic bomb", as I put it to him, a bomb that would implode any minute. I was surprised that he was still alive. He had untreated congestive heart failure, pancreatitis, COPD, asthma, peripheral vision loss, cataracts, and unmanaged blood pressure, which was putting him at much higher risk of morbidity, mortality, and sudden death.

In my opinion, this bogus medical note that he showed me, was another scheme to lower Kylo's care level to shut him up for good from chronic complaining. This phony medical note was written by the same person who had written other bogus notes. His name was Mr. Camacho R., an MLP. (It seems like MLP stands for mid-level practitioner, a designation that is invented by the Bureau of Prisons and then presented officially as some kind of diploma or degree). Any healthcare provider not writing his or her actual medical degree next to his or her name, such NP, or PA, and calling himself/herself an MLP instead is forbidden by law in all 50 states in the United States. No mid-level healthcare practitioner out in the civilian population writes MLP next to his/her name; they must identify themselves with a qualifying degree, and they all do without exception, because they are required by their licensing Boards to do so. Medical and nursing boards forbid the use of vague, obfuscating designations to hide one's real credentials. Healthcare providers in the civilian population with genuine credentials have no incentive or motivation to hide or obfuscate their qualifications by not writing their medical diploma or degree next to their names; in fact, they proudly do so.

I re-reviewed the BOP policy to see what kind of medical staff it is supposed to have. I was shocked to learn that the BOP also designates its medical assistants as their healthcare providers. This explains why the FBOP chooses to use designations such as MLP to mask the true qualifications of its healthcare staff. A medical assistant has six weeks to a maximum of six months of medical training as opposed to a physician who has a minimum of 12 to 20 years of medical training depending on his specialty before he or she is considered qualified to see patients independently without supervision from an attending physician. So calling both of these health professionals "care providers" is as suspicious as things can get. The highest technical task a medical assistant is qualified by training to perform is to take a patient's blood pressure; he or she is not a healthcare provider in any sense of the word.

I sought after the 77-year-old dental surgeon, Walter, to get a last-minute update from him, but he was still in solitary confinement somewhere, so I had no access to him. I did, however, have a chance to review all his remaining documentation, which I had hidden in locations in the dorm (with assistance from several other inmates) in a manner that prison guards could not easily detect, and if they did, they would not be able to easily put two and two together to figure out who put those documents in those locations. They certainly could not trace it back to me. When I reviewed Walter's paperwork piece by piece, I saw repetition of the same thing over and over. He wrote request after request for the release of information but the prison officials refused to give him copies of his OSHA report, a report from the Safety Department, Workman's Comp, hospital records, his prison medical records, or his imaging and laboratory records. It was clear that these mandatory reports required by government agencies in the event of an injury on the job were nonexistent in prison, a clear violation of several healthcare and federal law statutes that are strictly imposed in the civilian population on all doctors, hospitals, and nearly all healthcare entities without exception. Citizens are often put behind bars for violating these statutes, but the government is exempt from obeying the same laws that we healthcare workers are all expected to obey. My best guess is that the BOP likely forges phony reports to show that it complies with all these statutes if a court ever requests copies of OSHA, work injury, and other statutory reports, and the BOP probably does it only on an as needed basis and waits till it legally gets challenged. This theory clearly explains all the reasons why the BOP will refuse to release to injured prison workers their 'on the job injury' reports and all other mandatory reports to which they are entitled by law, prison or no prison, despite multiple written requests by the injured prisoners. The DOJ's double standard is that it would immediately shut down a hospital or a doctor's office that violated any of these government agency statutes, rules, and regulations but has no problem violating the same governmental agency regulations in an institution under its own jurisdiction. In this sense, the DOJ and FBOP are apparently above the laws that they impose on the rest of the American population.

I also found out that injury reports had been swept under the rug and medical records falsified in the case of all other prisoners who had on-the-job injuries. I went back to Grey, a forklift operator who had serious spinal injury while operating heavy machinery in prison camp, to see if he was given an injury report when he made a written request. He laughed like I had told him a joke when I asked him this and stated, "I am lucky if they give me Motrin once a month," he replied with some sense of humor while he felt pain in his back as he attempted to laugh. Grey was still in a wheelchair one year after his spinal injury when I left the prison with still no injury report given to him. A prison doctor also told him one week after his injury that he must return to work after acknowledging to him that he was incontinent (losing urine) due to his spinal injury and had tremendous pain due to crushed L4 and L5 vertebrae of his spine.

Four weeks before I left the prison, my own supervisor inmate, who was in charge of the grounds, broke his knee and told me that no injury report was given to him. They wrapped a cast around his leg without finding out what was broken, made him go back to work in two days with arm supports and his left leg hanging in the air, and refused him any more pain medication after giving him some Motrin once.

I also found out that no injury report or safety report existed or was given to Arthur when he requested it. He thanked me for writing the BP-9 to the warden for him, but then said that if they caught me doing it, they would have found a way to keep me in prison for much longer with new sanctions imposed on me. He advised me not to do it for anyone else, not even for himself, because he said that they would soon detect a pattern if I tried to do the same for another inmate, which he knew I was trying to do. He said, "They would easily detect a new emerging pattern of writing complaints being filed with the warden, suspected to have been written by one person, and they would trace it back to you by getting into the business of interrogating all prisoners one at a time like they do when they are trying to investigate an incident to find out who is behind something. In this case, it would be you. They will break someone down, someone you tried to help, who will let it all out to save himself from the SHU." After this point, I did not write BP-9s for anyone else. I particularly wanted to help Arthur in writing his BP-9 because I had seen him being abused by a prison guard despite his severe disability. He was to me an example of how disability or severe illness received no mercy from the prison officials and prison guards.

Prison guard, McClinton assigned Arthur to weed whack with a six-foot-long heavy shovel for 8 hours a day for three days on the Labor Day weekend for having harbored a piece of bread from the chow hall, his leftover from lunch. Arthur had a broken hip, was severely disabled, walked with the most awkward twisting motion around his hip, and had lived with potential multiple hip fractures related to chronic pathology for two years. His hip locked at work while trying to shovel weeds on Labor Day and he stood against a propane tank on the dairy farm for two hours and could not move. I walked to the prison guard's office at the dairy farm where I was also being punished with the same "extra-duty" assigned to me and suggested to the CO on duty that Arthur be taken to the hospital ER to be seen by a doctor. He simply ignored me and said, "Get back to work right now or else you will be whacking weeds every weekend from now on." Arthur became more immobilized than ever before since that day. He also started showing signs of another impending heart attack triggered most likely by this "extra duty" that he was assigned by McClinton. I gave him some hope by telling him that if he survived the first heart attack, which was always the riskiest one, he might survive another due to the collateral circulation that he might have developed since the previous heart attack two years prior. I encouraged him to go to the clinic with his complaint of chest pain but he decided not to go, stating, "They won't do anything. They will ask me to start putting in applications for a Sick Call, so why bother." "Do it just for a paper trail to preserve your legal right," I advised him, but he was in so much pain that he simply ignored me.

The prison guards made him go to work every day despite his disability. One of the guards told him, "I want to see your ass working till 3:00 pm; I don't want to see you resting in the dorm during work hours." I am not sure what he would have done if it were not for the kindness of the prisoner in charge of the grounds who let him sit down on the bench out of sight of the prison guards during his work hours. The prisoner in charge showed him where to hide if the guard came around to inspect or what to say to the guard if he caught him not working. I am an eyewitness to this story because I was also sent weed whacking with him for a three-day Labor Day weekend as my punishment because the guard McClinton had found a wooden shelf in my locker (wooden shelves are forbidden; only metal is allowed). This extra shelf was given to me by my bunkie Franco, a US army sergeant, as an act of kindness to give me some extra storage space for my books and paperwork.

Mr. McClinton is also the same prison guard who, in my second week at prison, told me to use my left hand to work if my right hand was paralyzed when I was still recovering from right hand and arm paralysis. I was not even yet officially assigned to work. When he discovered me writing on my notepad in the chapel library, he said, "It does not matter if you are assigned, you better get to work and if your right hand does not work, use your left, if your left leg does not work, use your right." It is not uncommon for prison officials to make disabled prisoners work full-time. The only exceptions are those they know can barely move their bodies. I guess they do not want to squeeze blood out of stone. Thanks to them for being so kind.

Rule number one in prison is you never defy a prison guard's order. A prison guard has been given more power by the Department of Justice than the nine judges of the Supreme Court of the United States. A prison guard can single-handedly give any punishment to a prisoner including locking him up in solitary confinement for up to 18 months by accusing the prisoner of anything, and no one in prison including the warden will question him or ask him for evidence for his claim against the prisoner. There are formal procedures of hearing in prison to see if someone violated a rule after he is accused by a guard, but these procedures are a showbiz and a sham. In other words, the original accusation by the guard is almost always proven to be valid. It is rare that an inmate will not be found guilty once he is accused by the guard of some prison rules. Prison guard's word is his evidence. Appropriate paperwork will be generated by prison authorities to justify the punishment but the original decision of the prison guard will reign supreme in most accusations. This is called teamwork, solidarity in the BOP's prison culture. I can relate many stories that I witnessed that prove this fact, but I will not describe those stories because they are not the explicit subject matter of this book. If they can forge medical records, framing someone for violation of prison rules is a piece of cake. I am sure that most average Americans are aware that even the Supreme Court of the United States does not have the power to throw any American in solitary darkness for 18 months without at least some evidence of a crime having been committed by the accused—but a prison guard can.

A word or two about "extra duty" vs. a "shot." What does it mean in prison? An example of this occurred when Arthur and I were given a choice by the prison guard, Mr. McClinton, to accept "extra duty" or a "shot" for violating the prison rule by bringing bread from the chow hall to his locker, and in my case, by putting a wooden shelf in my locker. We both chose extra duty to avoid ruining our prison records. A "shot" means that a prisoner gets written up, which can ruin a prisoner's record for good behavior for which there are further sanctions or deprivation of privileges imposed on him. Almost any violation can bring about imposition of sanctions. And the definition of violation is what the prison guard says violation is or perceives as a violation; it has nothing to do with what the prison policy says violation is. For the prison guard, violation could mean, "I don't like you the way you look or sit or eat." For example, I was caught by another prison guard, Mr. Zepeda, a correctional counselor, who found me in prison's chapel library writing and asked, "Where are you assigned to work?" "I have been assigned to the grounds," I replied. "But what are you doing here, it is 2:00 p.m., work time?" he inquired. "I finished early because I finished all the tasks assigned to me for the day, and there was nothing else left for me to do," I reported. He proceeded to say sarcastically, "You have job security, don't you." I replied, "Yes, I have job security. I make six (6) cents an hour which pays my mortgage and my bills," which was just a spontaneous slip of the tongue response. I immediately realized that what I had said would sure land me in the SHU. I quickly laughed at it as though I was just joking to relieve him of his tense posture toward me. I commented, "You know I am kidding, you know that, don't you? You can change my assignment if you like, I don't mind if you reassign me to some other job." That was a very lucky day for me. He decided not to react and walked away. I guess I managed to jolt him with a touch of light humor. I could have faced sanctions for my behavior.

Back to my final update meetings with the inmates. In my final rendezvous with Noah who lived in the adjacent dormitory, he informed me that the prison officials had to take him to hospital because he started throwing up blood continuously, and this made them nervous. The local community hospital doctor who evaluated his bloodwork sent a note to the prison that he must be seen by the nephrologist (a kidney specialist) or he could lose his kidneys and would then have to go on dialysis. Even though this was the second recommendation from outside community physicians, the prison officials refused all his requests for a consult with a nephrologist. Noah was very aware that going on dialysis was an early sign of impending death because dialysis went only so far before his kidneys would completely shut down. He was only 36 years old, a type I diabetic from a very young age, which explained why his organ systems were already failing at such a tender age. He showed me a response he had received from the warden denying him all his medications. This denial letter from the warden was dated October 4. He told me that he was still hoping for a response from Congressman Campbell whom he implored for help in his letter to him, but so far there was no response from the congressman despite the involvement of his family constantly writing to him and calling his office regularly.

My last good-bye encounter with Samuel, who had a history of three hospitalizations in two different hospitals having almost died of drug-induced Stevens-Johnson syndrome, was disturbing. He showed me colored photographs of his Stevens-Johnson syndrome from his second hospital admission, which he obtained directly from the hospital. I took Samuel to one of the available rooms in the chapel and examined him. I noted that his entire body had extreme scarring after the weeping wounds and bullae dried up. All the major scars on his chest, back, and abdomen corresponded with the color photographs from the hospital, pictures taken when lesions were active, oozing, and infected. I could superimpose that picture on his body. He was constantly itching as I was examining him. The color photographs taken at the hospital were textbook pictures of a Stevens-Johnson syndrome extreme case scenario as I remember having seen in *Harrison's Principles of Internal Medicine* textbook when I was in medical school 25 years ago. He told me that due to the way his body looked, he was embarrassed to take showers in front of other inmates, so he took shower very late at night when everyone was asleep. Samuel was physically and emotionally scarred and continued to suffer from pain. He was deeply depressed and he wept in front of me. After a while, I could not help crying either, but I cried after I left the room when he was not looking to hide my feelings from him.

Samuel also told me that the medical clinic had gone back to its behavior of not refilling his Advair and he has to constantly fight to get any refill, which is not consistently given to him, and when it is given, it is filled late so he has gone without medication for days. When that happens, he has trouble breathing and sleeping. He told me that the nurses and doctors were still telling him that the Stevens-Johnson syndrome was not caused by the Asmanex that they gave him. I was shocked to hear that from him because I had reviewed his medical records in which the FBOP's regional director wrote himself that allergic reactions caused by the substitute Asmanex were costing the Federal Bureau too much money because the use of Asmanex resulted in expensive hospitalizations. Samuel was worried that if they put him back on Asmanex, the substitute, he would die either from a worse form of recurrent Stevens-Johnson syndrome or from not being able to breathe for not wanting to take the substitute. "I am doomed either way" he said.

I sat down with Kingsley, a physician incarcerated for some false tax filing charges, as he described it to me, for an update on his Job's syndrome, a rare autoimmune genetic disorder. He told me that the prison had refused to give him the requested medications and diet and it seems like even the court judge was about to give up on him.

He had not heard anything from the judge for two months; the one person who was expected to rule on his health issues within a matter of days due to the seriousness of his condition had now gone silent all of a sudden. The judge had gone completely reticent after I, a physician licensed to practice in the states of New York and California, had submitted an affidavit to the court on Kingsley's behalf. In this affidavit, I described, under my license no., what I saw as opposed to what prison officials were describing through falsified medical records about his health condition, thus essentially exposing the prison official's lies to the court for not noting his physical exam in his medical chart. I also informed the judge that the prison had no special diets available for sick prisoners who needed special diets, thus also exposing the government attorney's lies about special diets being made available to sick inmates in prison. Having seen my affidavit that refuted the government's false claims may explain why the judge had gone silent all of a sudden.

It seems that the incestuous relationships of federal judges with the Department of Justice is so strong that they never fail to follow the one rule: The government always speaks the truth; everyone else's testimony that contradicts the DOJ must be dismissed. Kinglsey informed me that the government attorney argued with the judge to disregard my affidavit based on the fact that I was a bad doctor serving prison time for having harmed my patients with a dangerous German-made IUD. Kingsley said that he believed that he would die a slow death over the next 42 months of his prison sentence. The judge's silence made him lose all hope that his request to be transferred to a medical facility where he could get the medical care he needed would ever be honored. But his family was continuing to fight, he told me. I had seen Kingsley in prison when he looked a lot worse than what he looked like in the colored photograph that he sent to the judge through his attorney. By the time he was able to find someone to take a photograph of him in prison (a very challenging task indeed), his swelling had gone down a bit due to having starved by avoiding all gliaden and gluten in his diet and living on three to four pieces of fruit a day, but he still looked like a different species in the picture. He lost 25 pounds in three weeks as a result of this starvation, but the prison doctor refused to write a notation about the weight loss in his chart. Instead he wrote, "no weight gain."

If the Department of Justice can manufacture hundreds of false documents to convict innocent people such as myself, it should be a piece of cake for any federal judge to discard an affidavit from any concerned citizen, physician or not. The federal judges are not always about justice, law, and order. And sadly, they have been given nearly infinite power to do anything they want to anyone, guilty or innocent, without any adult supervision at all. Evidence plays a role in our courts only if our government wants to use evidence; otherwise both prosecutors and judges can discard evidence at will. My affidavit was not only my testimony but was testimony of eye-witness evidence that the judge seems to have discarded. Our government can turn actual evidence into no evidence and vice versa, if it serves the government's purpose, and they can discard real evidence at will. The government of the United States does not care when it is bent on violating a human right to perpetuate the corruption in the establishment that it has become so comfortable with. In my own case that landed me in prison, the US government forged hundreds of pages of false evidence to convince the judge that I had committed a crime. And the criminal court federal judge, Ishii, accepted all of the manufactured evidence as the basis to incarcerate me. The most overwhelming, irrefutable, and flawless evidence that I provided was ignored by the federal judge or he pretended it did not exist. This explains why none of the atrocities I saw happening in prison came as a total surprise to me. I have come to understand that this is how the system works in this land of ours, the land of the free. It is not much different from a third-world country. The famous lawyer, Gerry Spence, the author of *With Justice for None* (1989), explains it best when he states that the difference between corruption in America and that in a third-world country is one of method, not substance.

I will wind up this chapter with some updates from Elijah, Jacob, and Joseph in terms of what was going on with them while I was frantically busy going from one inmate to another gathering as much investigative data as possible before I departed from the prison. Elijah explained that his hopes of hearing back from senators, Barbara Boxer and Feinstein were dashed to the ground. He had neither heard back from the senators nor from Vivek Murthy, the Surgeon General. I told him that I was sorry if his hopes and wishes never came true. It turns out that politicians usually do not help prisoners no matter how legitimate the complaint or worthy a cause simply because they have no political gain in helping someone who is locked up, someone who has no voice, someone who is not going to get them on TV to make them look like heroes. So why bother and waste your time? I told him not to bother pursuing it any further.

I spoke with Jacob, the wasting away, 60-pound-underweight, type I diabetic. He told me that the clinic had started giving him three test strips a day after he was found in another diabetic coma, but now they are back to giving him only two test strips per day. I reviewed a letter to the prison by Seventh Day Adventist Hospital written on behalf of Jacob that clearly stated that he needed to be tested several times a day due to his brittle type I diabetes and that continuation of an insulin pump was critically important to avoid wide fluctuations in blood sugar levels. But the prison was once again ignoring all instructions from his outside healthcare providers and specialists who took care of him prior to him being incarcerated.

Finally, when I faced Joseph to see if he had any new updates, he informed me that he had stopped seeking help from the prison's Health Services. He only hoped that he would not lose his other limb before he finished doing his time. He also told me that he believed the physicians directly employed by the federal prison to take care of prisoners using the prison's healthcare insurance enjoyed absolute immunity so he could not do anything to sue them for criminal behavior or malpractice for that matter. I am not sure of that to this day. I do believe, however, that they have at least qualified immunity, which they often try to use in the court of law to defend themselves against their malpractice and unethical pursuits. It is also up to the courts as to how they interpret the law. What I do know for sure is that any prisoner who intends to sue the FBOP while still in custody of the Bureau of Prisons is like a person living in water under the mercy of the crocodile and pleading to the crocodile for justice in which the crocodile is not just the judge and the jury but also the one who is the accused, and therefore the defendant in the case. You can easily figure out what kind of justice lies ahead for a plaintiff living in water where the crocodile is the judge and the executioner who chewed off the plaintiff's limb.

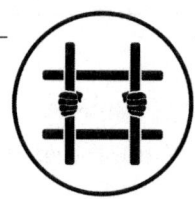

CHAPTER 23

# "CARE PROVIDERS" FROM HELL TRAINED TO TORTURE

THE FBOP OBSCURES FROM THE AMERICAN PUBLIC THE true qualifications of their Health Services staff that they announce to the world as the prison's "clinicians." A clinician in the medical community refers to someone who has appropriate clinical medical education and generally someone with the qualifications of a physician with added hands-on clinical experience under supervision for years to develop a sense of clinically detecting and deciphering medical signs and symptoms of a patient. It was only through diligent research that I was able to find detailed internal policies of the FBOP in terms of how they hire these clinicians. Most of these healthcare workers who are designated as "clinicians" by the prison system are not remotely qualified by any stretch of the imagination to provide

377

basic care to the very sick in prison who need ongoing care to stay alive, let alone provide them appropriate specialized medical care. For example, one of the health professionals that the FBOP lists as its clinician in its policy and programs is a medical assistant. I have been a physician for 25 years, and as I stated in the previous chapter, a medical assistant has anywhere from six weeks to six months of medical training after a high school diploma or GED as opposed to a general practitioner, who has a minimum of 12 years of medical training. I have dealt with, hired, fired, and worked with hundreds of medical assistants during my career as a private practitioner and I have found many to have a poor high school education and some of them cannot correctly read or write a sentence in English and many are functionally illiterate.

According to the FBOP, its nurses are also its clinicians and healthcare providers. These nurses, who sometimes have as little as two years of nursing training, are trained to do the nursing jobs such as cleaning, sterilizing, sanitizing, taking and reading doctors' orders properly, and giving medications and injections. They are neither clinicians nor healthcare providers. The physician's assistants often hired by the prison system are not clinicians either; by law they must work under the direct supervision of a licensed physician. The physician assistants (PA) are considered to be high-level clinicians by the prison system and are the mainstay of the prison system. They work independently without supervision, not to mention that those who work for the prison system are really the ones who are the bottom of the barrel, as I will discuss later in this chapter. These lesser qualified individuals, even in the civilian population, who are undoubtedly much better trained than those working for the prison, cannot tell one heart sound from another on a physical exam. So technically they are not clinicians, but at least the ones in the civilian population have a better sense of medicine having gone to school for as long as two to three years and being properly licensed to qualify for a civilian job. But it should not matter, should it? There is no such thing as anyone doing a physical exam or taking medical history on a prisoner in the FBOP system anyway. This is a great equalizer for all prison healthcare employees; they are all FBOP clinicians. So why should it matter when no one is going to need to use clinical skills? And why should the FBOP worry about it, clinician or no clinician? Let us call everybody a clinician including nursing assistants whose jobs once upon a time were to clean beds, remove poop and piss, and clean up after patients to sterilize the areas for the nurse. That is precisely what the BOP does. It has officially designated its medical assistants as BOP's clinicians.

This Health Services hiring policy for staff clinicians by the BOP says a lot. The policy explains, at least in part, some of the secretive coded designations that the BOP uses for these clinicians such as Dr. 1 and 2 and health provider 1, 2, 3, and 4 (really meaning nurses, paramedics, and medical assistants without revealing their qualifications) to obscure the true qualifications of their clinicians, healthcare practitioners, or doctors. The FBOP will gladly tell you, if asked, that calling clinicians provider 1, 2, and 3 is an effective way of communication, an efficient administrative method for the large size of the BOP bureaucracy, or perhaps they will tell you it is a "security matter" as to why these clinicians are not identified by name or at least by their proper designation such as an MD or a PA. The one indisputable device that the FBOP uses when it wants to hide any information of any kind from the public is to call it a security or safety matter to shut up any investigator, because who wants to mess with the prison security, which is so important in the eyes of everyone who hears about it. No one can dispute that fact because we all know that security and safety are important.

A 3,000-inmate prison with only one physician and perhaps a couple of nurses or paramedics has no reason to assign practitioners numbers such as 1, 2, or 3. That would be more appropriate if there were 50 or 100 clinicians working in a place. The fact that the prison has so few (virtually none) healthcare providers gives it away that designating clinicians as 1, 2, and 3 is the FBOP's way of covering up their qualifications in that these people are not clinicians. For example, the FBOP also uses a designation such as MLP (mid-level practitioner), which, as discussed earlier, is illegal to use by healthcare professionals according to state laws in all 50 states.

I believe that the BOP has learned over its history of 100 years how to con the legal system and the courts as to the true qualifications of what they call their clinicians and healthcare providers. It turns out that almost no healthcare provider out there who is genuinely licensed and qualified in all respects with proper education and training is known to be working for the federal bureau of prisons today for reasons described later in this chapter. I have no doubt, however, that despite being unqualified or poorly qualified, there are many kind-hearted people out there who accidentally end up working for the prison system. Good people in this world are like water that flows everywhere and the BOP can do nothing to stop it. Healthcare workers, regardless of their qualifications, who are aware of their higher affirmative duty toward the sick do not last long in the FBOP system, however, because the prison officials always discover them empathizing with or helping the sick and therefore either they are fired or they quit, leaving behind the most tyrannical nurses and criminal-minded physicians who are often promoted to higher positions for demonstrating their ability to emotionally withstand brutality and barbarism. That is a requirement in prison culture as it is cultivated through systematic training by those in control of the FBOP under the blessings of the DOJ. A DOJ's training manual for employees of the Federal Bureau of Prisons published in *Prison Papers* supports the observations I made in prison. The most vicious, heartless tyrants, ones who can demonstrate their capacity to be inhumanly cruel loyalists of the FBOP, become the long-term employees who are promoted from within and rise to the top.

This is a mirror image of the hierarchy in the Department of Justice in the civilian world where corrupt prosecutors in the Department of Justice who work illegally, unethically, and unconstitutionally are promoted to higher positions within the criminal justice system. Good responsible employees are fired for intentionally or unintentionally disclosing to the prisoners well-guarded healthcare information that is supposed to be kept secret. They are like the whistle-blowers inside the system that the BOP has to deal with from time to time. Conscientious employees cannot stand the prison death culture that they are constantly told to take part in, and they always end up leaving their employment with the prison system. I learned some of this from a kind-hearted prison employee, a wonderful, young southern man who was working for the prison but was planning to quit because he was terribly bothered by what he saw was going on and the expectations of his superiors to hide and protect health information from the prisoners, information that he knew was concocted. He was going to quit, so he did not care if he shared this information with me as long as I did not tell anyone my source. And he knew that I wouldn't under any circumstances.

It goes without saying that truly qualified healthcare professionals by definition know that they have a duty toward the sick and they will not cooperate with prison's death cult. They will go only so far before they end up quitting. This young, kind-hearted, southern Christian with good work ethic and a sense of moral responsibility toward all other humans was going to quit.

The long and the short of this is that those who are willing to strictly execute unwritten rules of the prison culture of "civic death of all felons" are the ones who predominately work for the Federal Bureau of Prisons. Although it makes sense that they should have tough people working in prisons because after all they are dealing with many dangerous criminals, the problem is that this is a subculture the prison officials preach to their subordinates. According to them, all felons in federal prisons have lost their civic and human rights, which our Declaration of Independence states were endowed upon them by the creator.

The readers who do not quite believe what I have to say about the prison culture should read some of the stories that have been published in the *Rolling Stone* and *The New Yorker* to know that I am not the only one saying these things about the prison system. For example, in the May 2016 issue of *The New Yorker*, you can read about the fate of Harriet Krzykowski, a former counselor at the Dade Correctional Institution who faced retaliation after questioning inmate abuse. Others who have done diligent research have similar findings. My version should be even more credible, however, because I am speaking from the belly of the beast and from what I have seen happening in prison with my own eyes. Having said this, I cannot rule out the fact that there may be some dedicated workers working for the FBOP whose family member had been hurt by a criminal in real life and therefore they carry disdain in their heart for all criminals under their custody. They see it as their chance to seek vengeance or redemption by treating every prisoner harshly and inhumanly. I can understand why these people will act that way.

None of this changes the fact that most criminal-minded health-care workers are working for the BOP for one reason, and one reason alone. They are not employable elsewhere; no one else will give them a job for reasons that I am about to describe at some length. In this sense, they themselves are very vulnerable. Abysmally underqualified healthcare workers in the federal prisons who rise to the top automatically learn, without formal coaching (although there is plenty of formal training), how to internalize a culture that manufactures medical records and to execute medical cruelty with flawless precision to please their superiors whose winks and nods they readily understand. Prison staff including healthcare workers and contractors are all too aware that they have qualified immunity and certain employees know that they have absolute immunity, so they don't have much to fear if they are caught engaging in criminal activities against the most vulnerable population inside the four walls of the prison. The worst thing that can happen is that they will lose their job or perhaps retirement benefits, but nobody is going to send them to jail.

I reviewed a 2016 Level of Care Memo dated August 12, 2006, exchanged between the Department of Justice and the BOP. There is a great deal of omission of facts and lies throughout the back and forth communication between the OIG and FBOP. For example, in this memo, when a federal judge asks the FBOP what judges could do to help the situation for medical care of sick prisoners, the FBOP replies: "Until the inmate comes into the prison and is evaluated by the prison's healthcare provider, the Presentence Report is the BOP's principle source of initially assessing medical conditions."

As you have learned from many of the true stories in this book, the FBOP disregards what is documented in the presentence reports about the medical condition(s) or care levels of incoming prisoners, not to mention that the FBOP does not do its own medical evaluation, which makes our government even more hypocritical. The prison doctor only fills in some bogus electronic medical records paperwork to give it the appearance of a genuine doctor's account and a prisoner's face-to-face encounter with a healthcare provider. I did not find a single example of a case in my investigation where judge's orders or official care level court designation were remotely respected or honored by the FBOP. The probation department's documentation with regard to the prisoner's health status is readily dumped in the DOJ's unfathomable garbage bin once the prisoner is removed from the court and taken to the prison.

I reviewed a 2016 OIG investigation report on the BOP in which the BOP presents to the OIG a list of benign logistical administrative issues that the FBOP is currently facing as the sole cause of all the FBOP's health management difficulties. These health administrative ailments are presented to the OIG as easily resolvable issues that would just require some tender loving care in terms of simple measures of revamping the hiring process for the BOP's Health Services staff. The FBOP presents the entire problem as not having enough money in the budget to hire enough qualified healthcare staff or competent workers. I do not doubt for a second that not being able to hire qualified healthcare workers is due to budgetary constraints. There is no denying that this may be one of the BOP problems, and it is a legitimate concern.

One of the common defenses for barbarism by the FBOP in the courts is one of the financial constraints on the BOP. This defense has been decisively repudiated as a financial issue with some courts threatening to close down a jail or prison if it cannot be run in a constitutional manner regardless of the stated cause. Although fiscal consideration is no basis for the complete denial of constitutional rights, it can be taken into consideration by the courts in fashioning the appropriate relief for the injured. This pretext, however, seems to become a basis to mitigate and justify all FBOP crimes regardless of the nature and cause of the crime.

However, from the viewpoint of someone who knows the prison culture from the inside, not having enough money to hire competent staff is only a very small fraction of the overall prison crises. The biggest issue is the global problem of death culture that plagues our federal prison system. Death culture is a cultural issue, a major part of the medical cruelty; it is not a money issue. This is also the direct consequence of government policies to perpetuate slave labor and keep the institution of slavery alive in the twenty-first century. I will disregard the philosophical discussion about the government's mass incarceration program and instead focus on the prison culture that was carefully cultivated and has been cherished by the Department of Justice for a century. When things are not running well in any institution in America, it is always a "not enough money" problem, whether it is our education, healthcare, or environment, never mind the trillions of dollars of taxpayers' money constantly being transferred from the US Treasury into the pockets of the wealthy and the privileged in corporate welfare.

The FBOP, a subdivision of the Department of Justice, supervises and trains the prison's Health Services staff to imbibe and celebrate a culture of civic death to all inmates, which has resulted in inhumane treatment of prisoners, and it has been carefully hidden from the American people since the inception of the FBOP in 1892. Although the idea of civic death has been legally repudiated, it continues to be perpetuated and nourished by the Department of Justice. This death culture story becomes public only once in a while through a rare court case and then is quickly forgotten because the American people think of that as an isolated case of brutality perpetrated by some bad apples. Little does the American public know that this is true across the board, as it relates to every human being locked up behind federal bars. The DOJ is actively hiding all the real issues from the public and covering for crimes actively being committed in violation of the fundamental human rights guaranteed to every American, including federal inmates by the Supreme law of the land, the Constitution of the United States of America.

The FBOP in the aforementioned OIG report mainly focuses on staffing problems and then prepares reports for the OIG based on its own analysis and self-investigations and comes up with a list of solutions. Then the OIG graciously accepts those reports and concludes that all problems have been discussed and resolved and the story of the OIG's investigation of the Bureau of Prisons concludes with a happy ending. Like a fairy tale, everyone goes home and lives happily ever after. It is clear that government agencies, including the overseeing agencies of the government, corruptly cooperate with each other to keep the American people deluded with incomplete and superficial news while keeping from the public eye the underlying ailments of the FBOP that are ostensibly classified secrets. Overseers of the government agencies have become part of the deep state instead of doing the job that the American public hired them for.

I'd like to give credit to some factual statements made by the BOP in the OIG's investigative report: "BOP's greatest recruiting challenge is attracting candidates that are also qualified to work in private healthcare organizations ... salary gap of BOP vs the outside world is 60% salary gap for physicians, 102% for pharmacists, 133% for dentists and 34% for nurses ... one-time bonus offered to a physician hire for BOP job is $403, for a nurse is $603," and so on. All of this is true. What the FBOP does not tell the OIG, however, is that deliberate medical cruelty, prisoners' abuse, and violation of their human rights is at the heart of the problem, not necessarily underpaid employees, although that is a factor. Being underpaid does not and should not automatically lead to the brutalization of human beings. One has nothing to do with the other. If the BOP were given all the money it needs, it might make employees happier due to better compensation for their work, but it will make no difference to the prison's death cult promoted by the Department of Justice. The BOP may be able to hire qualified staff with more money, but it would not solve the problem of active training sessions carried out for healthcare workers to teach them how to practice barbarism by experimenting on prisoners. Talking about lack of money and staffing issues barely scratches the surface and gives the FBOP an opportunity to mask real issues ailing the prison industrial complex under the cover of "budgetary constraints." I believe that the sick prisoners could get reasonable medical attention despite budgetary issues and the government's limited financial resources if the prison healthcare staff was trained to believe that the sick prisoners are human beings and not animals. If the BOP's claim that its healthcare workers went through some medical training to become licensed to practice medicine is true, then these workers must have learned in medical or nursing school that, first and foremost, they have a higher affirmative duty as doctors and nurses to take care of the sick and that every sick person is to be treated as a patient first and not as a prisoner or a criminal who deserves to be tortured. A sick patient is a patient, according to the Hippocratic oath that all health professionals take many times during their careers.

It is apparent that medical cruelty in prison is the result of the deeply ingrained prison culture of punishment and torture fostered by the Bureau of Prisons. You can pour as much money into the prison system as you want, but the problem will remain if the underlying culture does not undergo some kind of reform. Pouring in money will be like patch work. All it will do is raise employee's salaries and nothing will change. Torture will probably increase because now employees are really well fed and want to be more loyal to the well-kept internal policies of the Department of Justice because they are paid well enough to do so. The following demonstrates a remarkable precedence of this in the state of California in recent history that underscores my point:

Judge Thelton Henderson of the 9th Circuit Court forced the California prisons to solve the overcrowding and staffing problems several years ago to which the California's prison business lobbyists first resisted and then obliged under pressure. This resolved the medical cruelty in California only temporarily. Pouring in more money and reducing budget constraints did not help at the end of the day. Even the temporary improvements that were done were because California prisons were under scrutiny for any violations of mandatory Health Services after this landmark decision. Releasing 40,000 sick inmates resolved the overcrowding issue, but the prisoners had no respite from medical cruelty. Prisoners had more access to health staff only temporarily and a few inmates benefited from it during the active federal government audits. The medical cruelty and inhuman treatment never improved and quickly went back to where it started, because the issue presented to the court by the California prison system was framed solely in terms of an "overcrowding problem" and a problem of "lack of resources and money." The element of prison culture was kept from the court. As expected, the California prison system hid from the federal court that the real underlying problem was that the prison officials were trained to treat prisoners as sub-humans who did not deserve medical attention. It goes without saying that it would have been suicidal for anyone in the California prison system to portray this to the federal court as a problem of prison abuse and human rights violations. The discussion about the prison's death culture—culture that is practiced in both federal and state prisons to this day—was left out of the California Prison system investigation. As a result, the California prisons' horrible healthcare problem is now back to its original abysmal levels within a few years of the release of 40,000 inmates. It did not automatically help sick prisoners get better healthcare. It was a show biz for a brief period when federal audits were occurring and California prisons were being closely watched. All California prisons have miserably failed in all recent healthcare audits. Of the 35 prisons audited, only 1 barely passed the test set of healthcare standards by the federal overseer who was appointed for this purpose.

That is what one can expect to happen when prisons pretend that a problem does not exist or hide the real crux of the problem from the American public. We face the same problem today in the Federal Bureau of Prisons and we probably always had, but no one has ever written about it. Overcrowding and lack of resources is only part of the problem. The elephant in the room is a deliberate violation of human rights that is fostered by the institution of the Bureau of Prisons with full participation and blessings from its parent agency, the Department of Justice. Overcrowding and understaffing are two sides of the same coin. The most important take home lesson, however, is that if we resolve one or both of these issues, the real issue remains, that is, the medical cruelty. It will continue unless the education and training of the prison staff changes and they begin to learn the value of human life in this age of enlightenment, which is different from our medieval understanding of human rights and justice. Many third-world countries have learned this lesson of human dignity in the age of enlightenment. To catch up with the rest of the civilized world, America can learn this too.

In the aforementioned report, the FBOP in its responses to the OIG states by way of suggestion that it has to sometimes hire unlicensed physicians and healthcare workers, including hiring those who will just say "yes" to a job offer, because of this humungous problem of not being able to find people who are willing to work for the prison system at a fraction of the customary salaries in those professions. One prison administrator makes this comment in such a way in this report that it is clear from her statement that the FBOP will hire anyone who is willing to accept the job regardless of their background, pretending that these people have credentials and no criminal background. If you read between the lines, there is a clear suggestion that they will hire just about anyone and pretend that there is no need to check the hired's background or training level. Now that Obama has bragged that federal job applicants will not be required to tell if they have a criminal past, this could then mean that the BOP could now hire ex-criminals to provide healthcare to current criminals. Diamond cuts diamond. That should nicely work out for the DOJ to fulfil its intended goals.

The FBOP does not disclose, assuming that it must have the knowledge, that many of these healthcare worker hires might have been barred from practicing medicine in the outside world or may simply be considered unqualified to be allowed to practice medicine for one reason or another. This could include incompetency, history of malpractice, lack of medical license, suspended or revoked license, lack or total absence of prior training, and worst of all, no medical license at all. The FBOP also often hires those who have unverifiable foreign medical degrees and sometimes with little or no medical training and those whom no one would hire or trust to take care of their patients in a world outside the four walls of the prison.

One has to ask this question: Why would someone want to take a job with the FBOP at half or one-third of the standard salary? Would you take a job for $33,000 with the prison when plenty of healthcare jobs (two jobs for everyone applying) in the outside world offer you a standard salary of $100,000? The average sign-on bonus for a physician in the outside world can range from $25,000 to $250,000 just for a three-year commitment, the amount largely depending on your specialty, and the nurse's average sign-on bonus can range between $5,000 and $25,000. What sane physician will accept a sign-on bonus of $403 instead of $100,000, not to mention accepting half the amount of a physician's annual salary, year after year? Why would a nurse take a job with a bonus of $603 instead of $20,000, not to mention half the normal salary of a nurse for the rest of the his/her life? There has never been a dearth of jobs for nurses and physicians; there are often shortages. There are certainly shortages in underserved areas where hospitals offer doctors and nurses higher-than-average salaries and extraordinary bonuses in addition to student loan forgiveness and repayments to attract them to work in their smaller towns. The answer to all these questions is simple. These people are working for the prison not because they love to volunteer to help the unfortunate in our prisons but because something is seriously wrong with their qualifications or background. This explains why the people are willing to bend all medical ethics they were taught in school and unleash their personal anger and frustration for not being able to make a proper living against the prison population to keep a job that brings in a paycheck on a regular basis to feed their families. They are ready to please and appease their superiors in the prison because this only solidifies their long-term prospects for job and advancement up the ladder of prison bureaucracy.

Many of them are foreign graduates without residency training, with fake credentials, or even without a medical license. I asked the physician, Dr. Dhaliwal, at the Lompoc Prison camp in California if he had done three to five years of medical residency training like other physicians in the United States before working for the prison. His answer was, "You know how it is with foreign graduates; it is hard to get a residency spot anywhere." Dr. Dhaliwal has an MBBS degree from India, which is 4 years of medical training as opposed to a minimum of 12 years of medical training in the United States that one must undergo before calling himself a practicing physician. And one can do premedical requirements to go to a four-year MBBS degree program in India right after high school, called matriculation, which is just 10 years of schooling unlike the 12 years of high school education in the United States. In other words, in India, a person is already a physician with the years of education that is required to apply to a medical school here in the United States; it does not even include the additional 4 to 8 years of schooling in academics and hands-on clinical training required in the United States before an individual is considered to be qualified enough to see his or her first patient independently of an attending physician watching over. Here is this man, Dr. Dhaliwal, the prison physician who is considered to be qualified by the FBOP to see and diagnose a variety of complex patients with one year of student internship from India, which is the equivalent of a medical student's first year training here in the United States. I verified Dhaliwal's qualifications from the California Medical Board website where the public is allowed to go and verify, during the last stages of the publication of this book. It is extremely rare for a medical student to be able to practice medicine independently just after passing a licensing exam without any actual clinical training. Dhaliwal has a position that would ordinarily require a combined residency academic training in scores of medical specialties adding up to a 100 years of clinical training before he can take on the task of diagnosing and treating a 3,000-inmate population of very unique and complex medical issues. In addition, unqualified healthcare workers, such as medical assistants who are trained to be orderlies or nurse's assistants, are allowed to act as clinicians and perform the job of qualified physicians by the FBOP. The highest level of medical training a medical assistant receives is to be able to give an injection to a patient and keep the area for the doctor or nurse sterile and clean or to room a patient before the nurse comes in to take vitals.

The net result is that the FBOP neither gives diagnoses nor treatment to prisoners because it can't. No wonder the FBOP has turned the entire prison healthcare system into a massive scam. Some of the prison's healthcare practitioners would certainly be criminally prosecuted for independently practicing medicine without a license or without the supervision of an attending physician in the civilian world. DOJ's double standard is ironic in that it violates the healthcare laws in wholesale in BOP, the laws that it mandates the outside world must follow, and it enforces those laws with an iron fist on all healthcare professionals in all healthcare institutions in the civilian population. One should ask, is it ok for the BOP to do this simply because these healthcare workers, whom the prison calls their clinicians, are taking care of people who just happen to be prisoners and criminals? Is it because our government thinks that prisoners do not deserve the same healthcare as our civilian population?

One Health Services administrator of a prison complex informed the OIG during its investigation that the "BOP is sending us the sickest of the sickest of guys to take care of." This statement from a prison official only supports the stories of prisoners in this book. I like to further testify as a prisoner physician myself who has witnessed everything firsthand that an overwhelming number of federal prisoners are elderly, terminally ill, severely mentally ill, or mental drug addicts and this demographic population is rapidly increasing. These people belong in hospitals and need medical care and mental health attention. They do not belong in prisons; they belong in rehabs. They are thrown in facilities with nonexistent medical care and most of them have not even committed any violent crimes, in some cases committed no crime at all. It is cheaper for the government and its private prison profiteers to have mentally ill patients to provide free slave labor for them in prisons rather than be in costly rehabs and mental health facilities.

There is not the slightest hint or suggestion of deliberate indifference, cruel punishment and torture of prisoners in the 31-page OIG report. There is no mention of how the prison health workers and doctors receive their prison employee training and by whom. There is no mention about the prison subculture, cultish beliefs, and healthcare experimentation that is secretly practiced on sick prisoners. The difference between the government's classified information and the BOP's secret is that classified information, by definition has a risk of becoming pubic knowledge if it somehow leaks, or for some reason has to be made public through declassification or court order. The BOP secrets, on the other hand will never become public because it is unwritten and does not exist on paper; it is transmitted through a wink and a nod. They are prison policies that do not exist in paper but are enforced by corrupt officials. When this information does exist in written form, it can easily disappear because it was not official in the first place. The information in the government's possession, although sometimes classified, at least follows some principles of preservation in some form, but the prisoners' information in the FBOP follows no rules of preservation or filing, therefore these secrets are sometimes worse than classified information simply because parts of it are never going to be revealed to anyone ever, not even to the government itself. You can say this mysterious information exists, but does it? And if it does, where it might be hidden, no one will ever know.

The only hope is a rare whistle-blower or an insider willing to come forward and testify eye witness accounts to the American people. Whistle-blowers are becoming an extremely rare species now because the BOP employees who would love to expose the inside story of prisoner's mistreatment are too afraid to come forward because they have seen too many whistle-blowers being punished by the government for exposing corruption in governmental institutions. One would expect that a whistle-blower that exposes corruption should be rewarded for wanting to do the most patriotic thing to help restore our democratic values, but that is not the case in America. The kind of evidence and exposure you have seen in this book is as good as it is going to get. This is the best you can hope to get even with undercover work, which would not be possible for any journalist to undertake unless he or she was a prisoner at one time. Just as whistle blowers in the CIA, NSA, and FBI are aware, the potential whistle-blowers in the FBOP are too well aware of the reprisals from the Department of Justice if they were to come forward. They don't want to be in a situation where they have to go through the same thing that prisoners endure every day, or worse. That is what tyrannical governments do; they make an example of one person so that all others who have seen the consequences will never dare speak. Laws like the espionage and patriot act, and National Defense Act are now the government's new devices that are being vaguely applied to silence dissidents and to put them in jail if they don't stop exposing corruption. It has sent a chill down the spine of others who would like to speak their minds.

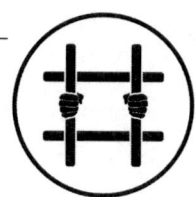

CHAPTER 24

# EAVESDROPPING AT THE PILL-CALL LINE

I DECIDED TO EAVESDROP AT THE PILL-CALL LINE EVERY morning and afternoon. I was hoping to get information from the prisoners by overhearing their conversations and to warm up to some of them so that they would share their documents, stories, or testimonies with me and the stories they knew about or experienced in their past during their long incarcerations. This pill-call line had prisoners with amazing stories; some of them had been in prison up to 50 years and had been to most prisons in the United States. So there was a wealth of information to be had. I could not let this pass.

When I started going to the pill-call line, it seemed like an insurmountable task to earn the trust of prisoners to get them to share any information at all. Some of them thought I was a spy from the FBI, CIA, or DOJ. This rumor was already going on just one week after I joined the pill-call line. This suspicion about me among some prisoners lingered till the day I left the prison on October 26, 2016. Many who became friendly with me on the pill-call line were too afraid of retaliation from the prison officials if they shared information. Some wouldn't even talk to me, and others would not give me anything in writing. Prisoners waiting in line outside the clinic window informed me that just a few months prior to my arrival at the prison, guards had discovered a group of prisoners trying to communicate with one another to organize a class action against the FBOP for deprivation of healthcare and for withholding medications. As a result, the prison officials sent the leader of this group to solitary confinement and transferred others who were complicit to different unknown federal facilities to scatter them so they could not reorganize.

It was not till I became known as a physician involved in helping the sick in prison when some inmates started to approach me for help with their medical issues. My positive attitude and willingness to help at every opportunity I had finally led to some prisoners in the pill-call line to start opening up to me.

Despite my best efforts, I was not able to get two-thirds of the prisoners in the pill-call line to talk to me. It was in the pill call line that Kye, the prisoner referred to early in the book told me: "Take my word for it. They will find you one of these days and you will find yourself in the SHU. I am telling and I am telling you, stop going to the pill line every day, it is only a matter of time. Time is ticking." I told him that I would take his advice but asked him if he would at least share with me his own documentation. He advised me to watch every step and watch my back at the same time, especially watch out for snitches in response to my question. He showed me the BOP handbook, page 75, which suggested that I could be sent to solitary confinement for up to 18 months for violating a prison policy that "carrying or sharing or photocopying another prison's personal document or prison's official document" was considered to be one among the most serious of all prison policy violations.

I managed to recruit from this pill-call line only a very small fraction of inmates to get to talk with me on a regular basis. A few of those I recruited from the pill-call line are already mentioned in this book. Some were so sick and deprived of healthcare that they had nothing left to lose so they did not care about retaliation from the prison guards. They were sick enough that they would rather be in solitary confinement than not talk about the medical cruelty they had been suffering at the hands of the prison doctor and nurses for such a long time. And yet there was another set of prisoners who trusted me enough to talk with me about their illnesses and the treatment they had been denied, but not trust me enough to share any written information corroborating their stories. They did not want to take the risk of their documents being discovered in my locker and vice versa and then be faced with the consequences.

I met a 66-year-old chiropractor at the pill-call line who had been begging to see a cardiologist for five years for a blood clot that traveled to his heart from varicose veins in his leg. He had a hugely swollen leg giving the appearance of elephantiasis, and he said he had [had] no luck with any care at the prison. He had rectal bleeding and varicose veins of the size that I had never seen in my entire career as a physician. He told me that he had no valves in his veins, which also caused the blood clot to travel to his heart causing his heart problems since the clot formation. He complained to me every day he saw me but did not want to share any documentation to discuss his medical documents. He told me that he was also one of those prisoners to whom the prison doctor, Dr. Dhaliwal, had said, "You have to pay for your sins," every time he asked for medical help.

Many prisoners who would not share their documents gladly shared their stories and the stories of others they knew closely: those who had died or were locked up in other federal prisons from where they had been transferred. Some of these federal inmates had been to various prisons around the country as part of their long sentences. I met with Wilder who had been a marine once upon a time and a former Hollywood star who appeared in several movies with Chuck Norris. He also had a history of ties with Manuel Noriega and knew the inside story of many of the CIA's hits and assassinations in Central America to install US-backed dictators. I personally cannot verify the truthfulness of this history, but some of this is now publicly known. What I can verify is what Wilder told me about his healthcare treatment in prison. Wilder had had surgery and chemoradiation for his prostate cancer in Butner Prison two years prior. He was serving 15 years on some drug trafficking charges. He told me that the FBI set him up by planting a bag of drugs in his car while distracting him in a conversation. Again, I cannot verify that this story is accurate, but it is plausible based on what I know what our government does.

What is believable, however, is the story he told me about his struggle with the FBOP for five years at Toussaint Prison Camp, Arizona, despite intervention from his family and friends and with the help of Congressman Juarez Bercera from the Los Angeles district to try to get treatment for his prostate cancer. After five years of political intervention, the prison officials finally transferred him to Butner Prison, North Carolina (Care Level IV facility, the highest care level in prison system) for surgery and 42 treatments of chemoradiation that were long overdue for his prostate cancer. He said that the cancer had spread considerably because of the long delay and he was lucky that he was still alive. Wilder promised to share his medical records with me almost every day until the last day I was in prison but never gave me anything to review. He always said, "I will show you my paperwork, I am not afraid of them," but he never did. I could tell that he knew too much and had inside information regarding how the US government operated in Panama. So even though he *said* he was not afraid, he was terrified and suspicious of everyone, including me, so I never received the records from him. I had already given up on him after two months of cajoling and being unsuccessful to lay my hands on his prison medical records. So most of the information I am describing is verbal, but every bit believable based on what I know about the prison. He told me that now, two years after his chemoradiation, he believed that his cancer had come back but they (prison health staff) were not willing to reevaluate him. He was 73 years old at the time.

While waiting in the pill-call line, I again heard the story of this baseball player who came to prison, contracted MRSA (the same bug that infected Joseph, who lost his leg), and died in five months from the infection because they refused to give him antibiotics. MRSA and scabies outbreaks in prisons are all too common. MRSA and fungal infections are often (not always) contracted from work-boots if you have the bad luck of getting an old pair with holes in them or nails sticking out from the inside due to wear and tear, all because they don't yet have a new pair for you. For example, I was given a very old pair of work-boots and was promised to be given a new pair, but that promise never became reality. I had a constant fungal infection on my feet along with blisters from the nails inside the shoes puncturing my skin, so I had to take meticulous care of my feet, sterilizing them every night. My bunkie on the top bunk, a former army sergeant, helped me take care of my feet better than a doctor would; I believe he was trained for this. So I got lucky. I was concerned that I might be the next victim of MRSA infection if I allowed even the smallest sign of infection to linger on my foot. Alas, most prisoners are not that lucky and not every prisoner gets a new pair of work-boots, but it is mandatory for inmates to wear those boots at work or on the grounds any hour during work hours. Wearing sneakers is a violation of prison policy. Some of these stories of loss of lives and limbs in prison were definitely caused by simply refusing to give these inmates a clean pair of work-boots. I heard of a Hispanic gang member who "dropped dead," as one of his friends put it, on the prison's clinic floor due to a mouth abscess he had growing for eight months for which he kept begging for treatment. They refused to attend to him and the infection traveled to his brain. The prison never disclosed the cause of his death to his family.

I heard some stories from the prisoners themselves and others from their friends, stories that I could not verify for accuracy because it was secondhand information, and I have no written documentation in my possession to back it up. However, I had every reason to believe those stories were true based on what I observed in prison every single day. For example, someone was saved from internal bleeding because a newly hired nurse chose to be proactive and insisted on calling the ambulance. She was someone who had not yet been baptized into the macabre BOP's prison culture. I learned about another prisoner who died of lung cancer because they were too late in finally transferring him to Butner after years of appealing to the prison officials.

I met a 53-year-old American Indian, Alistair, who told me that he was lucky to be alive because it took years of suffering before they had a cardiologist do ablation on his heart with Wolff-Parkinson-White (WPW) syndrome. He gave me a written testimony but later asked me not to publish it. He could not make up his mind if I could publish it or not. I have the testimony in my possession to this day in his own handwriting with his signature underneath and I have decided to publish anonymously without revealing his name to anyone. It is published under miscellaneous in *Prison Papers*. He was concerned that he would be retaliated against if I published his testimony because he was yet to serve a long sentence and would have to deal with the prison officials if they found out. "My life will be hell if they find out." He was not willing to share any other documents.

Native Americans, African Americans, Hispanics, and many small ethnic groups are particularly targets in prisons. I saw the prison guard, McClinton go to the native Indians' sweat lodge every week and throw around their sacred objects; I know that he would dare not do that to the religious objects of Christians or Muslims who had their own niche inside the chapel. Alistair gave me a copy of a U.S. Senate's resolution in 1982 that allowed American Indians to be recognized as a religion for the first time, and as a result the native Americans were allowed to build their sweat lodges in the federal prisons. I did not know this and I was shocked. The colonial settlers first exterminated an entire civilization of the original inhabitants on the two American continents and then did not even recognize religious rights of native Americans up until a few decades ago. It has never ceased to surprise me each time I learn more about the true history of the United States of America.

I met three people at the pill-line who were in dire need of hip replacements, but who had given up on the system and stopped trying to seek help. Then I met some people at the halfway house in Salinas in Northern California where I was transferred. There I met with Mr. Zyaire, an African American man who had come from Sheridan Prison Camp in Oregon and was two weeks away from being finally released by the BOP after 27 years of incarceration, an early release due to Obama's clemency. He was sentenced to 35 years in prison for selling drugs in the street, a crime for which some suburban white kid would serve six months, if that, for the same offense. This tells you how just our federal judges are. We Americans believe that punishment should fit the crime. Zyaire told me that he begged the prison officials for 12 years to treat the medical condition of his throat because he was losing his voice box year after year but they refused to evaluate him. Finally, after telling him for 12 years that nothing was wrong with him, they told him he had heartburn. When I saw Zyaire at the halfway house for the first time, it took me literally 30 seconds after he started talking to recognize that he suffered from spasmodic dysphonia, which is a specific form of an involuntary movement disorder called dystonia that affects only the voice box. (It is a neurological movement disorder evidenced by sustained muscular contractions.) Any physician in the civilian population, including those who are not particularly competent, can easily recognize this condition as some sort of dysphonia and call for immediate medical attention. In fact, you do not have to be a physician to tell that something is seriously wrong with the person speaking the way Zyaire did. This is the same disorder that Robert Kennedy Junior has. Those who have heard Robert Kennedy Junior speak should know exactly what I am talking about. That the prison doctors had been writing Zyaire's worsening disorder as heartburn in his prison medical records for over a decade, or telling him, "Nothing is wrong with you," once again confirmed everything that I had already known about falsification of medical records by prison doctors. Even if the prison doctor does not understand this disorder, he has an affirmative duty to have this prisoner evaluated by a specialist; how can he write in the medical chart that nothing is wrong with the patient in good conscience is beyond me. I am sure your jaw will drop if you are one of my readers who have heard Robert Kennedy Junior speak then imagine that such a person would not be allowed to be seen by a doctor to find out what was wrong. A three-year-old child could not miss this medical condition. Although good treatments for this disorder do not exist, it is a criminal misconduct to falsify records and to tell the prisoner that nothing is wrong with him except some heartburn. Indeed, someone with such a disorder is at higher risk for heartburn, and lingering chronic heartburn can lead to Barrett's esophagus culminating in throat cancer if not treated on time. I strongly advised Zyaire to have himself evaluated by an ear, nose, and throat (ENT) specialist and to request a biopsy from his esophagus as soon as possible to rule out Barrett's esophagus or throat cancer. Zyaire alleges that prison doctors never looked into this for 12 years.

Two weeks after my first meeting with him, Zyaire was released from the halfway house. I wish I could find out before he left if he had an esophageal biopsy done and what the results showed. There was no way I was going to be able to get any prison documentation from Zyaire in this regard in the two-week short encounter with him. I did try, however, and failed. Zyaire was too afraid to share his medical documents with me because he was so close to his final release after 27 years of imprisonment and did not want to take any chances. Besides he was too busy planning a trip to Obama's White House for an interview with John Vance of CNN just two days before Trump won the election. Zyaire was very optimistic on his way to the White House that Hillary Clinton would win the election and a prison reform would ensue, but he was disappointed to learn that just 48 hours after his visit to the White House, Trump won the presidential election. Little did the innocent Zyaire know that Hillary's Democrats and Trump's Republicans both worked for the prison industrial complex and could not care less about the prison reform.

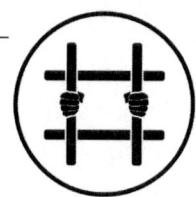

CHAPTER 25

# PRISON CULTURE: THE GOVERNMENT'S PERSPECTIVE

THE OFFICIAL DOJ TRAINING OF THE FBOP SUPERVISORS that stresses the importance of denying medical attention to sick prisoners because they are all "liars or malingerers" says it all. The title page of this training manual along with some excerpts that are published in *Prison Papers* is the confirmatory source of my belief and of what I have seen and experienced in the federal prison. I have also learned that it is not uncommon in some state and federal prison complexes to assign to the healthcare staff the role of security guards—sometimes officially, sometimes unofficially. A report by the *Los Angeles Times* in 2015 that the nurses and doctors are given the duty of prison guards in California prisons is not isolated to one prison, but it is true across the board in many federal prison facilities

407

in that most healthcare staff are trained to act primarily like prison guards and less as health service providers. Although it is quite understandable why the health staff has to have some training as guards because they are dealing with the prison population, sometimes with hard core criminals, what is not understandable is that healthcare is denied to prisoners as a tool for punishment above and beyond the incarceration. The common attitude federal prison doctors and other healthcare workers demonstrate in denying medications and emergency help is more consistent with a guard's behavior and inconsistent with the professional training of healthcare employees who have taken the Hippocratic oath.

The US government clings to a century-old practice that anyone who has been convicted of a crime has met his or her civic death, although this has been long declared unconstitutional and a violation of the Bill of Rights. The DOJ proactively instructs prison employees that prisoners must be deprived of all civil and human rights. The title page photograph, "Supervision of Inmates Training Session" (published in *Prison Papers*), is an internal document of the Federal Bureau of Prisons of the United States under the seal of the Department of Justice, which reflects the prison's death cult that subjects the sickest and the deathly ill inmates to the most heinous and inhumane treatments. This is despite the many supreme court decisions to the contrary, constitutional rights, the Eighth Amendment, international conventions, the United Nations (UN) Charter, and laws of our own land that forbid the US government from subjecting prisoners to medieval torture. Even the Geneva Conventions, to which the United States is a party, that govern the treatment of war criminals, and the International Criminal Court (ICC) does not allow any government to engage in the practice of deadly neglect of the emergency medical needs of prisoners of war, which is a routine practice in our federal prisons carried out on our own citizens.

Please read the language in the select portions of this training manual that the Department of Justice published. This is a training manual that instructs prison employees and contractors how to supervise inmates. This will clearly make you suspect that the root cause of the death cult that plagues our prison industrial complex may originate from the policies of our own government, not from simply a bunch of heartless bad apples who happen to be working for the Federal Bureau of Prisons.

The DOJ internal document, which has never been seen by the American public, which the prisoners are not allowed to possess if they ever see it or find it, corroborates the culture that I directly witnessed during my incarceration. This subculture has led to the deprivation of prisoners' civic and human rights, resulting in cruel and unusual punishment and a deliberate indifference to the most vulnerable population in our prisons. Medical cruelty, emotional abuse and violence, and the deadly neglect of terminally ill patients by prison guards and prison healthcare workers is part of the systematic cultural training sessions provided to prison staff and officials, healthcare workers, and private contractors. One of the air force officers at the Vandenberg Air Force Base who was overseeing inmate supervisors working under him said this confidentially: "The difference between what they teach us and what I have experienced is unbelievable. I would rather trust some of these guys (referring to inmates working for him) who are incredibly decent people than the folks who hold the training session, who steal food and equipment and lie about everything." He took a big risk in making this statement. I admire his courage.

I was told by an insider (a nonprisoner) that the excerpts in the prison's Training Manual (that I published in *Prison Papers*) are the hallmark of training for prisons' employees and contractors. "This is all they talk about for the most part," he said. I have no doubt that many prisoners are dangerous and should be on watch for their manipulative behaviors, and the training instructions in the DOJ Training Manual would easily apply to them. How these instructions apply to the very sick and elderly in prison is hard to understand. Prison staff are trained, however, to apply these principles of governance to all prisoners by trying to always remember one thing: Always say no, because all inmates are liars and malingerers, not to be trusted and must be told no for everything. There are no exceptions to this. These excerpts that I published are emphasized to prison officials and supervisors in these training sessions conducted under guidelines for training established by the Department of Justice. It is like a schoolteacher telling the kids what is important to remember from the textbook to pass the test. "These are the questions that will be asked on the test. So, memorize the highlights if you want to pass the test. Don't worry about the rest of the material, that is just for your information" ("the rest of the material" meaning prisoners have some human rights too). This kind of secretive systematic coaching has led to inhuman conditions for all prisoners held in custody of the US Federal Bureau of Prisons. How long has this culture existed? Your guess is as good as mine; although my guess is that it has always existed but will never be allowed to become public knowledge and will be kept hidden from those few left in the judicial system who still care about justice, human rights, and human dignity.

Prisoners and others (nonprisoners) who shared or obtained the documents published herewith are the bravest. Some of them (the prisoners) took the risk of being thrown in solitary confinement. Some of these inmates are so physically ill that they would rather take the risk of going into solitary confinement to get their medications than stop fighting for the medical care for the sake of being able to enjoy the freedom of minimum security prison camp and live a life as good as death. Freedom means nothing when you are very ill. When a person's health fails, everything else fails. Most prisoners described in this book would rather be transferred to higher security prisons; in fact, they beg to go into more dangerous environments, even solitary confinement, if they could only get their life-saving medications.

The problem gets worse. Not only do the sick not receive medication refills but also, they are thrown in solitary confinement if they show the slightest hint of aggressive behavior by repeatedly demanding medications or medical attention. Nearly every country on the planet officially recognizes solitary confinement as a form of mental torture and has outlawed it as an inhuman act of mental torture except one country on earth, and that is the United States. I ask you to try living in a closet-size dark room for a day and see what happens to your psyche. In US federal prisons, inmates are often thrown into solitary confinement for six months or more for minor prison rule violations, not to mention those who are confined to cages like animals simply because treating them for mental illness will cost the government too much. This is not to mention that the majority of them do not belong in prisons in the first place. They are mentally ill and not criminals. I met a few in prison who had had a history of being locked up in solitary confinement for as long as 42 months at a time, and many times over during decades-long incarceration. These are hard-core criminals however. We still have to ask the question though, is it ok to lock someone, anyone, in a dark room for four consecutive years? Even a dog or a cat could not handle that. And then the federal law requires that those thrown in solitary confinement be given one hour a day to get some sunlight and exercise, but that does not have to happen once you are in prison and they've got you. It depends on the prison guard that day. If a healthcare worker can have you sent to the SHU for demanding medications, the guards can certainly choose not to let you out for an hour a day. And this happens frequently to those who are being punished and being made an example of.

If I were to tell you that a regular prison guard, a prison nurse, a prison physician, or a correctional counselor has more judicial power than the entire panel of nine judges of the Supreme Court of the United States, you would think I was joking. I hope, however, that this book has convinced you that this is true. Any prison employee can put a prisoner in solitary confinement and keep him isolated in a tiny, dark room for months at a time, and they can do it at will, for pleasure or for fun. They can send an immobile crippled prisoner, who can barely walk ten steps, to a weed-whacking assignment for days on end, on an unstable terrain on the prison dairy farm filled with cow dung because he ate a piece of bread, a leftover that he brought from the chow hall, a violation of the prison policy. They say that the "punishment should fit the crime." That rule does not apply in the criminal justice system, let alone when you are in a prison's custody, away from public scrutiny. You don't have a chance. They can do almost anything to any prisoner at any time of their choosing. The game is over for you once you are locked up behind bars.

The next chapter, "Legal Considerations and Case Law," quotes historical legal cases that have exposed from time to time the medical cruelty, emotional violence, and deadly neglect of inmates in our prisons, which are blatant violations of the Eighth Amendment of the US Constitution and many other laws of the land. It is an important read for advocates and criminal justice organizations as well as for those attorneys who are representing the sick inmates who are trying to get the medical help they need. The relevant case law and historical precedence are quoted.

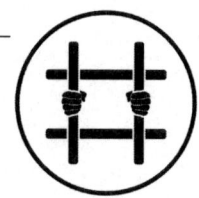

# LEGAL CONSIDERATIONS AND CASE LAW

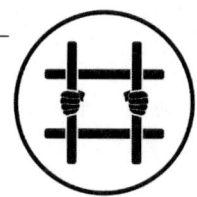

PER PRISON'S WRITTEN POLICY, EXHAUSTION OF ADMIN-
istrative remedies, 42 USC § 1997 e(a), means raising your issues
in the grievance system in your institution and pursuing them to the
fullest extent. Courts have held that a prisoner needs to raise issues at
the administrative level, which prohibits the prisoner from litigating
them until all remedies are exhausted. What the courts and the American people do not know, however, is that the government's vicious
circumvention of these administrative options ironically adopted
by the Department of Justice sarcastically says to the prisoners in
its custody, "Aha, I've got you. Let me show you how I am going to
'remedy' your complaints." An ingenious system has been devised
by the Bureau of Prisons to make sure that it never has to remedy
anything for anyone. The net result of a well-crafted prison policy
is that a prisoner would never be allowed to "exhaust" the remedy
filing requirements to ever become eligible to sue the government.
The BOP is like a five-year-old without adult supervision making
mocking gestures at the prisoners under its complete autonomous
tyrannical control. Justification for denial of requests is often drawn
from prisoners' health records, which were manufactured or forged
for the most part by the prison doctors, nurses, and prison officials.
Sometimes responses are given by using vague, deceptive language
and almost always end with the statement, "You should attend the
next Sick Call." The responses are made with a precalculation to

generate a vast treasure trove of bureaucratic legal paperwork for defense if any prisoner were to ever try to bring a case to the court for denial of medical care. The Federal Bureau of Prisons knows that the courts will have no choice but to believe the prison's version of the health history of the prisoner, while the prisoner's version, which is the true history, will carry little weight in the court. This explains the luckiest of the lucky ones—1 out of every 10,000—who are suffering will emerge as the winner who finally manages to sue the BOP with no guarantees that he will find justice in the end. With this in mind, let us discuss the cases of some lucky winners.

Every court case in this legal section will be a déjà vu of the stories that you have already read in the Trail of Tears Section. Nothing should come as a surprise to you after what you have already read. Considering the magnitude of the problem, you will also realize that these isolated court cases, including class actions where prisoners were vindicated, are only the tip of the iceberg in the sense that the legitimate complaints won in the court of law represent one hundredth of one percent of the overall number of prisoners suffering from the same lack of medical care in our prison system. After reading this section you will be left with no doubt that every prisoner whose documented case in this book (and tens of thousands of others whose cases will never be documented) deserve the same court decisions (or better) as these very few lucky prisoners did after their excruciatingly long legal battles against the Federal Bureau of Prisons.

The most interesting part of the following case law discussion for me personally is that during my research of legal literature on the subject of prison torture, I was able to find a court case of almost every type of prison medical torture discussed in this book, which includes courts finding federal prisons guilty of falsifying medical records, delaying or denying treatments, denying medications, using solitary confinement as punishment, and sending inmates back to work while they suffered from life-threatening medical conditions or on the job physical injuries. Every court case you read about in the next chapter will sound familiar.

One of the major differences between what you will find in these court cases and what you have read in the book is sheer volume, meaning that the American public is not aware that there are wholesale violations in prison, the sort that you see in these court cases, and that 99.9 percent of the inmates in federal prisons will never see any justice for violations of their human rights that are far worse than those that came before the courts. In other words, these court cases barely touch the surface of the magnitude of the problem, so much so that unless we have a major reform that brings our country out of the dark ages, multitudes of human beings will continue to suffer and will be greatly hidden from the view of the civilized world.

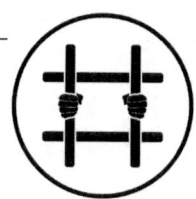

## CHAPTER 26

# THE FIRST CIVIL RIGHTS ACTION: *ESTELLE V. GAMBLE*

THE MAIN SOURCE OF INFORMATION FOR THIS LANDMARK court case is Legal Bulletin of *Lewisburg Prison Project*, 2011. *Estelle v. Gamble*, 429 U.S.C. 97 (1976), was the first case in 1976 in which the US Supreme Court established for the first time the standard of what a prisoner must plead in order for a claim violation of his Eighth Amendment rights under 42 U.S. § 1983. It is a case of a prisoner in the Texas State Prison who instituted a civil rights action on February 11, 1974, under 42 U.S.C. § 1983, against certain prison officials, including the chief medical officer of the prison hospital, in the US District Court for the Southern District of Texas, alleging that the defendants had violated the cruel and unusual punishment clause of the Eighth Amendment by failing to provide adequate medical treatment after the prisoner had sustained a back injury on November 9, 1973, while performing prison assignment.

According to plaintiff Gamble's complaint, a bale of cotton fell on him when he was unloading a truck. He continued to work, but after four hours, he became stiff and was granted a pass to the unit hospital. At the hospital, a medical assistant, Captain Blunt, checked him for a hernia and sent him back to his cell. Within two hours the pain became so intense that Gamble returned to the hospital where he was given pain pills by an inmate nurse and then was examined by a doctor.

The following day, Gamble saw a Dr. Astone, who diagnosed the injury as a low-back strain, prescribed Zactritin (a pain reliever) and Robaxin (a muscle relaxant) and placed Gamble on "cell-pass, cell-feed" status for two days, allowing him to remain in his cell at all times except for showers. On November 26, Gamble again saw Dr. Astone, who continued the medication and cell-pass, cell-feed for another seven days. He also ordered that Gamble be moved from the upper bunk to the lower bunk for one week, but the prison authorities did not comply with that directive. The following week, Gamble returned to Dr. Astone. The doctor continued the muscle relaxant but prescribed a new pain reliever, Febridyne, and placed Gamble on cell-pass for seven days, permitting him to remain in his cell except for meals and showers. On November 26, the Gamble again saw Dr. Astone, who put him back on the original pain reliever for five days and continued the cell-pass for another week.

On December 3, despite Gamble's statement that his back hurt as bad as on the first day, Dr. Astone took him off cell-pass, thereby certifying him to be capable of work. At the same time, Dr. Astone prescribed Febridyne for seven days. Gamble then went to a Major

Muddox and told him he was in too much pain to work. Muddox had Gamble moved to administrative segregation (another term for solitary confinement.) On December 5, Gamble was taken before the Prison Disciplinary Committee because of his refusal to work. When the committee heard his complaint of back pain and high blood pressure, it directed that he be seen by another doctor.

On December 6, Gamble saw defendant, Dr. Gray who performed a urinalysis, blood test, and blood pressure measurement. Dr. Gray prescribed the drug Ser-Ap-Es for the high blood pressure and more Febridyne for the back pain. The following week, Gamble again saw Dr. Gray, who continued the Ser-Ap-Es for an additional 30 days. The prescription was not filled for four days, however, because the "staff lost it." Gamble went to the Unit Hospital two more times in December; both times he was seen by Captain Blunt, who prescribed Tignolos (described as a muscle relaxant). For all December, he remained in administrative segregation.

In early January, Gamble was told on two occasions that he would be seen in the farm if he did not work. He refused nonetheless, claiming to be in too much pain. On January 7, 1974, he requested to go to Sick Call for his back pain and migraine headaches. After an initial refusal, he saw Captain Blunt who prescribed sodium salicylate (a pain reliever) for seven days and Ser-Ap-Es for 30 days. Gamble returned to Captain Blunt on January 17 and then on January 25, and received renewals for the pain reliever prescription both times. Throughout these months, he was kept in administrative segregation.

On January 31, Gamble was brought before the Prison Disciplinary Committee for his refusal to work in early January. He told the committee that he could not work because of his severe back pain. Captain Blunt testified that Gamble was in "first class" medical condition. (This should remind you of Grey's story in this book who walked around with untreated "crushed vertebrae" but was deemed physically fit to work.) The committee, with no further examination or testimony, placed Gamble in solitary confinement as punishment.

Four days later, on February 4 at 8:00 a.m., Gamble asked to see a doctor for chest pain and "blank outs." It was not until that night that a medical assistant examined him and ordered him to be hospitalized. The following day, Dr. Hector performed an EKG; one day later Gamble was placed on Quinidine for treatment of irregular cardiac rhythm and moved to administrative segregation. On February 7, he experienced pain in his chest, left arm, and back and asked to see a doctor. The guards refused. He asked again the next day. The guards again refused. Finally, on February 9, he saw Dr. Heaton, who ordered the Quinidine continued for three more days. On February 11, he swore out his complaint and in instituting a civil rights action under 42 U.S.C. § 1983.

The previous case was argued on October 5, 1976, and decided on November 30, 1976. The defendants were J.W. Estelle Jr., Director of Department of Corrections, Warden of the Prison; and Dr. Ralph Gray, Director of the Department and the Chief Medical Officer of the prison hospital. The District Court initially dismissed the complaint for failure to state a claim upon which relief could be granted. The US Court of Appeals for the Fifth Circuit reversed and remanded with instructions to reinstate the complaint (516 2d 937).

On certiorari, the US Supreme Court reversed and remanded. Seven out of nine supreme court judges held that (1) deliberate indifference to a prisoner's serious medical needs constituted cruel and unusual punishment under the Eighth Amendment and gave rise to civil rights cause of action under 42 USCS § 1983, regardless of whether the indifference was manifested by prison doctors in their response to the prisoner's needs or by prison guards in intentionally denying or delaying access to medical care or intentionally interfering with treatment once prescribed; (2) the prisoner's complaint in the case failed to state a cognizable U.S.C. § 1983 claim against the prison's chief medical officer and thus had been properly dismissed as to him by the District Court, since the allegations showed that the prisoner had been treated by medical personnel on 17 occasions spanning a three-month period following his injury and since the failure to employ additional diagnostic techniques (such as an ordinary X-ray) or additional form of treatment was a matter for medical judgment and amounted at most, to medical malpractice cognizable in state courts; and (3) the case would be remanded to allow the Court of Appeals to consider whether a cause of action was stated against the other prison officials, since the Court of Appeals had focused primarily on the alleged action of prison medical personnel and had not separately considered whether the allegations against the other officials stated a cause of action.

The Eighth Supreme Court Judge, Blackmun J., concurred, but Stevens J., the ninth judge, dissented. Stevens expressed the view that (1) the proposed complaint against the prison medical officer should not have been ordered dismissed, since it was impossible, on the basis of the complaint to assess the quality of the medical attention that was furnished to the prisoner, and thus, evidence should have been received; (2) certiorari should not have been granted based on the pleadings in the case at bar; and (3) in any event, by its reference to "deliberate indifference," and the "intentional" denial of adequate medical care, the court improperly attached significance to the subjective motivation of the defendant as a criterion for determining whether cruel and unusual punishment had been inflicted, whereas such determination should instead turn on the character of the punishment rather than the motivation of the person who inflicted it.

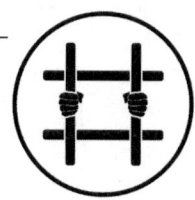

## CHAPTER 27

# EIGHTH AMENDMENT VIOLATIONS: COURT CASES OF CRUEL AND UNUSUAL PUNISHMENT

THE HISTORY OF CONSTITUTIONAL PROHIBITION OF "cruel and unusual punishment" has been recounted at length in prior opinions of the court. For example, in *Gregg v. Georgia*, 428 U.S. 153, 169–173 49L Ed 2d 859, 96 S ct 2909 (1976): The primary purpose of the drafters was to proscribe "tortures" and other barbarous methods of punishment. Accordingly, the court in the case of *Estelle v. Gamble* first applied the Eighth Amendment by comparing challenged methods of execution to concededly inhuman techniques of punishment.

The oldest case reference to prison torture and punishment I was able to find is from 1890 that refers to cruel punishment as follows: "Punishments are cruel when they involve torture or lingering death" (Kemmler, 136 U.S. 436 447 34L Ed519 10S [t930] [1890]). Following are some historical quotes from court cases that define prison torture as a violation of the Eighth Amendment. These are presented in the best possible chronological order as follows:

The Eighth Amendment embodies "broad and idealistic concepts of dignity, civilized standards of humanity and decency ... against which we must evaluate panel measures" [Jackson v. Bishop 404 F. 2d 571, 579 [ca8 1968]).

Violation of the Eighth Amendment Right has been found when there is intentional denial of needed medical care, or when a prison official's conduct indicates deliberate indifference to the medical needs of the prisoners (Bishop v. Stoneman, 508 F. 2d 1224 [2nd Circuit 1974]; Russell v. Sheffer, 528 F. 2d 318 [4th Circuit 1975]).

It is safe to affirm that punishment of torture ... and all others in the same line of unnecessary cruelty, are forbidden by the Eighth Amendment" (Gregg v. Georgia, 428 U. S. 153, 169–173 49L Ed 2d 859, 96 S ct 2909 [1976]).

We have held repugnant to the Eighth Amendment punishments which are incompatible with evolving standards of decency that mark the progress of a maturing society (Top v. Dulles).

More recent cases have held that the amendment proscribes more than physical barbarous punishments. The *Gregg v. Georgia* case of 1976 is one of these cases. Punishment that "involves the unnecessary and wanton infliction of pain" is a violation of the Eighth Amendment.

Other notable cases of Eighth Amendment violations include medical treatment of prisoners as cruel and unusual punishment, 1 Cap. U.S. Rev. 83 (1972); *Burks v. Teas*, 492 F. Supp. 650 (W.D. Mo 1980); *Hampton v. Holmburg Prison Officials*, 546 F. 2d 1077 (3rd Circuit 1979); *Duncan v. Duckworth*, 644 F. 2d 653 (7th Circuit 1981).

The "unnecessary and wanton infliction of pain" constitutes cruel and unusual punishment forbidden by the Eighth Amendment" (Whitley v. Albers, 475 U.S. 312, 319 [1986]).

These elementary principles establish the government's obligations to provide medical care for those whom it is punishing by incarceration. An inmate must rely on prison authorities to treat his medical needs. If the authorities fail to do so, those needs will not be met. In the worst cases, such a failure may actually produce physical "torture or a lingering death." In less serious cases, denial of medical care may result in pain and suffering, which no one suggests will serve any penological purpose. The infliction of such unnecessary suffering is inconsistent with contemporary standards of decency as manifested in modern legislation codifying the common view that "it is but just that the public be required to care for the prisoner, who cannot by reason of deprivation of his liberty, care for himself."

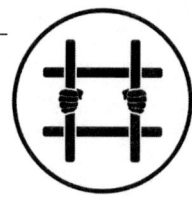

## CHAPTER 28

# DELIBERATE INDIFFERENCE: COURT VERDICTS

DELIBERATE INDIFFERENCE IS: *THE CAREFUL PRESERVATION of one's ignorance despite awareness of circumstances that would put a reasonable person on notice of an essential fact to crime* – Black's Law Dictionary, 9th Edition, 1990

Following is a list of cases in which the courts decided against prison officials who were found guilty of deliberate Indifference to the needs of sick prisoners. This is by no means a comprehensive list.

- *Gregg v. Georgia*: "We therefore conclude that deliberate indifference to serious medical needs of prisoners constitutes unnecessary and wanton infliction of pain."

- *Gregg v. Georgia*: "Deliberate indifference is true whether the indifference is manifested by prison doctors in response to the prisoner's needs or by prison guards in intentionally denying or delaying access to medical care, or intentionally interfering with the treatment once prescribed."

- *Gregg v. Georgia*: "Deliberate indifference to a prisoner's serious illness or injury states a cause of action under § 1983."

- *Bass by Lewis v. Wallenstein* (769 F. 2d 1173 [7th Cir. 1985]): A 15-minute delay in a doctor's response to an inmate's cardiac arrest was described as "deliberate indifference" by the court.

- *Payne v. Lynaugh* (843 F. 2d 177 [1988]): The 5th Circuit found an Eighth Amendment violation when an inmate who required oxygen for his emphysema was not transferred to an equipped facility.

- *Maryland v. New Jersey* (719 F. sup. 292, 293 [D. N. J 1989]): "We will no longer tolerate prison officials' deliberate indifference to the chronic pain of an inmate than we would a sentence that required an inmate to submit to such pain."

- *Reed v. Dunham* (893 F. 2d 285 [10th Circ. 1990]): A two-hour delay in treating serious stab wounds was considered to be "deliberate indifference" by the court.

- *Borretti v. Wiscomb* (930 F. 2d 1150 [6th Cir. 1991]): A nurse's interruption of prescribed treatment constituted "deliberate indifference," according to the court despite the fact that the inmate's wound eventually healed.

- *Whitley v. Albers*: According to Ninth Circuit instructions, "there is a *two-pronged test* for evaluating a claim for *deliberate indifference* to a serious medical need. First, the plaintiff must show a serious medical need by demonstrating that failure to treat a prisoner's condition could result in further significant injury or cause just unnecessary and wanton infliction of punishment for it to be "deliberately indifferent." The second prong is satisfied by showing (1) a purposeful act or failure to respond to a prisoner's pain or possible medical need and (2) harm caused by the indifference. Prison officials have often used "inadvertence" or "error in good faith" as their defense against inmate lawsuits. However, it is "obduracy and wantonness, not 'inadvertence' or 'errors made in good faith' that characterizes the conduct prohibited by the Eighth Amendment."

Prison officials and the US government have used other devices to defend their behavior in the court system, such as "prison officials were not 'subjectively deliberately indifferent'" or it was not a "purposeful act or failure to respond" to a prisoner's pain or medical need. But according to *McGuckin v. Smith* (974 F. 2d 1050, 1059–60 [9th Cir. 1992]), deliberate indifference is as simple as an "indifference to a prisoner's serious medical needs" that violates the Eighth Amendment.

- *Charles v. District of Columbia* (834 Supp 439 [D. C. 1992]): Regular denials of refilling glaucoma medication stated a claim of deliberate indifference.
- *Benner v. Peck* (825 F. Supp 1411 [S. D. Iowa 1993]): The court stated that refusal to provide glasses to a seriously near-sighted 20–400 inmate (virtually blind) was deliberate indifference.

An example of a prototypical case of deliberate indifference is seen in *Brooks v. Celeste* (39 F. 3d 125, 128 [6th Cir. 1994]) in which the court stated, "Allegations that prison officials ignored an inmate's repeated requests for medical treatment and complaints of excruciating pain should satisfy the deliberate indifference standard." The court in this case further stated, "While a single instance of medical care denied or delayed, viewed in isolation, may appear to be the product of mere negligence, repeated examples of such treatment bespeaks a deliberate indifference by prison authorities."

- *Green v. Branson* (108 F. 3d 1296 [10th Cir. 1997]): The court decided that evidence of falsification of medical records showed "deliberate action."

- Barry and Ratella (985 F. Supp 1235 [S. D. Cal 1997]): Case law explains prison doctors who knew of an inmate's hernia, which required surgery, and who nonetheless allowed the inmate to suffer for two years without surgery were showing "deliberate indifference."

- *Moore v. Jackson* (123 F. 3rd 1082 [8th Cir. 1997]): Defendant (dentist's) failure to extract a prisoner's infected tooth for seven months demonstrated "deliberate indifference"

- *Simmons v. Cook* (154 F. F. 3d 805 [8th Cir. 1998]: The court decision was that the prison officials who were aware that paraplegics in solitary confinement were denied medical care showed "deliberate indifference."

- *Rivera v. Sheehan* (1998 WL 531875 [ND III 1998]): The defendants, prison officials, who knew the inmate had AIDS and needed daily medication responded to her condition only when she lay in coma in her cell. The court condemned "this treatment as criminal," noting defendants had "put themselves on a limb and refused to appreciate the sawing sound underneath them."

- *Parkinson v. Columbia County District Attorney* (679 N. Y. S 2d 505 [Supp. Ct Columbia City, 1998]): An inmate's artificial leg was confiscated when he was arrested and not returned to him till after his conviction on the theory that it (the leg) might be the evidence in his appeal. The result for the inmate was his confinement to his cell. The court found both the Eighth Amendment violation and the Fourteenth Amendment violation of deprivation of property without due process.

- *Ralston v. McGovern* (167 F. 3d 6160 [7th Cir. 1999]): The court gave a verdict in which it said that the failure to treat an inmate with cancer who was in great pain was "deliberate indifference."

- *Broch v. Wright* (315 F. 3d 158, 163 [2nd Cir. 2003]): Deliberate indifference has been defined simply as untreated "existence of chronic and substantial pain" that violates the Eighth Amendment.

- *Sealock v. Colorado* (2000): Inmate with symptoms of heart attack and severe pain suffered delay of several days before being taken to a hospital where he was found to have in fact suffered a heart attack was "deliberate indifference" by the court.

- *Jeff v. Penner* (439 F. 3d 1091, 1096 [9th Cir. 2006]): Deliberate indifference "may appear when prison officials deny, delay or intentionally interfere with medical treatment, or it may be shown by the way in which prison physicians provide the medical care."

The list of court cases of deliberate indifferences to the Eighth Amendment is extensive and includes refusing to give medications, denying treatment for drug addiction, not accommodating medications for the disabled, denying access to shower, not providing interpreting services to the deaf and the hearing impaired, and denying care to the mentally and physically disabled. It includes most but not all scenarios that you are familiar with from reading stories in the Trail of Tears.

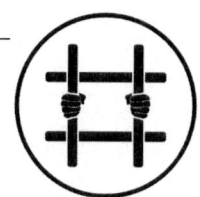

## CHAPTER 29

# BEST ADVICE FOR CIVIL LIBERTIES AND PUBLIC SERVICE ATTORNEYS AND HUMAN RIGHTS GROUPS

THE BOP WILL SOMETIMES IGNORE COURT ORDERS TO release medical records and then release only the portions of manufactured records that it wants to release. Since obtaining true medical records from the BOP is the largest problem, the best thing for plaintiff attorneys to do is to have their prisoner clients keep a very meticulous and comprehensive record of their own, which should include a detailed account of photocopies of all paperwork filed; handwritten notes of conversations; medical incidents, including dates, names, and symptoms; medications requested; written Sick-Call Requests; any paperwork with handwritten notes of all communications with the medical staff; photocopies of informal and formal Administrative Remedy Request records, including receipts and rejection notices and the BOP responses/denials; circumstances of any work injuries; attempts to get treatment; formal and informal communications, electronic or paper; any diagnosis acknowledged and verbally given; refusal to give a diagnosis; all written requests made for release of medical records without response from prison officials; any slip-of-the-tongue statements made to the prisoner by the prison's healthcare workers; and records and the dates of responses or lack thereof to the inmate's remedy requests kept in a chronological order. Ask your client prisoner to send copies of everything to someone outside the prison for safekeeping in case prison guards confiscate his only paperwork and destroy it. Rest assured that at one point or another, the prison guards will confiscate your client's paperwork if they know that you or your client intend to put the prison at risk of a liability by filing a lawsuit.

Presentation of these records to the court will show the court much of the relevant evidence that is being withheld or not disclosed by the prison officials during the course of the lawsuit. You can bet your life that if you depend on the prison officials to release your client's genuine medical records (which are either nonexistent on paper/electronics or are already altered by now) upon order from the court in a lawsuit that you have filed, the prison will not reveal any information that supports your case or is inculpatory to the FBOP. The FBOP will conceal as much information as it thinks it could get away with. There is not a thing the judge can do (or simply won't do) even if he senses that the BOP is withholding relevant records. He will pretend that the BOP has provided all the records in its possession simply because BOP says so.

Pay attention to *Ramos v. Lamont Lamm* (639 F. 2d 559 [10th Cir. 1980]) that provides an overview of a successful lawsuit alleging various constitutional problems with a correctional system, including medical treatment. Prisoners' rights organizations may take class actions, which can be powerful ways of changing widespread problems in a prison facility.

The US Supreme Court has held that to create liability for Eighth Amendment purposes, "the prison official (must) know of and disregard an excessive risk to inmate health and safety." Deliberate indifference can be demonstrated by an act of omission that was either a one-time incident or part of an ongoing situation. The fact of the matter is that there is no such thing as an isolated one-time violation in prison, which is the reason for you to keep all your records. Prison staff does not believe in a one-time violation; it believes in wholesale violations with no exceptions made, which can be proven only with a good paper trail, a paper trail that will strongly and clearly suggest that BOP is not divulging many parts of the inmate's healthcare story.

Courts have defined through case law the State of Mind Requirement for deliberate indifference. For example, high-level prison officials were not entitled to the dismissal of a prisoner's complaint where inferences could be drawn from the pleadings that a prison official threw away the inmate's doctor-prescribed orthopedic shoes and canes, the inmate could not get treatment from the prison doctor, and standard prison-issued shoes caused him constant pain, and where the inmate had written to officials about those problems (*Sanders v. Horn*, 960 F. Supp 893 [E. D. Pa 1997]). Rest assured that if you do not insist that your inmate client keep photocopies of all his remedy requests and every little piece of information, verbal or written, that he exchanges with the prison officials, this information will forever be lost and the prison officials will never show that information to the courts. This information in the hands of prison officials will then be permanently destroyed as though it never existed. No court in the world will force the BOP reveal the information that is vital to your case.

In *Miltier v. Beorn* (896 F. 2d 848 [4th Cir. 1990]), doctors failed to respond to an inmate's complaint of chest pain, blackouts, and breathing problems and the inmate later died of a heart attack. Tell your prisoner clients to make every complaint, major or minor, in written form, even if they write one sentence, and then keep a photocopy of that for their records in their locker and ship one photocopy of everything to loved ones or family as a backup in case paperwork is destroyed by prison guards or stolen from your client. If an inmate made a million verbal complaints, "he never complained" is what the prison officials will say, so always do it in writing even if it is one single sentence and systematically keep a record.

- *Kelley v. Borg* (60 F. 3d 664 [9th Cir. 1995]): Although a prisoner told guards (verbally) that fumes were coming into his cell, he was made to stay in the cell and passed out as a result. The prisoner was lucky to prove his case without written evidence.

- *Yarbaugh v. Roach* (736 F. Supp. 318 [D. KYE 1990]): A prisoner with multiple disabilities made an Eighth Amendment claim that officials failed to provide medical care when he showed that he had not been seen by a doctor since entering the facility 18 months earlier, had received no physical therapy or assistance with daily needs, and was housed in a cell with a malfunctioning call-button.

- *Madrid v. Gomez* (889 F. Supp 1146 [N. D. Cal 1995]): The court found the FBOP in an Eighth Amendment violation when an untrained staff member performed emergency medical treatment.

Have your clients find out about the qualifications of those who are supposedly their "care providers" in prison. It is extremely common for the prison to have staff with little or no qualifications treat prisoners. The prison healthcare workers often do not write their medical degree or diploma against their name; they call themselves Provider 1, 2, 3, and so on to conceal from prisoner patients their true medical qualifications. It is not unusual to see inmates more qualified to know what to do under a certain circumstance to treat their own medical condition than their prison health service providers. Prison policy allows the prison to use "medical assistants" as their clinicians. In the outside community, a medical assistant is the equivalent of someone in the doctor's office who is qualified to room a patient and take blood pressure if he or she is well trained by the physician to do so through on-the-job training. And medical assistants in prison certainly do not know how to take blood pressure. You are lucky if the prison doctor knows how to take blood pressure properly.

- *Williams v. Ward* (553 F. Supp. 1024 [W. D. N. Y. 1983]: Section 1983 Cause of Action case against the head of corrections in which an unlicensed doctor was hired to treat inmates and the doctor displayed gross negligence in his amputation of the inmate's leg.
- *Carty v. Farrelly* (957 F. Supp. 727 [D. V. 7. 1997]): Staff unqualified to identify mental illness was found to have violated the Eighth Amendment.

- *Casey v. Lewis* (834 F. Supp 1477 [D Ariz 1993]): An Eighth Amendment violation was found to have occurred where mentally ill inmates were put on lockdown because there wasn't staff qualified to make a diagnosis.

Imagine a scenario out in the civilian population in which someone pretending to be a doctor without a medical license amputates your leg; he will be in jail for life for doing so. The rule of law does not apply to those working for the prison system or the Department of Justice. Per BOP's own literature, it reserves the right to hire physicians without medical licenses under the guidelines of the same DOJ that will send anyone in the civilian population to prison for life for practicing medicine without a license. The federal government enjoys self-proclaimed exemptions to all the laws that it enforces on the American people. This is what we call above the law. The idea of equality before the law is just a philosophical theory in the United States. The reality of it all is very different. Therefore, I recommend that your inmate client, who is seriously hoping to sue, knows the qualifications of the health service provider assigned to him because that knowledge might help a great deal in making a good case. Additionally, you, as the inmate's attorney, may want to look into it by checking the background history of these health providers by going to license verification on medical board and nursing board websites and dental or optometry board websites. This information is publicly available to anyone. You can search under name.

Following are cases that are particularly useful for public service attorneys who are representing inmates in a lawsuit again the BOP.

- Bazelon, Implementing the Right to Treatment (26 U. S. Chi. L. Rev. 742. 748-749 [1969]): "If a society confines a man for the benevolent purpose of helping ... then its 'right' to so withhold his freedom depends entirely upon whether help is in fact provided ... when the legislature justifies confinement by a 'promise of treatment,' it thereby commits the community to provide the resources necessary to fulfil the promise."

- 42 U.S.C. § 1983: "Every person who under color of law ... subjects or causes to be subjected any citizen of the United States to the deprivation of any rights, privileges, or immunities secured by the constitution ... shall be liable to the party injured in an action at law, suit in equity or other proper proceeding for redress."

- *Johnson v. Duffy* (588 F. 2d 740, 743 [9th Cir. 1978]): "A person subjects another to the deprivation of a constitutional right, within the meaning of §1983, if he does an affirmative act, participates in another's affirmative acts or omits to perform an act which he is legally required to do that causes the deprivation of which complaint is made."

- *Casey v. Lewis* (834 F. Supp. 1477 [D. Ariz 1993]): Courts have held that an adequate medical system will conduct an initial health screening of inmates and have a reasonable Sick-Call procedure.

- *Occoqum v. Bary* (717, Supp 854 [D. KYE 1989]): "Lack of adequate initial screening contributes to constitutional violation."

- *Benavides v. U. S. Bureau of Prisons* (995 F. 2d 269, 273 [KYE Circuit 1993]): "Guaranteed the ultimate disclosure" of medical records to the prisoner requesting them.

## ADDITIONAL RESEARCH REFERENCES
## AND FEDERAL STATUTES

- Federal Constitutional Guarantee against cruel and unusual punishment, 33L Ed 2d 932

- Prison conditions as amounting to cruel and unusual punishment, 51 AL R 3d 111

- Criminal Law § 76, 78, Cruel and Unusual Punishment clause, standards

- Criminal Law § 78, Cruel and Unusual Punishment, what constitutes

- Criminal Law § 76, Cruel and Unusual Punishment, medical care for prisoners

- 15 Am Jur 2d, Civil Rights § 14, 23.1; 21 Am Jur 2d, Criminal Law

- §610-612; 60 Am Jur. 2d, Penal and Correctional Institutions §52

- Federal Procedural Forms L. Ed, Civil Rights § 10:151 et seq

- Am Jur. Pl & Pr Forms (Rev. ed.), Penal and Correctional Institutions. Form 11

- Am Jur. Trials 1, Prisoners' Rights Litigation

- 42 USCS § 1983; Constitution, 8th and 14th Amendments

- U.S. L Ed Digest, Civil Rights § 10; Criminal Law § 78

- A L R Digests, Civil Rights § 1.3; Criminal Law § 170

- L Ed Index to Annos, Civil Rights; Cruel and Unusual Punishment; Prisons and Prisoners

- ALR Quick Index, Cruel and Unusual Punishment; Discrimination; Prisons and Convicts

– Federal Quick Index, Civil Rights; Cruel and Unusual Punishment; Prisons and Prisoners

– Pleading § 179, Medical treatment of injured prisoners, Sufficiency of Civil Rights Complaint

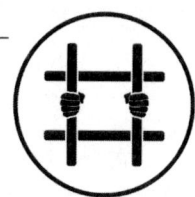

CHAPTER 30

# U.S.C.§516.29 FEDERAL STATUTES AND REGULATIONS

FEDERAL TORT CLAIMS ACT (FTCA) (28 U.S.C. 1346 [B], 2671-2680): A waiver of sovereign immunity, which in certain exceptions makes the United States liable for tort claims in the same manner as a private individual.

Federal Employees Liability Reform and Tort Compensation Act of 1988 (FELRTCA or the Westfall Act; Pub L. No. 100–694, 102 Stat. 4563 [codified at and amending 28 U.S.C. 2671, 2674, 2679]): Amending the Federal Tort Claims Act makes the FTCA the exclusive remedy for common law tort claims arising from actions taken by federal employees acting within the scope of employment. The law was passed to eliminate problems caused by *Westfall v. Erwin* (484 U.S. 292 [1988]).

10 U.S.C. 1089 (Defense of certain suits arising out of medical malpractice): The provision, commonly referred to as the Gonzalez Act, makes the FTCA the exclusive remedy for suits alleging medical malpractice against a military healthcare provider.

28 CFR 50.15 (Representation of federal officials and employees by Department of Justice attorneys … in civil, criminal, and congressional proceedings in which federal employees are sued, subpoenaed, or charged in their individual capacities): The DOJ regulations set out the policy and procedures for requesting representation in individual liability cases. See also 28 CFR part 15 (Defense of certain suits against federal employees).

28 CFR 50.16 (Representation of federal employees by private counsel at federal expense) (59 FR 38 243, July 27, 1994).

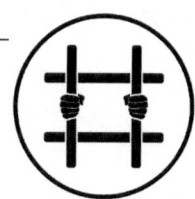

CHAPTER 31

# QUALIFIED AND ABSOLUTE IMMUNITIES AND THE GOVERNMENT'S COMMON DEFENSE

FEDERAL LAW CREATES A BODY OF IMMUNITY THAT protects state officials against claims of monetary damages. Immunity is of two types.

1. Qualified immunity: Most prison officials have qualified immunity against federal civil rights money damages claims. This means that even if the plaintiff has alleged violations of a clearly established right, the government official is entitled to qualified immunity if a reasonable person could have believed that the conduct in question was lawful. But the

catch is that prison officials are almost always able to prove their conduct against sick prisoners as lawful because they manage to conceal prisoners' true medical records from the courts. They present to the court manufactured medical records that give the appearance of a reasonable conduct by a reasonable person while hiding documentation that clearly suggests criminal misconduct. A prison official can be held liable for money damages only if the conduct violated "clearly established (federal) statutory or constitutional rights of which a reasonable person would have known" (Harlow v. Fitzgerald, 457 U. S. 800 [1982]). It is a piece of cake for prison officials to prove reasonable conduct to the court because the court is devoid of all the details and facts of the case. Prisoners' testimonies are ignored because, after all, they are "felons." And then there must be a precedence of a court decision that has explicitly held the conduct unconstitutional, or prior court decisions from which it can be reasonably inferred that the challenged conduct was unconstitutional. A court that determines whether a defendant can rely on qualified immunity is expected/required to consider all relevant legal precedent not just cases cited by the parties.

2. Absolute Immunity: State officials who perform traditional judicial functions have absolute immunity from damage actions even if their actions violated clearly established law. Thus, investigating government agents, judges, prosecutors, and parole board members sued as individuals can never be held liable in Section 1983 actions for acts performed as part of their official duties. Thus, it should not be surprising to understand why certain government officials are not

particularly concerned about committing crimes against prisoners at will, for business or for pleasure, because they know they have been literally endowed with the power of gods. They have absolute power. Lord Acton was right then and he is right today that "power corrupts and absolute power corrupts absolutely."

It is true that prison employees, such as correctional officers and prison Health Services employees, do not enjoy absolute immunity; the prison's disciplinary committee is also not protected by absolute immunity even though it adjudicates facts. This explains why this category of employees working for the federal government in prison system feels the need to systematically cover up information and create false records, because they want to be able to defend themselves if their qualified immunity is ever challenged.

The important point to understand is that the defenses of qualified and absolute immunity are available only when a person is sued in an individual capacity. These defenses cannot be asserted when a person is sued in an "official" capacity. It is also important to remember that the absolute and qualified immunity defense can only be asserted when money damage is requested and not when declaratory or injunctive relief is sought.

This reminds me of my attorney explaining to me that we would need the government's permission to present any evidence that incriminates the government because the US government itself cannot be sued unless it consents to be sued. Now why would the government consent to be sued or allow any evidence that incriminates it to be presented? This government freedom from being sued is called "sovereign immunity" (United States v. Sherwood, 312 U.S. 584 [1941]), and the United States can define the terms and conditions under which it can be sued (Honda v. Clark, 386 U.S., 484, 501 [1967]). The FTCA (Federal Tort Claims Act) waives the federal government's sovereign immunity when its employees are negligent or wrongful within the scope of their employment; however, the waive of sovereign immunity is limited and the terms of the FTCA define the boundaries of suits against the United States (United States v. Orleans, 425 U.S. 807 814 [1976]).

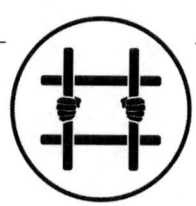

# SECTION V
# CONCLUSION

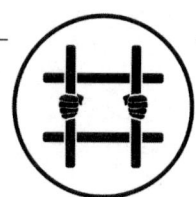

THE US COURTS HAVE CALLED IT "CRUEL AND UNUSUAL punishment," but I call it prison torture for reasons unknown to the courts. The US Supreme Court and federal courts believe that cruelty exists in isolated cases that show up from time to time in court cases, but the truth is that court cases of prison torture reflect one-hundredth of one percent of all cases that will never make it to the court system. Do not overestimate what our supreme court or federal judges know; there are some things they are clueless about and yet other things they know well but pretend they don't know, simply because they feel obligated to serve the interests of the elite, the lobbyists, and the wealthy of this nation that nominated them, the ones who hold the prison contracts, and not the people of this country. A corrupt Supreme Court is one of the reasons prison torture in the United States is unlikely to change anytime soon just as money in politics is unlikely to change anytime in the future. In fact, the situation has been worsening and is likely to continue to deteriorate due to the rising prison population and the prison profit model of the US corporate government. The problem of prison human rights abuse in the United States runs across the board because of the unwritten law of the termination of civil and constitutional rights of prisoners that is promoted by the Department of Justice. Thus, prisoners, tens of thousands of them, are faced with the same medical cruelty, emotional violence, and deadly neglect in every federal prison in America.

Prison's death cult is part and parcel of the active training programs designed for Federal Bureau of Prisons employees under the guidelines of the Department of Justice. This book has been about exposing the prison's death culture as it affects the sickest and the most vulnerable of prisoners held in the custody of the Federal Bureau of Prisons.

I always thought that a prison was a place where criminals were held to protect society from their crimes. I never once thought that a prison could be a place where the government committed crimes against criminals. One can imagine the American people having less sympathy for criminals being tormented, after all they committed crimes against society and perhaps deserved this retribution. That is not the issue however; the sickest of the sick in our prisons are often elderly, nonviolent criminals, mentally ill, drug addicts, the poorest of the poor, homeless, and many who committed minor crimes that did not warrant confinement by any standards of the civilized world. So we have to ask ourselves: Are we a civilized nation, a country that has proclaimed itself the leader of the civilized world? What makes it worse is that we also have people locked up for dissidence, political reprisals, whistle-blowing, and many of our American heroes who took their civic duty most seriously as citizens in divulging crime and corruption in our government and its ownership by the profiteers. Add to that a significant number of the innocent incarcerated, good responsible citizens sent to federal prisons through coerced guilty confessions obtained by ambitious, narcissistic, and unethical prosecutors. Many of those suffering in prisons desperately need medical attention, and many among them belong in hospitals, doctors' offices, and mental health institutions, not in prisons by any stretch of the imagination. The story of every nonviolent criminal published in this book speaks loud and clear. I hope that some of these stories have sent a chill down your spine. Perhaps you understand this book better if one of your family members who was incarcerated, and perhaps rightfully so, for a minor crime such as smoking marijuana is now being denied medical attention for a terrible work-related injury that he or she suffered in prison while subjected to slave labor at 6 cents an hour wage for years or decades.

America's true "exceptionalism" in this sense, that we Americans are not aware of, is clear in that our elected government simply refuses to be a part of the civilized world. We refuse to be a party to international laws or we first become a party but then refuse to obey those laws that parties are expected to follow. While we impose human rights rules on the rest of the world with an iron fist, we have exempted ourselves from following the same rules that the Supreme Court described as "evolving standards of decency that mark the progress of a maturing society and broad and idealistic concepts of dignity, civilized standards of humanity and decency … against which we must evaluate panel measures." We have also exempted ourselves from the UN Charter that nearly 200 nations signed, the charter that says in Article 5, "No one shall be subjected to torture or a cruel, inhuman or degrading treatment or punishment."

In title 28 of USC, Congress saddled the Bureau of Prisons and the Department of Justice with the obligation, not the option, to provide adequate medical care to prisoners compared to medical care one would receive outside. Program statement § 10.32 states a prisoner has the "Right to be free from affliction of cruel and unusual punishment as guaranteed by the Eighth Amendment." Violation of the Eighth Amendment rights have been found where there is an intentional denial of needed medical care, or when a prison official's conduct indicates deliberate indifference to the medical care of prisoners.

Prisoners' testimonies in their own words corroborated by the official internal documents that are evidence of their medical history and denial of care as revealed in this book screams out cruel, indifferent, unjust, unfair, unethical, inhuman, barbaric, unconstitutional, illegal, and criminal. These true stories from inside the federal prison are just another black mark among many others on the failing caricature of capitalism that we have masked as a democracy to try to dupe the rest of the world, our own people being the primary target of this deception, because without the approval of its own people, our government will not be able to brutalize its own people and the rest of the world. These stories expose the hypocrisy of a nation that is a self-proclaimed beacon of equality, liberty, fairness, and justice for everyone else around the world. Our children "pledge allegiance to the flag of the United States of America and to the republic for which it stands, one nation under God, indivisible, for liberty and justice for all." Do we have justice for all? Or do we have justice for a select few? We have been a nation that superimposed our definition of *democracy* (the definition of democracy being "democracy is what we say democracy is") on other nations and invaded countries on the slightest hint of a human rights violation, killing millions of innocent people, while at home we dispense our own people medieval justice. Our behavior is appalling in the sense that even in many third world countries, people are able to enjoy at least some fundamental human rights at the dawn of the twenty-first century.

I came from a third-world country four decades ago. India was a true third-world nation when I left. Perhaps it is a lot different now, I don't know. I remember when I was about eight years old, my father, a senior police officer, was assigned to be in charge of guarding arrangements for a sick prisoner inside the hospital ward, so he would not escape. The prisoner, who was in his early 60s, was admitted to the hospital for almost three months. Even though this prisoner was convicted of a murder, he was able to exercise his right to healthcare when he needed it. And the inmate did not have to beg for medical care, he was just admitted to the hospital because he was noted to be sick. One has to think that would be just the right thing to do in any civilized society. Physicians came on their rounds and examined him twice a day like they did other patients; nurses gave him medications and took care of him as they did other patients in the ward in performance of their affirmative duty to the sick that they were trained to do. The prisoner did not return to his prison cell until he was found to be completely well as determined by his attending physicians at the hospital. These were the rights available to a convicted murderer, someone who had been found to have committed a heinous crime, in a third-world country half a century ago. It is hard to believe that the same rights are not available to even nonviolent offenders 50 years later in the United States, a self-appointed "role model" for democracy for the rest of the world. Where is this democracy and where is this justice? We have yet to look under our own carpet.

The situation at hand in our prisons today can be summarized in one sentence: If a civilian physician were to violate one-tenth of a single violation acted out by a prison doctor or healthcare worker, his or her medical license would be summarily suspended as an emergency measure by a medical board and he or she would face criminal charges. What goes on in prison's healthcare system is not simple malpractice; it is a crime by all legal definitions and scholarly consensus as described in criminal law, jurisprudence, the Constitution of the United States, amendments, case laws, common laws, domestic and international law, and Geneva Conventions. The number of healthcare crimes that a healthcare worker in the Federal Bureau of Prisons commits in a day (or is capable of committing) exceeds the seriousness of all the crimes by all the criminal-minded, civilian healthcare workers put together in the United States in a year. In fact, the kind of mistreatment and brutalization of humans that I witnessed in the federal prison is simply not seen to exist in the civilian population. Even the worst of the worst physicians in the community cannot conceive of perpetrating medical cruelties of the magnitude that the prison staff carries out as a routine practice. Such violations are second nature to healthcare workers in prison; it is business as usual. This is a double standard of law and order engineered by the same Department of Justice that claims to uphold it. It is worse than a simple double standard in the sense that there are no rules whatsoever. Anything goes; almost any behavior is permitted as long as no one will ever find out. Some of these violations are infractions of human rights equivalent to war crimes committed against those who have nowhere else to go to seek help because they are locked up with no access to outside doctors or healthcare facilities. Most violations and illegal acts are committed in the name of prison security or safety, when in fact these are not security or safety matters but matters of civil, constitutional, and basic human rights secured for every human on the planet through domestic and international laws in our modern-day world that is guided by awareness of the value of human life. The kind of wanton misconduct that will cause public outrage of immeasurable proportions in a civic society at large is regarded as normal conduct in a prison's subculture cultivated and nourished by unwritten prison policies implemented by the FBOP under the guardianship and the protection of the Department of

Justice's conventional wisdom. And who has the guts to tarnish the image of the Department of Justice except someone crazy like me whom they will send back to prison for doing so?

As I have repeatedly stated earlier, a large majority of these sick prisoners are nonviolent criminals and many of them are elderly, alcoholics, mentally ill, disabled, homeless, and got addicted to substances. Many of these drug addicts are the product of our own society that Big Pharma and complicit medical community got them addicted to oxycontin, by telling them, 'don't worry, it is not addictive at all', which snowballed into opioid addiction followed by other kinds of addictions and crimes to financially support their habit. And then putting the sickest of patients and drug addicts begging for medical care in solitary confinement by calling it a safety issue is not justifiable by any measure of human civilization; it is a criminal act, and the falsehood of such a justification should be easily perceivable by the American people. The FBOP Administrative Remedy policy is worthless if it exists only on paper. The BOP makes every attempt to violate its own written promises in ways that are undetectable by the legal system and that are designed to deceive and break the law through unwritten rules, conventions, and a very deeply entrenched prison culture of death, domination, coercion, and deprivation. It is unlikely that the FBOP well-kept secrets will ever officially become public except through rare sources such as this book or an occasional whistle-blower of which none seem to exist at this time in our prison system due to the fear of reprisals. The DOJ has made it clear during the Obama rule that if anyone tries to blow the whistle on the government corruption, the consequences will be immeasurably harsh. Obama's DOJ has made good this threat by incarcerating many whistle-blowers to long sentences more than any previous president in the history of the United States. This has sent a chill down the spine of potential whistle-blowers working for the prison system.

Many sick prisoners die of unnatural causes because of denial of healthcare, and the American people will never find out because these prisoners are incarcerated for so long that they have lost their families, families who could have questioned the FBOP as to the cause of the death of their loved ones. This makes the BOP's job of concealing its acts of obstruction of justice and the commission of crime very easy. There is no adult supervision because the prison supervisors and those in the upper echelon are part of the dominant culture. And the supervisors of supervisors, the DOJ, is part of the culture too. The DOJ has made this culture the official policy of the FBOP.

The DOJ's and government agencies' double standards are self-evident when it comes to law, order, or justice. For example, the DOJ will prosecute and imprison members of any medical practice, healthcare organization, or hospital found to be in violation of OSHA regulations, safety regulations, or Workers' Comp regulations, but the DOJ (FBOP) considers itself exempt from committing the same violations. It is a norm in any federal prison to make a total mockery of any of these government agencies' rules and regulations, literally. Prison officials have no problem with showing you their middle finger if you remind them of any of these legal obligations that they have toward the inmates, or toward the American taxpayer for that matter. The DOJ (FBOP) is free to violate any law of the land as long as it is done within the four walls of the prison with no one watching. Any details of this information will never get out because it is guarded like government's state's secret privileges like those of the CIA. We, the public, do not see inside the prisons; therefore, out of sight is out of mind. We all assume that our government must be "doing the right thing" inside those prisons; it is the Department of Justice after all. How can it violate the same laws that it upholds so dearly? How is that possible when it dispenses justice and enforces law and order for the well-being of an entire nation? This is what the business cartel of the prisons' industrial complex, of which the Department of Justice is a vital part, would like you all to believe. Any conscientious prison employee who dares divulge any inside information to the American people will pay a very heavy price and face reprisals and serious consequences. Most prison employees don't reveal this information because they have adopted the prison culture of medical cruelty and deeply internalize those values. They are brainwashed to believe that their behavior is justified because, after all, these inmates are nothing but a bunch of criminals and perhaps they deserve harsher punishment with no upper limits for torture.

Savvy prisoners who understand what is going on can't reveal this information either. Many prisons have a history of blocking the mail from going out if they find out that the prisoners have started writing stories of prison abuse to the outside newspapers and media. There have been many cases like this even though the prison policy forbids the prison officials from reading the outgoing mail. They are allowed to read only the incoming mail. Pages 75 and 76 of the BOP policy manuals discuss sanctions of solitary confinement for up to 18 months for any prisoner who is caught photocopying and smuggling any internal document that belongs to the government's official, classified, or "guarded" information. By the same token a prisoner cannot photocopy medical records or any document related to the healthcare history of another prisoner. Prisoners are also thrown in solitary confinement if they are found to be discussing or sharing any healthcare records or documents that could potentially expose the FBOP's illegal actions of perpetrating medical cruelty on those who they know are genuinely very sick.

Once imprisoned, a citizen becomes one of the weakest members of the society—on purpose. Inmates are stripped of their personal freedom to a large degree and their few remaining options are managed by their jailors to "minimize security risks" and to optimize "penological value." It is obvious and has been recognized for centuries that a prisoner's welfare is under the sole control of his jailor(s) and that control creates a requisite duty. Shaping an institution that can make the punishment fit the crime has long been a theoretical goal of the criminal justice system with widely varied results. The arc of history in free societies has moved away from requiring "a pound of flesh" in payment for a debt to society and instead has integrated the variables of time, levels of security, and forms of restitution. None of these variables contemplate any type of corporeal punishment beyond confinement. The court said in *Maryland v. New Jersey* (719 F. sup. 292, 293 [D.N.J. 1989]): "We will no longer tolerate prison officials' deliberate indifference to the chronic pain of an inmate than we would a sentence that required an inmate to submit to such pain."

In a country inspired by the idea that every person has a God-given endowment of life and liberty toward a pursuit of happiness, forced confinement is itself a severe penalty. The Eighth Amendment of the US Constitution provides the boundary of our social contract forbidding cruel and unusual punishment. For more than 50 years, the Supreme Court has held that the Eighth Amendment stands squarely against "barbarous" physical punishments. And stands for "broad and idealistic concepts of dignity, civilized standards, humanity and decency." The practice of medicine should seamlessly support those ideas because it is inadvertently bound to higher standards of ethical behavior.

It has been said that "government is force." The medical services of the BOP show the erosion of principle that can occur when those axioms act in combination. The prison setting and arbitrary administration process should be enough power, but the BOP benefits from the blind eye of the court system, which defers to the presumed correctness of the medical records that the BOP routinely falsifies and provides it with a number of additional protections. The results are medical providers who operate with little concern for accountability instead of with a moral obligation and affirmative duty towards the sick and the disabled.

Only in the most depraved social misadventures in history has medicine been hijacked by a state and in essence turned against those it was intended to aid. It is of course little consolation for captives suffering from medical neglect that the system espouses itself to be enlightened in a way that would surely be attentive to their needs.

Some criminals approach their sentences with the hope that the prison might afford the time and opportunity to begin the process of piecing their lives together. For those with serious health concerns in an environment of neglect, confinement engenders cycles of suffering, hopelessness, desperation, and isolation as they feel their lives come apart at the seams. Superintending over this suffering is the Federal Bureau of Prisons of the Department of Justice. As you might imagine, the FBOP is a huge bureaucracy and has reams of policy manual and program statements. These documents express nothing like the ideas behind Germany's Final Solution, yet the system's capacity to enable crimes against humanity are undeniable.

To understand how such a disparity between expressed intent and manifest institutional performance can exist, all you have to do is read the testimonies and the real-life stories backed up with the actual inside documentation regarding those prisoners published in *Prison Papers.* Much of the information that I have provided through the publication of original documentation is always kept concealed from the American people or from the courts.

I have said this before and will say it again: you have to see it for yourself to believe that a prison guard in a federal prison is given more power than a judge on the Supreme Court of the United States. This guard, often a former soldier from the army or an equivalent, with a compromised high school education, in some cases compromised in terms of functional literacy for reading or writing, can put any prisoner in solitary confinement for months at a time if the prisoner looks at him the wrong way. A nurse in prison, who often has no idea as to what the nursing profession is all about, can and will put a prisoner in solitary confinement for months at a time for insisting on receiving his medications. All she has to do is to call the prison guards and inform them how the prisoner became a security threat and write a report with a narrative of her choice, a report that no one will question; the rest is automatically taken care of. There are so many devices a prison employee is equipped with in this unwritten prison training manual, the rules of which are conveyed only verbally in prison employee training sessions to prove that the prisoner was a security or safety risk to the institution and therefore must be held in a dark hole the size of a parking lot guard booth with barely any light coming in. Then the guards have the power to keep the prisoner inside that hole for months or for as long as they wish without ever letting him see the sunlight. No warden will question a guard's decision; those guards who do this routinely are considered to be good employees who know how to run the prison effectively. How can the warden be mad at such good employees? He depends on them and their loyalty; they know how to rule with an iron fist and keep everyone in check.

One of the long-term prisoners who had been in different prisons for 30 years told me a story when there was a government talk about cutting the prison budget and firing some excess prison guard positions. When the guards learned of this in prison where this inmate was held, they planned and purposely left open the cell doors of two arch rival gang members, which led to a prison battle between two gangs and two people died and scores got injured. Thus they made the prison warden and the government rethink firing guards because cutting guard duties was now a prison security issue. No one got fired and no budgets were cut. He informed me that it was reported on television and newspapers but only prisoners knew, not the media or the newspapers, that the riot and killing was orchestrated by prison guards to keep their jobs.

I believe that our legal system has to revisit the legal concepts such as the idea of absolute immunity granted to some prison and public officials. Common sense dictates that if people, no matter who they are, are given unlimited power, they will abuse it in unlimited ways. After all what is the point of having absolute power if you not going to enjoy some. Perhaps we need a constitutional amendment that will reduce absolute power granted to the government officials in the Department of Justice and some in the Federal Bureau of Prisons. Even police officers out in the community are granted only qualified immunity even though they put their lives at much greater risk every day. Prosecutors and public officials linked to the prison system who work inside the four walls of their protected systems are not risking their lives nearly as much as police officers patrolling the streets and yet they are granted the powers that only gods possess. They enjoy total discretion and sovereignty, which invariably translates into unchecked autonomous tyranny.

Even the qualified immunity doctrine was a desire to ensure that the insubstantial claim against government officials will be resolved prior to discovery. The immunity doctrine was not meant to allow government officials to use the color of the law to commit crimes against prisoners and then claim immunity if they were to ever get caught breaking our domestic laws.

The US Supreme Court has emphasized that when a government official's conduct has violated clearly established laws, the "existing precedent must have clearly placed the statutory or constitutional question beyond debate" (Ashroft v. Al-Kidd, 2011). It is, however, not possible to establish precedent(s) in these situations. The collusion among government employees of the DOJ, BOP, and other government agencies involved in revolving-door relationships make it impossible for incidents to become precedent(s) because the government manages to keep everything away from the public radar by using its unlimited power and influence to keep info in the dark.

The way our system works reminds me of a true story of my wife who is a very kind-hearted, compassionate nurse. She worked at a nursing home in Poughkeepsie, New York, where she noted that all the nursing staff was abusing elderly residents in many ways including unnecessarily tying them up at night and not changing their diapers, leaving them to defecate and writhe in feces and urine in their beds for hours during the night shift when there was no supervision. My wife felt outraged and she said to the rest of the nursing staff at the nursing station, "We need to talk about this. This has to change." My wife did not realize who she was messing with. Ever since then, she was terrified to go to the parking lot after she finished her shift because they told her, "We will meet you outside in the parking lot," giving winks and nods to one another suggesting that they would kick her (my wife's) ass. My wife had to quit that job of course. This is what our DOJ, FBOP, and other government agencies have become: gangsters, that is, if anyone dare expose their inner workings.

I must emphasize again that a number of prisoners are older and, no matter their age, many have serious and overlooked health concerns. The histories of some of the prisoners described in the Trail of Tears Section allow you to enter the plight of criminals suffering in confinement from deliberate medical neglect. These men live in punishing health conditions in a setting that creates intractable strategies to obtain humane medical care. What you find most alarming is that these prisoners aren't held in a third-world prison nor are they the victims of tyrannical regimes bent on making their enemies suffer. These men are imprisoned in the United States where law of the land purports to guarantee them basic levels of medical care.

An extraordinarily high percentage of prisoners in custody of the Federal Bureau of Prisons today has an ever-increasing older population with each decade that has passed by since the 1980s, when the government started the mass incarceration program. They are terminally ill, disabled, and helpless. Only an uncivilized medieval society can be expected to hold such a high percent of its population in its prisons; these are patients who need doctors first and then social, economic, and cultural rehabilitation. This is not to mention that an approximate whopping 20 percent of this prison population is made up of innocent prisoners who never committed any crime, those who were thrown into federal prisons by ambitious, unethical, and corrupt prosecutors at gunpoint, often without discussion, due process, or the option of a trial. This category includes all those who did not have the money to defend themselves, and even if they did, the pressure and threats of much harsher punishment from the prosecutors were overwhelming and relentless until they gave in to the demands of the prosecutors. Unethical prosecutors are given unlimited power and unlimited means by the government to threaten ordinary citizens unchecked in any manner with no questions asked. Any ordinary citizen will easily bog down under such oceanic pressure and plead guilty to whatever they are accused of. This category includes dissidents or whistle-blowers of government and corporate corruption. In the former Soviet Union, anyone who disagreed with the government was considered to be mentally ill and was sent to the Gulag. Today in America, anyone who disagrees with our government and its owners—the corporations and drug companies—is similarly branded as mentally ill and sent to prison. These innocent people need to be immediately released from US prisons. Those who need help or better training or a boot camp to straighten out their lives should get help, motivation, encouragement, and training—not incarceration. I will not dwell on this aspect of our prisons as this is a topic that is vastly important and is a discussion for another book for another day that I am currently working on.

Suffice it to say that the acts of medical cruelty in our prisons against criminals no matter what their offense, including those who are violent criminals, are criminal acts in themselves. These acts are crimes against humanity (International Criminal Court, Art. 3 [37 ILM 999]). Crime in international law is a crime against the law of nations to which the United States is a willing party. The US government and its echo chamber, the mainstream media, jumps up with praise for the International Criminal Court (ICC) when it finds any nation liable for violation of human rights but keeps itself immune to blame and above reproach for similar violations and crimes of much greater magnitude. In other words, the ICC, the UN, and human rights organizations and what they have to say is used as a tool by the US government to find fault with the enemy governments while avoiding investigations of its own war crimes and human rights abuse by the international overseers. The United Nations knows that it must not criticize the United States, and if it does, it is immediately branded as an ineffective organization incapable of doing anything right. And the United Nations dare not protest when the US government decides to invade other countries against strong advice from the entire international community. The crime of unilateral aggression has long been regarded as the greatest crime of all because hidden inside it is all other crimes known to man put together in one package.

The Geneva Conventions denote agreements of 1949 that extensively defined the basic rights of wartime prisoners and established protections for the wounded and the sick. One has to ask: Don't the prisoners, most of whom are citizens of the United States, many nonviolent prisoners in our Federal Bureau of Prisons and our states, deserve at least the rights of prisoners of war? What I saw in prison was not simply ignoring the health needs of these prisoners but cruel and barbaric punishment physically, emotionally, and psychologically by using war crime strategies to further punish them more than what they already have had imposed on them through incarceration. Many core elements of the war crimes such as willful killing and causing great suffering or severe injury to body or health, torture, and inhuman treatment are essentially part of the prison culture adapted by the DOJ that believes that anyone who is sent to jail has met his or her civil death, even though our constitution, the supreme law of the land, says otherwise. The civil rights endowed on all US citizens through First, Fourth, and Fifth amendments are not circumstantial; they are not subject to discussion or exception under our Constitution, the supreme law of the land, and yet they are violated by our government like they don't even exist. The court decisions on prison cases in the last few decades opposing the idea of "civic death" of prisoners have met with such resistance from what is ironically called the Department of Justice. Whenever a bill has been introduced in the US Senate that is intended to eradicate corruption in the Department of Justice that is strongly and overwhelmingly supported by every concerned organization in the country, including lawyers, judges, bar associations, defense lawyers, law schools, and renowned scholars of legal ethics, it has met with tough resistance from only one organization—the US Department of Justice. The latest one in this series is a bill introduced to stop the Brady violations by the Department of Justice. The Department of Justice wishes to continue to be treated as an exception to the rule of law expected to be fully adhered to by the rest of the world population—that is, it wants to be above the law simply because it is the enforcer of the law. It is like a cop who gives you a speeding ticket for driving at unsafe speed but he feels free to drive at 100 miles an hour even when he is not chasing a criminal but simply driving for a weekend fun ride.

America can choose to describe itself as the beacon of human rights and democracy around the world, but this hypocrisy is revealed when it treats its own citizens as though they were imprisoned in a third-world country or captives of European barbarism before the age of enlightenment. That makes our democracy a hypocrisy. The *Economist* (June 20–26, 2015) reported that with less than 5 percent of the world's population, the United States now holds roughly one-quarter of the world's prisoners, about two and half million altogether. The incarceration in the federal prisons has gone up 800 percent since the early 1980s. The US prison population today includes 1.6 million in federal and state prisons and over three-quarters of a million in local and immigration pens. That number rises to 7 million if you count everyone on probation or parole, halfway houses, or other ways of incarcerating or isolating people before or after jail time. The incarceration rate in the land of the free has risen several-fold since the 1920s and is now 5 times Britain, 9 times Germany, and 14 times Japan. At any one time, 1 in every 35 adults in America is in prison, on parole, or on probation. One in every three African American men can expect to be locked up in jail at one time or another in their lives, and one in four black children have a parent behind bars. I saw no difference between a prisoner in an American prison camp today and a black slave described in history 150 years ago working on a Southern plantation. The only difference I noted is that now we have not just black slaves (although the majority are Blacks and Hispanics), but poor Whites, American Indians, and other minorities all pitching in together for free slave labor to enrich the owners of the prison's criminal industrial complex.

The number of prisoners over the age of 50 in federal prisons has tripled since the 1980s. Research shows that the elderly in prison are not dangerous, especially those who have had nonviolent pasts. It is unconscionable to break up families of even younger nonviolent criminals. The recidivism among the elderly with a violent past is about 2 percent and those nonviolent elderly is nearly zero (0) percent, as opposed to an overall recidivism rate of 77 percent. Our prison system represents the ultimate moral decadence of any Western society, an early sign of a civilization on a rapid decline. The high recidivism rate among the young is also the consequence of a culture of damnation. Recidivism is also purposeful in that the system makes sure that when a person gets out of prison, he continues to be deprived of all human rights in some form or another so he/she is forced to commit crime again in order to physically survive.

The Thirteenth Amendment to the Constitution declared that slavery was illegal *except* as a punishment for crime. Soon after the emancipation of slaves after the Civil War, the black slaves were shoved right back into free labor slavery in prisons with the pretext that they looked at white women the wrong way and therefore committed a crime of rape just by looking. Blacks struggled for another century leading up to the Civil Rights Movement, which finally freed them from free slave labor, at least for a decade or two, only to be put right back into prisons under the new government mass incarceration program called the War on Drugs—a novel idea to put the Black and the poor in prison to retrieve its long-lost chattel slavery. And to dupe the public that we no longer have free slave labor in this country, we now pay these free laborers in prisons 3–10 cents an hour for harsh labor, so now we can say, 'hey look, they are getting paid for their work.' The slavery has also expanded in that it no longer is confined to Blacks but to other poor minorities and poor Whites. So the outdated Thirteenth Amendment is still being used in one form or another to mass incarcerate the poor for the dual purpose of social cleansing and to obtain free enslaved labor to enrich private corporations and prison contractors.

The constitution that we wrote in 1787 gave to the already-haves everything but gave the have-nots nothing. It gave the poor no economic rights or rights to a job or healthcare or housing; it gave us no rights to live with basic necessities of life. The Bill of Rights was only added later due to popular demand. The Declaration of Independence did say, "Right to equality, liberty and the pursuit of happiness," but in reality, what was practiced throughout our history was "equality, liberty and right to property"—that is, the right to property for the rich, the elite, and the bond holders. Our Constitution legitimized bringing back slave fugitives to their masters by force. And when the Constitution talked about equality, it meant equality only among the white elite; the rest of us, including the poor whites, never had rights of citizenship. It is not hard to see that we started a tradition of injustice for the poor from day one of the adoption of our Constitution. Most American lawyers, including my own defense lawyers, missed that part when they learned the Constitution of the United States, taught to them as a "sacred document," as one of the ten commandments that must be strictly followed by everyone. The law professors teach this to their students because their own professors had been taught the same propaganda a generation prior and so on and so forth. There is nothing new about our legal system run by the corporations that continues to criminalize the working class to this day. It is the brain child of the same "holy tradition" of our "sacred constitution" from 230 years ago that was designed by the wealthy for the wealthy to protect the wealthy. Ronald Reagan wrote an essay in 1987 at the bicentennial of our Constitution calling it a "marvelous document" that could have been written only by the guiding hand of God. One wonders if Ronald Reagan read the Constitution. And if he did, did he understand it with his Hollywood head? The bottom line is that it does not matter what the Constitution says; and it does say lot of wonderful things, the Constitution will not protect us even if it is perfected with all the amendments we could want added to it. What matters is what the people do with this document. You can have a wonderful document that can sit on the shelf collecting dust for 230 years. Adding more amendments or new legislation may be a good start but is not the be all and end all. Our problems, inside and outside the prisons, are cultural and value problems, and the culture must change or else we have no hope.

I end this book with the hope that it will ignite a discussion among the millennials and the Y generation and generations yet to come and will continue to remind them that the time has come to bring about change in America and that we need to take our country back from profiteers. Ours is a country that has been masking as the democratic leader of the world while violating the human rights of its own population, a wolf in a sheep's clothing serving the interests of the powerful while ignoring us, the masses, "We the people." They call us "the riffraff" behind closed doors. I cannot emphasize enough that the ultimate sovereignty lies with us, "we the people," and not with our corrupt leaders in both parties who take our votes and then wake up to a new reality the moment they land in Washington, DC, to realize that the betrayal of promises is the way to go for personal success. *Apre moi, le deluge* becomes their motto. Thence on, they only look forward and never look back at those who voted for them in exchange for their promises.

I am grateful to prisoners and others, whose true names I cannot divulge at this point, who made this investigation possible and worked relentlessly to make documents available for me to publish. Some of the prisoners who helped me with my investigation most likely committed some crime somewhere, sometime in their lives, the exact details of which I do not know, and some of them claim that they are innocent. What I do know for sure is that they are all nonviolent criminals except one. Helping me with this vital project was their way of redeeming themselves by doing something good for themselves and for those suffering in prison—that is, to help expose corruption and crimes in our government establishment that is withholding medical care from the sick in our prisons. In this sense, our government is no better than them. A crime is a crime no matter who commits it.

I want Americans and the rest of the people in the civilized world to know that I cannot fight the injustice and violation of human rights in our prison system by myself. Many have come before me and tried and failed. That is because we are dealing with the most powerful and the most corrupt establishment that human history has ever seen. To see any results, we all have to join hands and pitch in our time and energy. Hundreds of writers, authors, activists, whistle-blowers, and dissidents must start coming forward in droves, and millions of people must come out in the streets in civil disobedience before we can begin to pressure the government enough that it will consider reforms in all areas of rampant corruption, not just prison torture, which is probably the worst of all things a decadent society is capable of. It was because of the tremendous pressure from ordinary people that gave FDR the balls to stand up to the powerful wealthy corporations. If it were not for great solidarity among the working people, he would not have had the wherewithal to combat the power and influence of the rich. We live in a world of conflict of interest where the American ruling class has made our world more precarious every day for 99 percent of us inhabiting this planet. This is now becoming a worldwide phenomenon due to American corporate globalism that has brought this most powerful tsunami of crime and corruption to every corner of the planet. I can promise you that there is absolutely no solution to this problem except one and only one thing: organization and solidarity many times bigger than what was seen in the 1930s and again in the 1960s. That will bring about a new revolution, but this revolution may not occur in America, it will occur elsewhere, America may already have gone off the deep end heading in the direction of becoming a third-world nation of the future, with no hope of reversal of human values here at home. I will be thrilled if my readers could understand just one thing—no matter how big and strong the military-industrial congressional intelligence corporate criminal complex becomes, no matter how massive the shadow government, no matter how formidable the deep state and the corrupt corporate media, the ultimate power always rests in the hands of the people if they decide to wake up one morning and take charge.

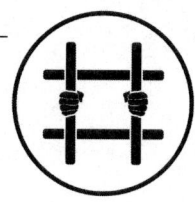

# INMATES' CONSENT

FOLLOWING IS THE WORDING OF THE INMATES' CONSENT whose stories are described in this book and medical health information published in *Prison Papers*. The original handwritten version of this consent, with inmates' signatures, registration numbers and dates of births redacted, is published towards the latter part of the book, *Prison Papers:*

> We, the prisoners at the South Federal Prison Camp, Lompoc, California authorize and assign power of attorney to Paul Singh, DO, MD to conduct business in terms of presenting our medical case reviews, medical records and medical history in class action or tort claims, or revealing the information to Congress, President of the United States, civil rights and healthcare organizations for the intent purpose of seeking justice from healthcare abuse at the hands of the Department of Justice. Federal Bureau of Prisons.

This information of personal medical records involving documentation of our administrative remedy process struggles at the BOP may be revealed in the form of an investigative report, medical case review(s), manuscripts, documentary, books, book reviews, print and audio-visual media, initially anonymously followed by an expose of documents and testimonies in the event Bureau of Prisons decides to deny the validity of claims that any harm is done to prisoners.

We certify that we have read, reviewed and discussed, and comprehended the above statement before signing and dating it. Granting this authority covers all aspects of HIPAA laws:

Name                              Signature

Date                              Registration #

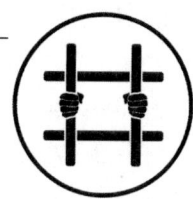

# ACKNOWLEDGMENTS AND GRATITUDE

I LIKE TO EXPRESS MY GRATITUDE TO VARIOUS INDIVIDUALS and organizations who supported me in putting my prison manuscripts on *Prison Torture in America* and *Prison Papers*, in their final form. I am thankful to several amendment attorneys who clarified the scope of law and its limitations as it pertained to my investigational journalism from inside the prison. I also feel indebted to those who read the manuscripts and did the fact checking for me in comparing my writings in *Prison Torture in America* with the actual evidence that I presented in *Prison Papers* in support of my claims. My special thanks to Sue Kauffman for her copy-editing of the manuscripts that I wrote in prison under very challenging and difficult circumstances.

What I am truly grateful to everyone involved is not just for their professional and often pro bono services but the moral support they provided me for making the publication of *Prison Torture in America* and its Companion Book, *Prison Papers* possible. I hope that this covert investigation from inside our Federal prison system is the beginning of a dialogue about what America is doing to its prison population, a form of enslavement and inhuman torture that continues to this day since the 13th and 14th amendments 150 years ago. Our hypocrisy is clear from these books, in that we do not practice what we preach the rest of the world about human rights and dignity.

This acknowledgment is not complete without giving full credit to Jonathan Kirsch, a First Amendment attorney with 40 years of experience specializing in this area of the law for vetting my manuscripts in terms of the current first amendment, copyright, libel and defamation statutes on the books.

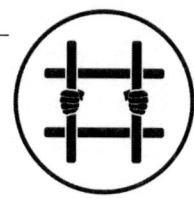

# RESOURCES AND CREDITS

Americans for Responsible
  Solutions
Americans United for Change
Ammera David RT
Amnesty International
Amnesty USA
Amy Goodman
Andrew Kreig
Angela Davis
Annie Machon
Antiwar.com
Arundhati Roy
Barret Brown
Benjamin Jealous
Bernie Sanders
Between the Lines Press Publishers
Bill Press
Bill Moyers
Black Commentator.com
Blogger.com
Blogs for Prisoners
Book TV CSPAN
Brandon Terry
Bruce Fein
CA PRA Public Records 1798
California Guardian
  photojournalists
California Prison Focus
*Canadian Dimension* magazine
  (Canadian Dimension.com)
Canadian Journalism Foundation
Cape Codders for Peace and Justice
Carol Anderson
Catalina Velasquez

Catherine Mackinnon
Cato Institute Prison Project
CCS Criminal Capture System
Cenk Uyger
Center for Constitutional Rights
  (CCR)
Center for Human Rights and
  Global Justice at NYU School of
  Law
Chad Joy (FBI's whistle-blower)
Child Welfare League of America
Chris Hedges
*CIA's Greatest Hits*
Code Pink: Women for Peace
Colonel Lawrence Walkerson
Committee to Protect Journalists
Common Sense magazine
Commonwealth Press Publishers
Counter Punch National Office
*Covert Action* magazine
Craig Murray
Crassely Senator
Criminal Justice Policy Coalition
Criminal Law Reporter
Critical Justice
*Crossing the Rubicon* documentaries
Daily Post Silicon Valley for First
  Amendment
Dana Priest (investigative journalist
  for *Washington Post*)
Daniel Ellsberg
Danielle Indian
Darren Smith, PhD

David Carr (*New York Times* columnist)
David Jolly
David Kaye
David Lat
David Rieff
David Warmely
Dean Corn
Deborah Parker
Democracy for America
Democracy Now
Doctors Without Borders
*Dollars and Sense* magazine
Donald Bostrom (Swedish investigative reporter)
Dorothy Rabinowitz
Dr. Baz Dreisinger of John Jay School of Criminal Justice
Dreams Publication
Edgar Cahn
Ellen Shrecker
Emily Ekins
Erin Bilbray
Errol Morris
Eugen Puryear
Eurim Pharm Germany Generic IUD Manufacturer
Family and Corrections Network
Federal Resource Center for Children of Prisoners
Franz Gayl
Free School
Freedom of the Press Foundation (Freedom.press)

FirstAmendmentCoalition.org
First Amendment Project
Freeman radio
Friends and Families of Incarcerated Individuals
Fund for Civil rights
Gary Johnson
Gary Null
Gary Ruskin
George Galloway
Gerry Spence
Get Canadian drugs.com
Glenn Greenwald
Global Mail Canada
Government Accountability Project (GAP)
Greg Palast
Harold Pinter
Hart House, Alberta, Canada
Harvey Silverglate
Haymarket Press Publishers
Heather Johnson
Henry Wallace (33rd Vice President)
*How the World Works* by Noam Chomsky
Howard Zinn
Hugh Aynesworth
Human Right Watch
Human Rights Watch Prison Project
*In These Times*
Independent Media Center

Institute of International
  Humanitarian Affairs at
  Fordham University
Inter-American Commission on
  Human Rights
International Justice Mission
Ira Sorkin
Jack Rice
Jackie Speier
*Jailhouse Lawyer's Handbook*
"Jailhouse Nation," *The Economist*
James Davis
James Duane
James Riser
Jane Mayer (journalist for
  *The New Yorker*)
Jeff Lamken
Jeff Merkeley Senator
Jeff Weaver
Jen Senko
Jennifer Reisch
Jeremy Scahill
Jerry Allen Baily
Jesse Ventura
Jill Stein
Jimmy Dore
John Bergman, DC
John Crane
John Emshwiller and Rebecca
  Smith
John Irk
John Kiriaku
John Nichols
John Pfaff

John Pilger
John Pilgrim
John Porter
Joie Chen
Jonathan Tasiri
Jordan Chariton
Journalists Without Borders
Judge Alex Kozinski
Judge Betty Fletcher
Judge Emmet Sullivan
Judge Napolitano, Fox News
Judge Sidney Thomas
Judge Stuart
Judge Thelton Henderson
Judge Wallace Tashima
Justin Porter
Justine Bamberg, esq
Kamala Harris (Senator)
Katrina Vanden Heuvel
Keith Best
Keith Ellison
Ken Karen
Ken Mesplay, PhD, Green Party
Kerry Kennedy
Kevin Johnson
Kevin Zeese
KFCF Free Speech radio
KGL Talk Radio
KGO radio
Kurt Eichenwald
Kyle Mercado
*L.A. Progressive*
Lannan Foundation
Larry Cohen

Laura Flanders
Law Schools Social Justice Projects
Lawrence B. Jones
Lawrence Lessig
Leana Sheryle Wen, MD, MSc
Lecture series at Stanford
  Continuing Education on
  Global Assault on Expression
Lee Camp
Legal Services for Prisoners with
  Children
Linda McQuaig
Links to Criminal Justice
  Resources and Organizations by
  Christopher Zoukis
Lisa Ling
Lucas Walker
Lucy Florez
BENICIO Asante
Madea Benjamin
*Manufacturing Consent* by Noam
  Chomsky
Marcia Angell, MD
Margaret Flowers, MD
Mariam Abusharkh
Marianne Udow
Marianne Williamson
Mark Godsey
Mark Hertsgaard
Martha Rosenberg
Maryl Steeple
Mass Freedom Project
Matt Taibi
Media Edge Channel

Megan Markle
Melinda St. Louis
Michael Adams
Michael Isikoff
Michael Marcot
Michael Moore
Michael Parenti
Michael S. Greco
Michael Sandle
Michel Dekort
Michelle Alexander
Miguel Francis Santiago
Mihael A. Kroll
Mike Moses
Mike Panpantonio
Molly Crabapple
Mollye Barros
Morris Berman
Mother Jones Magazine
NAACP
Naomi Klein
National Institute
National Lawyers Guild National
  Office
National Office
New Press Publishers
Newsmax TV
Nick Davis (investigative reporter
  for the *Guardian*)
Nina Turner
Noam Chomsky
Nora Weber, mother of a son who
  died in prison from medical
  torture

Occidental College

Oliver Stone

Open Secrets

Otis R. Taylor Columnist, *San Francisco Chronicle*

Our Revolution

Oxfam International

Pacifica Radio Stations

Parkland Press, Canada Publishers

Partnership for Safety and Justice, Oregon

Pattie Brassand

Paul George

Peter Cicchino Youth Project of the Urban Justice Center

Peter Joseph

Peter Singer

Pramila Jayapal

Prison Activist Resource Center

Prison Legal News

Prison Self-help Legal Clinic

Prisoner's Wives

*Prisoners Self-Help Litigation Manual* by John Boston & Daniel Manville

Prisoners' Families

Professor Harvey Kaye

Professor Heather Thomson

Professor Leif Wenar of King's College London

Professor Theodore Postol

*Profits Over People* by Noam Chomsky

Project Veritas undercover videos

Protect Our Care – Families USA

Public Citizen News

Public Citizen's Congress Watch

Rachel Kamel

Radio WZBC, Boston College

Ralph Nader

Ramparts.com

Rana Rao

Rand Paul

Ray McGovern

Reporters Without Borders

Resource Center of the Americas

Revolutiontruth.org

Richard Belzer

Richard Escrow

Rob Mariani

Robert Greenwald

Robert Reich

Robert Weissman

Ron Paul

Russ Feingold

Sanctuary Press Publishers

Sanders Institute

Sean Parker

Sean Stone

Senator Orrin Hatch, Republican from Utah

Seven Story Press Publishers

Seymor Hersh

Shannon Jackson

Sheik Aamer

Sidney Powell

Somerville Community Access Radio

Southend Press, Boston Publishers

Southern Center for Human Rights

Southern Poverty Law Center –
Sylvia Rivera Law Project

Spare Change News

Stephen Giller

Steven Bersstein

Steven Christian

Steven Molo

Steven Pinker

Stoppharmagreed.com

Stuart Taylor, Jr.

Susan Harley

Susan R. Estrich

Susan Sarandon

Tabatha Wallace

Tamara Draut

Tavis Smiley

Ted Devine

Ted Rall

TGI Justice Project San
Francisco, CA

The Commonwealth Club of
California

*The Guardian*, London

The Guerilla News Network

The Harvard Book Store

The Hawks TV Show

The Innocence Projects

*The Intercept*

*The Nation* magazine

The New Press

The New School

The New York Review of Books

*The Progressive* magazine

*The Times of Israel*, on Teva and Big
Pharma Corruption

*Thistle* magazine

*Thistle*, MIT

Thom Devine, Government
Accountability Act

Thom Hartman

Thomas Drake

Thomas Tamm Atty for DOJ
whistle-blower

Thomas W. Simon (*Ranking on
International Crimes*)

Thomas Wilner and Andy
Worthington

*Three Days of Condor*

Tim Canova

Tim Lynch

Transformative Justice Law Project
of Illinois

Trial Lawyers for Justice

*Trial Lawyers* magazine

Truthdig.com

Tulsi Gabbard (Sanders Institute
Fellow)

Tyrel Ventura

U.N.I.O.N. (United for No
Injustice, Oppression or Neglect)

U.S.C. § 516-29 Federal Statutes
and Regulations (refer to
Legal Section of the book for
comprehensive legal references)

Victor Sperandeo

Vinay Devnath

Vincent Emauele
Virginia Held
Vivienne Westwood
*Washington Spectator* magazine
WBAI
William Binny
William Hodes
*Wise* magazine
Women for Women International

Woody Harrelson
World Socialist Website
World Watch Institute
WorldPulse
*Yes* magazine
*Z Magazine*
Zahara Heckshcher
Zyphyr Teachout